1988/89 Edition

Accounting Standards

AF697310

Statements of Financial Accounting Concepts

Financial Accounting Standards Board

IRWIN

1988, Homewood, Illinois 60430

Published by the
Financial Accounting Standards Board

High Ridge Park, P.O. Box 3821, Stamford, Connecticut 06905-0821

Printed in the United States of America

FOREWORD

In the past, previous standards-setting bodies made periodic attempts to develop a framework of fundamentals on which financial accounting and reporting standards could be based. Significant accounting tools were developed in the period from the first formalization of a standards-setting hierarchy in 1938 to the creation of the Financial Accounting Standards Board, but no broadly accepted framework resulted. In 1973, based on the recommendations of the Study Group on the Objectives of Financial Statements (the "Trueblood" Report) and at the behest of the Financial Accounting Standards Advisory Council and others, the Financial Accounting Standards Board included a project on its initial technical agenda to develop "broad qualitative standards for financial reporting." That project was subsequently expanded to the development of a conceptual framework for financial accounting and reporting. The Board has published a number of Discussion Memorandums, a Statement of Tentative Conclusions, Research Reports, Exposure Drafts of Concepts Statements, and final Concepts Statements on parts of the conceptual framework project. Copies of those publications are available from the FASB.

This volume contains the full text of five of the six Statements of Financial Accounting Concepts issued to date:

- *Objectives of Financial Reporting by Business Enterprises* (No. 1)
- *Qualitative Characteristics of Accounting Information* (No. 2)
- *Objectives of Financial Reporting by Nonbusiness Organizations* (No. 4)
- *Recognition and Measurement in Financial Statements of Business Enterprises* (No. 5)
- *Elements of Financial Statements* (No. 6)

Paragraphs in those Concepts Statements that have been amended or superseded by subsequent Concepts Statements are shaded to alert the reader. *Elements of Financial Statements of Business Enterprises* (No. 3) no longer appears in this volume because it was replaced by Concepts Statement No. 6. A substantial part of the contents of Concepts Statement No. 3 was brought forward unchanged to Concepts Statement No. 6. To assist the reader who wants to find where a paragraph in Concepts Statement No. 3 may now appear in Concepts Statement No. 6, a cross-reference index has been included on pages 83-85 of this volume to indicate the location of identical or similar paragraphs in each Statement.

The existing Concepts Statements are intended to serve the public interest by setting the objectives, qualitative characteristics, and other concepts that guide selection of economic events to be recognized and measured for financial reporting and their display in financial statements or related means of communicating information to those who are interested. Concepts Statements guide the Board in developing sound accounting principles and provide the Board and its constituents with an understanding of the appropriate content and inherent limitations of financial reporting. That process provides the means for developing evenhanded financial and other information that, together with information from other sources, facilitates the efficient functioning of capital and other markets and otherwise assists in promoting efficient allocation of scarce resources in the economy.

Unlike a Statement of Financial Accounting Standards, a Statement of Financial Accounting Concepts does not establish generally accepted accounting principles and therefore is not intended to invoke application of Rule 203 or 204 of the Rules of Conduct of the Code of Professional Ethics of the American Institute of Certified Public Accountants. Rule 203 provides that a member of the American Institute of Certified Public Accountants shall not express an opinion that financial statements conform with generally accepted accounting principles if those statements contain a material departure from an accounting principle promulgated by the Financial Accounting Standards Board, unless the member can demonstrate that because of unusual circumstances the financial statements otherwise would have been misleading. Rule 204 requires members of the Institute to justify departures from standards promulgated by the Financial Accounting Standards Board for the disclosure of information outside the financial statements in published financial reports.

Norwalk, Connecticut
June 1988

Timothy S. Lucas
Director of Research and
Technical Activities

TABLE OF CONTENTS

No.		Page
1	Objectives of Financial Reporting by Business Enterprises.	1
2	Qualitative Characteristics of Accounting Information	26
3	Elements of Financial Statements of Business Enterprises	83
4	Objectives of Financial Reporting by Nonbusiness Organizations.	144
5	Recognition and Measurement in Financial Statements of Business Enterprises	177
6	Elements of Financial Statements (a replacement of FASB Concepts Statement No. 3—incorporating an amendment of FASB Concepts Statement No. 2).	227

Topical Index. 333

Statement of Financial Accounting Concepts No. 1 Objectives of Financial Reporting by Business Enterprises

STATUS

Issued: November 1978

Affects: No other pronouncements

Affected by: No other pronouncements

HIGHLIGHTS

[*Best understood in context of full Statement*]

- Financial reporting is not an end in itself but is intended to provide information that is useful in making business and economic decisions.
- The objectives of financial reporting are not immutable—they are affected by the economic, legal, political, and social environment in which financial reporting takes place.
- The objectives are also affected by the characteristics and limitations of the kind of information that financial reporting can provide.

  —The information pertains to business enterprises rather than to industries or the economy as a whole.

  —The information often results from approximate, rather than exact, measures.

  —The information largely reflects the financial effects of transactions and events that have already happened.

  —The information is but one source of information needed by those who make decisions about business enterprises.

  —The information is provided and used at a cost.

- The objectives in this Statement are those of general purpose external financial reporting by business enterprises.

  —The objectives stem primarily from the needs of external users who lack the authority to prescribe the information they want and must rely on information management communicates to them.

  —The objectives are directed toward the common interests of many users in the ability of an enterprise to generate favorable cash flows but are phrased using investment and credit decisions as a reference to give them a focus. The objectives are intended to be broad rather than narrow.

  —The objectives pertain to financial reporting and are not restricted to financial statements.

- The objectives state that:

  —Financial reporting should provide information that is useful to present and potential investors and creditors and other users in making rational investment, credit, and similar decisions. The information should be comprehensible to those who have a reasonable understanding of business and economic activities and are willing to study the information with reasonable diligence.

  —Financial reporting should provide information to help present and potential investors and creditors and other users in assessing the amounts, timing, and uncertainty of prospective cash receipts from dividends or interest and the proceeds from the sale, redemption, or maturity of securities or loans. Since investors' and creditors' cash flows are related to enterprise cash flows, financial reporting should provide information to help investors, creditors, and others assess the amounts, timing, and uncertainty of prospective net cash inflows to the related enterprise.

  —Financial reporting should provide information about the economic resources of an enterprise, the claims to those resources (obligations of the enterprise to transfer resources to other entities and owners' equity), and the effects of transactions, events, and circumstances that change its resources and claims to those resources.

- "Investors" and "creditors" are used broadly and include not only those who have or contemplate having a claim to enterprise resources but also those who advise or represent them.

- Although investment and credit decisions reflect investors' and creditors' expectations about future enterprise performance, those expectations are commonly based at least partly on evaluations of past enterprise performance.

- The primary focus of financial reporting is information about earnings and its components.

- Information about enterprise earnings based on accrual accounting generally provides a better indication of an enterprise's present and continuing ability to generate favorable cash flows than information limited to the financial effects of cash receipts and payments.

- Financial reporting is expected to provide information about an enterprise's financial performance during a period and about how management of an enterprise has discharged its stewardship responsibility to owners.

- Financial accounting is not designed to measure directly the value of a business enterprise, but the information it provides may be helpful to those who wish to estimate its value.

- Investors, creditors, and others may use reported earnings and information about the elements of financial statements in various ways to assess the prospects for cash flows. They may wish, for example, to evaluate management's performance, estimate "earning power," predict future earnings, assess risk, or to confirm, change, or reject earlier predictions or assessments. Although financial reporting should provide basic information to aid them, they do their own evaluating, estimating, predicting, assessing, confirming, changing, or rejecting.

- Management knows more about the enterprise and its affairs than investors, creditors, or other "outsiders" and accordingly can often increase the usefulness of financial information by identifying certain events and circumstances and explaining their financial effects on the enterprise.

* * * * *

Statement of Financial Accounting Concepts No. 1
Objectives of Financial Reporting by Business Enterprises

STATEMENTS OF FINANCIAL ACCOUNTING CONCEPTS

This is the first in a series of Statements of Financial Accounting Concepts. The purpose of the series is to set forth fundamentals on which financial accounting and reporting standards will be based. More specifically, Statements of Financial Accounting Concepts are intended to establish the objectives and concepts that the Financial Accounting Standards Board will use in developing standards of financial accounting and reporting.

The Board itself is likely to be the major user and thus the most direct beneficiary of the guidance provided by the new series. However, knowledge of the objectives and concepts the Board uses should enable all who are affected by or interested in financial accounting standards to better understand the content and limitations of information provided by financial accounting and reporting, thereby furthering their ability to use that information effectively and enhancing confidence in financial accounting and reporting. That knowledge, if used with care, may also provide guidance in resolving new or emerging problems of financial accounting and reporting in the absence of applicable authoritative pronouncements.

Unlike a Statement of Financial Accounting Standards, a Statement of Financial Accounting Concepts does not establish generally accepted accounting principles and therefore is not intended to invoke the application of Rule 203 of the Rules of Conduct of the Code of Professional Ethics of the American Institute of Certified Public Accountants (or successor rule or arrangement of similar scope and intent).* Like other pronouncements of the Board, a Statement of Financial Accounting Concepts may be amended, superseded, or withdrawn by appropriate action under the Board's *Rules of Procedure.*

The Board recognizes that in certain respects current generally accepted accounting principles may be inconsistent with those that may derive from the objectives and concepts set forth in this Statement and others in the series. In due course, the Board expects to reexamine its pronouncements, pronouncements of predecessor standard-setting bodies, and existing financial reporting practice in the light of newly enunciated objectives and concepts. In the meantime, a Statement of Financial Accounting Concepts does not (a) require a change in existing generally accepted accounting principles, (b) amend, modify, or interpret Statements of Financial Accounting Standards, Interpretations of the FASB, effective Opinions of the Accounting Principles Board, or effective Bulletins of the Committee on Accounting Procedure, or (c) justify either changing existing generally accepted accounting and reporting practices or interpreting the pronouncements listed in (b) based on per-

*Rule 203 prohibits a member of the American Institute of Certified Public Accountants from expressing an opinion that financial statements conform with generally accepted accounting principles if those statements contain a material departure from an accounting principle promulgated by the Financial Accounting Standards Board, unless the member can demonstrate that because of unusual circumstances the financial statements otherwise would have been misleading.

sonal interpretations of the objectives and concepts in the Statements of Financial Accounting Concepts.

To establish objectives and concepts will not, by itself, directly solve financial accounting and reporting problems. Rather, objectives and concepts are tools for solving problems. Moreover, although individual Statements of Financial Accounting Concepts may be issued serially, they will form a cohesive set of interrelated concepts and will often need to be used jointly.

The new series of Statements of Financial Accounting Concepts is intended and expected to serve the public interest within the context of the role of financial accounting and reporting in the economy—to provide evenhanded financial and other information that, together with information from other sources, facilitates efficient functioning of capital and other markets and otherwise assists in promoting efficient allocation of scarce resources in the economy.

Contents Paragraph Numbers

Highlights
Introduction and Background .... 1—31
  Financial Statements and Financial Reporting .... 5— 8
  Environmental Context of Objectives .... 9—16
  Characteristics and Limitations of Information Provided .... 17—23
  Potential Users and Their Interests .... 24—27
  General Purpose External Financial Reporting .... 28—31
Objectives of Financial Reporting .... 32—54
  Information Useful in Investment and Credit Decisions .... 34—36
  Information Useful in Assessing Cash Flow Prospects .... 37—39
  Information about Enterprise Resources, Claims to Those Resources, and Changes in Them .... 40—54
    Economic Resources, Obligations, and Owners' Equity 41
    Enterprise Performance and Earnings .... 42—48
    Liquidity, Solvency, and Funds Flows 49
    Management Stewardship and Performance .... 50—53
    Management Explanations and Interpretations 54
The Conceptual Framework: A Perspective .... 55—56
Appendix A—Background Information .... 57—63

This Statement contains no conclusions about matters expected to be covered in other Statements resulting from the Board's conceptual framework project, such as objectives of financial reporting by organizations other than business enterprises; elements of financial statements and their recognition, measurement, and display; capital maintenance; unit of measure; criteria for distinguishing information to be included in financial statements from that which should be provided by other means of financial reporting; and criteria for evaluating and selecting accounting information (qualitative characteristics).

INTRODUCTION AND BACKGROUND

1. This Statement establishes the objectives of general purpose external financial reporting by business enterprises. Its concentration on business enterprises is not intended to imply that the Board has concluded that the uses and objectives of financial reporting by other kinds of entities are, or should be, the same as or different from those of business enterprises. Those and related matters, including whether and, if so, how business enterprises and other organizations should be distinguished for the purpose of establishing objectives of and basic concepts underlying financial reporting, are issues in another phase of the Board's conceptual framework project.[1]

2. This Statement is the first of a planned series of publications in the Board's conceptual framework project. Later Statements are expected to cover the elements of financial statements and their recognition, measurement, and display as well as related matters such as capital maintenance, unit of measure, criteria for distinguishing information to be included in financial statements from that which should be provided by other means of financial reporting, and criteria for evaluating and selecting accounting information (qualitative characteristics). Accordingly, this Statement contains no conclusions about matters such as the identity, number, or form of financial statements or about the attributes to be measured[2] or the unit of measure to be used. Thus, although designation in the objectives of certain information as relevant has implications for communicating the information, the Statement should not be interpreted as implying a particular set of financial statements. Nor should the Statement be interpreted as suggesting that the relative merits of various attributes, such as historical cost/historical proceeds or current cost/current proceeds, have been resolved. Similarly, references in it to measures in units of money should not be interpreted as precluding the possibility of measures in constant dollars (units of money having constant purchasing power).

3. This Statement also does not specify financial accounting standards prescribing

---

[1]In August 1977, the Board announced its sponsorship of a research study on the objectives and basic concepts underlying financial reporting by organizations other than business enterprises. The Board published the research report, *Financial Accounting in Nonbusiness Organizations: An Exploratory Study of Conceptual Issues,* by Robert N. Anthony, in May 1978. It issued a *Discussion Memorandum,* "Objectives of Financial Reporting by Nonbusiness Organizations," in June 1978 and held public hearings in October and November 1978.

[2]"Attributes to be measured" refers to the traits or aspects of an element to be quantified or measured, such as historical cost/historical proceeds, current cost/current proceeds, etc. Attribute is a narrower concept than measurement, which includes not only identifying the attribute to be measured but also selecting a scale of measurement (for example, units of money or units of constant purchasing power). "Property" is commonly used in the sciences to describe the trait or aspect of an object being measured, such as the length of a table or the weight of a stone. But "property" may be confused with land and buildings in financial reporting contexts, and "attribute" has become common in accounting literature and is used in this Statement.

accounting procedures or disclosure practices for particular items or events; rather it describes concepts and relations that will underlie future financial accounting standards and practices and in due course serve as a basis for evaluating existing standards and practices. Its effect on financial reporting will be reflected primarily in Statements of Financial Accounting Standards (please see "Statements of Financial Accounting Concepts" on page 4). Until the FASB reexamines its pronouncements, pronouncements of predecessor standard-setting bodies, and existing financial reporting practices, pronouncements such as *APB Statement No. 4,* "Basic Concepts and Accounting Principles Underlying Financial Statements of Business Enterprises," or the *Accounting Terminology Bulletins* will continue to serve their intended purpose—to describe objectives and concepts underlying standards and practices existing before the issuance of this Statement.

4. This Statement includes a brief exposition of the reasons for the Board's conclusions.[3] It therefore includes no separate Appendix containing a basis for conclusions. Appendix A to this Statement contains background information for the Statement.

Financial Statements and Financial Reporting

5. The objectives in this Statement pertain to financial reporting and are not restricted to information communicated by financial statements. Although financial reporting and financial statements have essentially the same objectives, some useful information is better provided by financial statements and some is better provided, or can only be provided, by means of financial reporting other than financial statements. The following paragraphs briefly describe some major characteristics of financial reporting and financial statements and give some examples, but they draw no clear distinction between financial reporting and financial statements and leave extremely broad the scope of financial reporting. The Board will draw boundaries, as needed, in other parts of the conceptual framework project or in financial accounting standards.

6. Financial statements are a central feature of financial reporting. They are a principal means of communicating accounting information to those outside an enterprise. Although financial statements may also contain information from sources other than accounting records, accounting systems are generally organized on the basis of the elements of financial statements (assets, liabilities, revenues, expenses, etc.) and provide the bulk of the information for financial statements. The financial statements now most frequently provided are (a) balance sheet or statement

---

[3]The Board has previously provided a more detailed discussion of the environment of financial reporting and the basis underlying the Board's conclusions on objectives of financial reporting by business enterprises in Chapters 1-3 of *Tentative Conclusions on Objectives of Financial Statements of Business Enterprises* (Stamford, CT: Financial Accounting Standards Board, December 2, 1976). The Board may reissue pertinent parts of that discussion, and perhaps other related material, in a more permanent publication.

of financial position, (b) income or earnings statement, (c) statement of retained earnings, (d) statement of other changes in owners' or stockholders' equity, and (e) statement of changes in financial position (statement of sources and applications of funds). To list those examples from existing practice implies no conclusions about the identity, number, or form of financial statements because those matters are yet to be considered in the conceptual framework project (paragraph 2).

7. Financial reporting includes not only financial statements but also other means of communicating information that relates, directly or indirectly, to the information provided by the accounting system— that is, information about an enterprise's resources, obligations, earnings, etc. Management may communicate information to those outside an enterprise by means of financial reporting other than formal financial statements either because the information is required to be disclosed by authoritative pronouncement, regulatory rule, or custom or because management considers it useful to those outside the enterprise and discloses it voluntarily. Information communicated by means of financial reporting other than financial statements may take various forms and relate to various matters. Corporate annual reports, prospectuses, and annual reports filed with the Securities and Exchange Commission are common examples of reports that include financial statements, other financial information, and nonfinancial information. News releases, management's forecasts or other descriptions of its plans or expectations, and descriptions of an enterprise's social or environmental impact are examples of reports giving financial information other than financial statements or giving only nonfinancial information.

8. Financial statements are often audited by independent accountants for the purpose of enhancing confidence in their reliability. Some financial reporting by management outside the financial statements is audited, or is reviewed but not audited, by independent accountants or other experts, and some is provided by management without audit or review by persons outside the enterprise.

Environmental Context of Objectives

9. Financial reporting is not an end in itself but is intended to provide information that is useful in making business and economic decisions—for making reasoned choices among alternative uses of scarce resources in the conduct of business and economic activities. Thus, the objectives set forth stem largely from the needs of those for whom the information is intended, which in turn depend significantly on the nature of the economic activities and decisions with which the users are involved. Accordingly, the objectives in this Statement are affected by the economic, legal, political, and social environment in the United States. The objectives are also affected by characteristics and limitations of the information that financial reporting can provide (paragraphs 17-23).

10. The United States has a highly developed exchange economy. Most goods and

services are exchanged for money or claims to money instead of being consumed by their producers. Most goods and services have money prices, and cash (ready money, including currency, coins, and money on deposit) is prized because of what it can buy. Members of the society carry out their consumption, saving, and investment decisions by allocating their present and expected cash resources.

11. Production and marketing of goods and services often involve long, continuous, or intricate processes that require large amounts of capital, which in turn require substantial saving in the economy. Savings are often invested through a complex set of intermediaries which offer savers diverse types of ownership and creditor claims, many of which can be freely traded or otherwise converted to cash.

12. Most productive activity in the United States is carried on through investor-owned business enterprises, including many large corporations that buy, sell, and obtain financing in national or multinational markets. Since investor-owners are commonly more interested in returns from dividends and market price appreciation of their securities than in active participation in directing corporate affairs, directors and professional managers commonly control enterprise resources and decide how those resources are allocated in enterprise operations. Management is accountable to owner-investors, both directly and through an elected board of directors, for planning and controlling enterprise operations in their interests, including gaining or maintaining competitive advantage or parity in the markets in which the enterprise buys, sells, and obtains financing and considering and balancing various other, often competing interests, such as those of employees, customers, lenders, suppliers, and government.

13. Business enterprises raise capital for production and marketing activities not only from financial institutions and small groups of individuals but also from the public through issuing equity and debt securities that are widely traded in highly developed securities markets. Numerous, perhaps most, transactions in those markets are transfers from one investor or creditor to another with no part of the exchange price going to the issuing enterprise. But those transactions set the market prices for particular securities and thereby affect an enterprise's ability to attract investment funds and its cost of raising capital. Those having funds to invest normally assess the expected costs, expected returns, and expected risks of alternative investment opportunities. They attempt to balance expected risks and returns and generally invest in high risk ventures only if they expect commensurately high returns and will accept low expected returns only if expected risk is commensurately low. A business enterprise is unlikely to be able to compete successfully in the markets for lendable or investment funds unless lenders and investors expect the enterprise to be able to sell its output at prices sufficiently in excess of its costs to enable them to expect a return from interest or dividends and market price appreciation commensurate with the risks they perceive. Thus, well-developed securities markets tend to allocate scarce resources to enterprises that use them efficiently and away from inefficient enterprises.

14. In the United States, productive resources are generally privately owned rather than government owned. Markets—which vary from those that are highly competitive, including many commodities and securities markets, to those that involve regulated monopolies, including markets for telephone service or electricity—are significant factors in resource allocation in the economy. However, government intervenes in the allocation process in many ways and for various purposes. For example, it intervenes directly by collecting taxes, borrowing, and spending for its purchases of goods and services for government operations and programs; by regulating business activities; or by paying subsidies. It intervenes less directly through broad tax, monetary, and fiscal policies. Government also has a broad interest in the impact of business enterprises on the community at large and may intervene to alter that impact. Many government interventions are expressly designed to work through market forces, but even government actions that are not so designed may significantly affect the balance of market forces.

15. Moreover, government is a major supplier of economic statistics and other economic information that are widely used by management, investors, and others interested in individual business enterprises and are commonly included in news reports and other statistics and analyses in ways that may broadly affect perceptions about business and economic matters. Although government statistics are primarily "macro" in nature (pertaining to the economy as a whole or to large segments of it) and do not generally disclose much about individual business enterprises, they are based to a considerable extent on information of the kind provided by financial reporting by individual business enterprises.

16. The effectiveness of individuals, enterprises, markets, and government in allocating scarce resources among competing uses is enhanced if those who make economic decisions have information that reflects the relative standing and performance of business enterprises to assist them in evaluating alternative courses of action and the expected returns, costs, and risks of each. The function of financial reporting is to provide information that is useful to those who make economic decisions about business enterprises and about investments in or loans to business enterprises. Independent auditors commonly examine or review financial statements and perhaps other information, and both those who provide and those who use that information often view an independent auditor's opinion as enhancing the reliability or credibility of the information.

Characteristics and Limitations of Information Provided

17. The objectives of financial reporting are affected not only by the environment in which financial reporting takes place but also by the characteristics and limitations of the kind of information that financial reporting, and particularly financial statements, can provide. The information is to a significant extent financial information based on approximate measures of the financial effects on individual business enterprises of transactions and events that have already happened; it cannot be provided or used without incurring a cost.

18. The information provided by financial reporting is primarily financial in nature—it is generally quantified and expressed in units of money. Information that is to be formally incorporated in financial statements must be quantifiable in units of money. Other information can be disclosed in financial statements (including notes) or by other means, but financial statements involve adding, subtracting, multiplying, and dividing numbers depicting economic things and events and require a common denominator. The numbers are usually exchange prices or amounts derived from exchange prices. Quantified nonfinancial information (such as number of employees or units of product produced or sold) and nonquantified information (such as descriptions of operations or explanations of policies) that are reported normally relate to or underlie the financial information. Financial information is often limited by the need to measure in units of money or by constraints inherent in procedures, such as verification, that are commonly used to enhance the reliability or objectivity of the information.

19. The information provided by financial reporting pertains to individual business enterprises, which may comprise two or more affiliated entities, rather than to industries or an economy as a whole or to members of society as consumers. Financial reporting may provide information about industries and economies in which an enterprise operates but usually only to the extent the information is relevant to understanding the enterprise. It does not attempt to measure the degree to which the consumption of wealth satisfies consumers' wants. Since business enterprises are producers and distributors of scarce resources, financial reporting bears on the allocation of economic resources to producing and distributing activities and focuses on the creation of, use of, and rights to wealth and the sharing of risks associated with wealth.

20. The information provided by financial reporting often results from approximate, rather than exact, measures. The measures commonly involve numerous estimates, classifications, summarizations, judgments, and allocations. The outcome of economic activity in a dynamic economy is uncertain and results from combinations of many factors. Thus, despite the aura of precision that may seem to surround financial reporting in general and financial statements in particular, with few exceptions the measures are approximations, which may be based on rules and conventions, rather than exact amounts.

21. The information provided by financial reporting largely reflects the financial effects of transactions and events that have already happened. Management may communicate information about its plans or projections, but financial statements and most other financial reporting are historical. For example, the acquisition price of land, the current market price of a marketable equity security, and the current replacement price of an inventory are all historical data—no future prices are involved. Estimates resting on expectations of the future are often needed in financial reporting, but their major use, especially of those formally incorporated in financial statements, is to measure financial effects of past transactions or events or

the present status of an asset or liability. For example, if depreciable assets are accounted for at cost, estimates of useful lives are needed to determine current depreciation and the current undepreciated cost of the asset. Even the discounted amount of future cash payments required by a long-term debt contract is, as the name implies, a "present value" of the liability. The information is largely historical, but those who use it may try to predict the future or may use the information to confirm or reject their previous predictions. To provide information about the past as an aid in assessing the future is not to imply that the future can be predicted merely by extrapolating past trends or relationships. Users of the information need to assess the possible or probable impact of factors that may cause change and form their own expectations about the future and its relation to the past.

22. Financial reporting is but one source of information needed by those who make economic decisions about business enterprises. Business enterprises and those who have economic interests in them are affected by numerous factors that interact with each other in complex ways. Those who use financial information for business and economic decisions need to combine information provided by financial reporting with pertinent information from other sources, for example, information about general economic conditions or expectations, political events and political climate, or industry outlook.

23. The information provided by financial reporting involves a cost to provide and use, and generally the benefits of information provided should be expected to at least equal the cost involved. The cost includes not only the resources directly expended to provide the information but may also include adverse effects on an enterprise or its stockholders from disclosing it. For example, comments about a pending lawsuit may jeopardize a successful defense, or comments about future plans may jeopardize a competitive advantage. The collective time needed to understand and use information is also a cost. Sometimes a disparity between costs and benefits is obvious. However, the benefits from financial information are usually difficult or impossible to measure objectively, and the costs often are; different persons will honestly disagree about whether the benefits of the information justify its costs.

Potential Users and Their Interests

24. Many people base economic decisions on their relationships to and knowledge about business enterprises and thus are potentially interested in the information provided by financial reporting. Among the potential users are owners, lenders, suppliers, potential investors and creditors, employees, management, directors, customers, financial analysts and advisors, brokers, underwriters, stock exchanges, lawyers, economists, taxing authorities, regulatory authorities, legislators, financial press and reporting agencies, labor unions, trade associations, business researchers, teachers and students, and the public. Members and potential members of some groups—such as owners, creditors, and employees—have or contemplate having direct economic interests in particular business enterprises. Managers and directors,

who are charged with managing the enterprise in the interest of owners (paragraph 12), also have a direct interest. Members of other groups—such as financial analysts and advisors, regulatory authorities, and labor unions—have derived or indirect interests because they advise or represent those who have or contemplate having direct interests.

25. Potential users of financial information most directly concerned with a particular business enterprise are generally interested in its ability to generate favorable cash flows because their decisions relate to amounts, timing, and uncertainties of expected cash flows. To investors, lenders, suppliers, and employees, a business enterprise is a source of cash in the form of dividends or interest and perhaps appreciated market prices, repayment of borrowing, payment for goods or services, or salaries or wages.They invest cash, goods, or services in an enterprise and expect to obtain sufficient cash in return to make the investment worthwhile. They are directly concerned with the ability of the enterprise to generate favorable cash flows and may also be concerned with how the market's perception of that ability affects the relative prices of its securities. To customers, a business enterprise is a source of goods or services, but only by obtaining sufficient cash to pay for the resources it uses and to meet its other obligations can the enterprise provide those goods or services. To managers, the cash flows of a business enterprise are a significant part of their management responsibilities, including their accountability to directors and owners. Many, if not most, of their decisions have cash flow consequences for the enterprise. Thus, investors, creditors, employees, customers, and managers significantly share a common interest in an enterprise's ability to generate favorable cash flows. Other potential users of financial information share the same interest, derived from investors, creditors, employees, customers, or managers whom they advise or represent or derived from an interest in how those groups (and especially stockholders) are faring.

26. Some of the potential users listed in paragraph 24 may have specialized needs but also have the power to obtain information needed. For example, both the information needed to enforce tax laws and regulations and the information needed to set rates for public utilities are specialized needs. However, although both taxing authorities and rate-making bodies often use the information in financial statements for their purposes, both also have statutory authority to require the specific information they need to fulfill their functions and do not need to rely on information provided to other groups. Some investors and creditors or potential investors and creditors may also be able to require a business enterprise to provide specified information to meet a particular need—for example, a bank or insurance company negotiating with an enterprise for a large loan or private placement of securities can often obtain desired information by making the information a condition for completing the transaction.

27. Except for management, and to some extent directors, the potential users listed in paragraph 24 are commonly described as "external users," and accounting and

reporting are sometimes divided conventionally into internal and external parts. That broad distinction more nearly suits the purposes of this Statement than does another common conventional distinction—that between managerial or management accounting (which is designed to assist management decision making, planning, and control at the various administrative levels of an enterprise) and financial accounting (which is concerned with accounting for an enterprise's assets, liabilities, revenues, expenses, earnings, etc.)[4] because management uses information provided by both management accounting and financial accounting. Management needs, in addition to financial accounting information, a great deal of management accounting information to carry out its responsibilities in planning and controlling operations. Much of that information relates to particular decisions or to particular cost or profit centers and is often provided in more detail than is considered necessary or appropriate for external financial reporting, even though the same accounting system normally accumulates, processes, and provides the information whether it is called managerial or financial or internal or external. Directors usually have access to at least some information available to management that is normally not provided outside an enterprise. Since management accounting is internal to an enterprise, it can usually be tailored to meet management's informational needs and is beyond the scope of this Statement.

General Purpose External Financial Reporting

28. The objectives in this Statement are those of general purpose external financial reporting by business enterprises. The objectives stem primarily from the informational needs of external users who lack the authority to prescribe the financial information they want from an enterprise and therefore must use the information that management communicates to them. Those potential users include most of the groups listed in paragraph 24.

29. Financial reporting has both an internal and an external aspect, and this Statement focuses on the external aspect. Management is as interested in information about assets, liabilities, earnings, and related elements as external users and, among its other requirements, generally needs the same kinds of information about those elements as external users (paragraph 25). Thus, management is a major user of the same information that is provided by external financial reporting. However, management's primary role in external financial reporting is that of communicating information for use by others. For that reason, it has a direct interest in the cost, adequacy, and understandability of external financial reporting.

30. General purpose external financial reporting is directed toward the common

[4]That distinction between managerial and financial accounting is made, for example, by Eric L. Kohler, *A Dictionary for Accountants,* 5th ed. (Englewood Cliffs, NJ: Prentice-Hall, Inc., 1975), pp. 208 and 303, and by Sidney Davidson, James S. Schindler, Clyde P. Stickney, and Roman L. Weil, *Accounting: The Language of Business,* 3rd ed. (Glen Ridge, NJ: Thomas Horton and Daughters, Inc., 1977), pp. 24 and 34.

interest of various potential users in the ability of an enterprise to generate favorable cash flows (paragraph 25). Thus, the objectives in this Statement are focused on information for investment and credit decisions for reasons that are largely pragmatic, not to narrow their scope. The objectives need a focus to avoid being vague or highly abstract. Investors and creditors and their advisors are the most obvious prominent external groups who use the information provided by financial reporting and who generally lack the authority to prescribe the information they want. Their decisions and their uses of information have been studied and described to a much greater extent than those of other external groups, and their decisions significantly affect the allocation of resources in the economy. In addition, information provided to meet investors' and creditors' needs is likely to be generally useful to members of other groups who are interested in essentially the same financial aspects of business enterprises as investors and creditors.

31. For convenience, *financial reporting* is used in place of *general purpose external financial reporting by business enterprises* in the remainder of this Statement.

OBJECTIVES OF FINANCIAL REPORTING

32. The following objectives of financial reporting flow from the preceding paragraphs and proceed from the more general to the more specific. The objectives begin with a broad focus on information that is useful in investment and credit decisions; then narrow that focus to investors' and creditors' primary interest in the prospects of receiving cash from their investments in or loans to business enterprises and the relation of those prospects to the enterprise's prospects; and finally focus on information about an enterprise's economic resources, the claims to those resources, and changes in them, including measures of the enterprise's performance, that is useful in assessing the enterprise's cash flow prospects. The reasons for focusing the objectives of financial reporting primarily on investment, credit, and similar decisions are given in paragraph 30. That focus and wording do not mean that the objectives apply only to investors and creditors and exclude everyone else. To the contrary, information that satisfies the objectives should be useful to all who are interested in an enterprise's future capacity to pay or in how investors or creditors are faring.

33. The objectives are those of financial reporting rather than goals for investors, creditors, or others who use the information or goals for the economy or society as a whole. The role of financial reporting in the economy is to provide information that is useful in making business and economic decisions, not to determine what those decisions should be. For example, saving and investing in productive resources (capital formation) are generally considered to be prerequisite to increasing the standard of living in an economy. To the extent that financial reporting provides information that helps identify relatively efficient and inefficient users of resources, aids in assessing relative returns and risks of investment opportunities, or otherwise assists in promoting efficient functioning of capital and other markets, it helps to create a favorable environment for capital formation decisions. However, investors, credi-

tors, and others make those decisions, and it is not a function of financial reporting to try to determine or influence the outcomes of those decisions. The role of financial reporting requires it to provide evenhanded, neutral, or unbiased information. Thus, for example, information that indicates that a relatively inefficient user of resources is efficient or that investing in a particular enterprise involves less risk than it does and information that is directed toward a particular goal, such as encouraging the reallocation of resources in favor of a particular segment of the economy, are likely to fail to serve the broader objectives that financial reporting is intended to serve.

Information Useful in Investment and Credit Decisions

34. Financial reporting should provide information that is useful to present and potential investors and creditors and other users in making rational investment, credit, and similar decisions. The information should be comprehensible to those who have a reasonable understanding of business and economic activities and are willing to study the information with reasonable diligence.

35. This Statement uses the terms investors and creditors broadly. The terms include both those who deal directly with an enterprise and those who deal through intermediaries, both those who buy securities from other investors or creditors and those who buy newly issued securities from the enterprise or an underwriter, both those who commit funds for long periods and those who trade frequently, both those who desire safety of investment and those who are willing to accept risk to obtain high rates of return, both individuals and specialized institutions. The major groups of investors are equity securityholders and debt securityholders. The major groups of creditors are suppliers of goods and services who extend credit, customers and employees with claims, lending institutions, individual lenders, and debt securityholders.[5] The terms also may comprehend security analysts and advisors, brokers, lawyers, regulatory agencies, and others who advise or represent the interests of investors and creditors or who otherwise are interested in how investors and creditors are faring.

36. Individual investors, creditors, or other potential users of financial information understand to varying degrees the business and economic environment, business activities, securities markets, and related matters. Their understanding of financial information and the way and extent to which they use and rely on it also may vary greatly. Financial information is a tool and, like most tools, cannot be of much direct help to those who are unable or unwilling to use it or who misuse it. Its use can be learned, however, and financial reporting should provide information that can be used by all—nonprofessionals as well as professionals—who are willing to learn to

[5]Debt securityholders are included in both groups because they are investors as that term is commonly used as well as creditors by contract and usual legal definition. Moreover, it is often convenient to refer to them as investors without making a precise distinction between "investors in debt securities" and "investors in equity securities." That distinction is made if it is significant

use it properly. Efforts may be needed to increase the understandability of financial information. Cost-benefit considerations may indicate that information understood or used by only a few should not be provided. Conversely, financial reporting should not exclude relevant information merely because it is difficult for some to understand or because some investors or creditors choose not to use it.

Information Useful in Assessing Cash Flow Prospects

37. Financial reporting should provide information to help present and potential investors and creditors and other users in assessing the amounts, timing, and uncertainty of prospective cash receipts from dividends or interest and the proceeds from the sale, redemption, or maturity of securities or loans. The prospects for those cash receipts are affected by an enterprise's ability to generate enough cash to meet its obligations when due and its other cash operating needs, to reinvest in operations, and to pay cash dividends and may also be affected by perceptions of investors and creditors generally about that ability, which affect market prices of the enterprise's securities. Thus, financial reporting should provide information to help investors, creditors, and others assess the amounts, timing, and uncertainty of prospective net cash inflows to the related enterprise.[6]

38. People engage in investing, lending, and similar activities primarily to increase their cash resources. The ultimate test of success (or failure) of those activities is the extent to which they return more (or less) cash than they cost.[7] A successful investor or creditor receives not only a return *of* investment but also a return *on* that investment (cash, goods, or services) commensurate with the risk involved. Moreover, investment, credit, and similar decisions normally involve choices between present cash and future cash—for example, the choice between the price of a security that can be bought or sold or the amount of a loan and rights to expected future cash receipts from dividends or interest and proceeds from resale or repayment. Inves-

---

[6]Several respondents to the Exposure Draft, "Objectives of Financial Reporting and Elements of Financial Statements of Business Enterprises," interpreted this objective as requiring "cash flow information," "current value information," or "management forecast information." However, the objective focuses on the purpose for which information provided should be useful—emphasizing the importance of cash to people and the activities they use to increase cash inflows that also help increase the productive resources and outputs of goods and services in an economy—rather than the kinds of information that may be useful for that purpose. The objective neither requires nor prohibits "cash flow information," "current value information," "management forecast information," or any other specific information. Conclusions about "current value information" and "management forecast information" are beyond the scope of this Statement. Paragraphs 42-44 note that information about cash receipts and disbursements is not usually considered to be the most useful information for the purposes described in this objective.

[7]Questions of measurement scale and unit of measure are beyond the scope of this Statement (paragraph 2). Therefore, the description in paragraphs 38, 39, and others ignore, for example, that a dollar of cash received as dividends, interest, or proceeds from resale or repayment is not necessarily equal in purchasing power to a dollar invested or loaned earlier, a dollar of cash collected from customers is not necessarily equal in purchasing power to a dollar spent earlier, and a dollar of cash paid to a creditor is not necessarily equal in purchasing power to a dollar received earlier.

tors, creditors, and others need information to help them form rational expectations about those prospective cash receipts and assess the risk that the amounts or timing of the receipts may differ from expectations, including information that helps them assess prospective cash flows to the enterprise in which they have invested or to which they have loaned funds.

39. Business enterprises, like investors and creditors, invest cash in noncash resources to earn more cash. The test of success (or failure) of the operations of an enterprise is the extent to which the cash returned exceeds (or is less than) the cash spent (invested) over the long run (footnote 7).[8] A successful enterprise receives not only a return *of* its investment but also a satisfactory return *on* that investment. The market's assessment of an enterprise's expected success in generating favorable cash flows affects the relative market prices of its securities, although the level of market prices of securities is affected by numerous factors—such as general economic conditions, interest rates, market psychology, and the like—that are not related to particular enterprises. Thus, since an enterprise's ability to generate favorable cash flows affects both its ability to pay dividends and interest and the market prices of its securities, expected cash flows to investors and creditors are related to expected cash flows to the enterprise in which they have invested or to which they have loaned funds.

Information about Enterprise Resources, Claims to Those Resources, and Changes in Them

40. Financial reporting should provide information about the economic resources of an enterprise, the claims to those resources (obligations of the enterprise to transfer resources to other entities and owners' equity), and the effects of transactions, events, and circumstances that change resources and claims to those resources.[9]

Economic Resources, Obligations, and Owners' Equity

41. Financial reporting should provide information about an enterprise's economic resources, obligations, and owners' equity. That information helps investors, creditors, and others identify the enterprise's financial strengths and weaknesses and assess its liquidity and solvency. Information about resources, obligations, and

---

[8]Descriptions of operations of business enterprises commonly describe a cycle that begins with cash outlays and ends with cash receipts. That description is not only straightforward and convenient but also generally fits manufacturing, merchandising, financial, and service enterprises whose operations comprise primarily activities such as acquiring goods and services, increasing their value by adding time, place, or form utility, selling them, and collecting the selling price. Cash receipts may precede cash payments, however, and commonly do in the operations of some service and financial enterprises. The order of cash flows does not affect the basic nature of operations but may complicate descriptions and analyses.

[9]Economic resources, claims to those resources, changes in resources and claims, and the elements that represent them in financial statements are the subject of the next phase in the Board's conceptual framework project on elements of financial statements of business enterprises.

owners' equity also provides a basis for investors, creditors, and others to evaluate information about the enterprise's performance during a period (paragraphs 42-48). Moreover, it provides direct indications of the cash flow potentials of some resources and of the cash needed to satisfy many, if not most, obligations. That is, some of an enterprise's resources are direct sources of cash to the enterprise, many obligations are direct causes of cash payments by the enterprise, and reasonably reliable measures of future net cash inflows or future net cash outflows are often possible for those resources and obligations. Many cash flows cannot be identified with individual resources (or some obligations), however, because they are the joint result of combining various resources in the enterprise's operations. Indirect measures of cash flow potential are widely considered necessary or desirable, both for particular resources and for enterprises as a whole. That information may help those who desire to estimate the value of a business enterprise, but financial accounting is not designed to measure directly the value of an enterprise.

Enterprise Performance and Earnings

42. Financial reporting should provide information about an enterprise's financial performance during a period. Investors and creditors often use information about the past to help in assessing the prospects of an enterprise. Thus, although investment and credit decisions reflect investors' and creditors' expectations about future enterprise performance, those expectations are commonly based at least partly on evaluations of past enterprise performance.[10]

43. The primary focus of financial reporting is information about an enterprise's performance provided by measures of earnings and its components. Investors, creditors, and others who are concerned with assessing the prospects for enterprise net cash inflows are especially interested in that information. Their interest in an enterprise's future cash flows and its ability to generate favorable cash flows leads primarily to an interest in information about its earnings rather than information directly about its cash flows. Financial statements that show only cash receipts and payments during a short period, such as a year, cannot adequately indicate whether or not an enterprise's performance is successful.

44. Information about enterprise earnings and its components measured by accrual accounting generally provides a better indication of enterprise performance than information about current cash receipts and payments. Accrual accounting attempts to record the financial effects on an enterprise of transactions and other events and

[10]Investors and creditors ordinarily invest in or lend to enterprises that they expect to continue in operation—an expectation that is familiar to accountants as "the going concern" assumption. Information about the past is usually less useful in assessing prospects for an enterprise's future if the enterprise is in liquidation or is expected to enter liquidation. Then, emphasis shifts from performance to liquidation of the enterprise's resources and obligations. The objectives of financial reporting do not necessarily change if an enterprise shifts from expected operation to expected liquidation, but the information that is relevant to those objectives, including measures of elements of financial statements, may change.

circumstances that have cash consequences for an enterprise in the periods in which those transactions, events, and circumstances occur rather than only in the periods in which cash is received or paid by the enterprise. Accrual accounting is concerned with the process by which cash expended on resources and activities is returned as more (or perhaps less) cash to the enterprise, not just with the beginning and end of that process. It recognizes that the buying, producing, selling, and other operations of an enterprise during a period, as well as other events that affect enterprise performance, often do not coincide with the cash receipts and payments of the period.

45. Periodic earnings measurement involves relating to periods the benefits from and the costs[11] of operations and other transactions, events, and circumstances that affect an enterprise. Although business enterprises invest cash to obtain a return *on* investment as well as a return *of* investment, the investment of cash and its return often do not occur in the same period. Modern business activities are largely conducted on credit and often involve long and complex financial arrangements or production or marketing processes. An enterprise's receivables and payables, inventory, investments, property, plant, equipment, and other noncash resources and obligations are the links between its operations and other transactions, events, and circumstances that affect it and its cash receipts and outlays. For example, labor is often used by an enterprise before it is paid for, requiring that salaries and wages payable be accrued to recognize the obligation and measure the effects on earnings in the period the labor is used rather than when the payroll checks are issued. Conversely, resources such as raw materials and equipment may be paid for by an enterprise in a period that does not coincide with their use, requiring that the resources on hand be recognized and that the effect on earnings be deferred until the periods the resources are used. Similarly, receivables and the related effects on earnings must often be accrued before the related cash is received, or obligations must be recognized when cash is received and the effects on earnings must be identified with the periods in which goods or services are provided. The goal of accrual and deferral of benefits and sacrifices is to relate the accomplishments and the efforts so that reported earnings measures an enterprise's performance during a period instead of merely listing its cash receipts and outlays.[12]

46. Earnings and its components relate to an individual enterprise during a particular period. Over the life of an enterprise (or other very long period), total reported earnings equals the net cash receipts excluding those from capital changes (ignoring changes in value of money noted in footnote 7), but that relationship between earnings and cash flows rarely, if ever, holds for periods as short as a year. The major

[11]"Cost" is the sacrifice incurred in economic activities—that which is given up or foregone to consume, to save, to exchange, to produce, etc. For example, the value of cash or other resources given up (or the present value of an obligation incurred) in exchange for a resource is the cost of the resource acquired. Similarly, the expiration of future benefits caused by using a resource in production is the cost of using it.

[12]The process described in this paragraph is commonly called the "matching of costs and revenues," and "matching" is a significant part of it, though not the whole. "Matching" is one of the subjects of the next phase in the conceptual framework project on elements of financial statements.

difference between periodic earnings measured by accrual accounting and statements of cash receipts and outlays is timing of recognition of the components of earnings.

47. Investors, creditors, and others often use reported earnings and information about the components of earnings in various ways and for various purposes in assessing their prospects for cash flows from investments in or loans to an enterprise. For example, they may use earnings information to help them (a) evaluate management's performance, (b) estimate "earning power" or other amounts they perceive as "representative" of long-term earning ability of an enterprise, (c) predict future earnings, or (d) assess the risk of investing in or lending to an enterprise. They may use the information to confirm, reassure themselves about, or reject or change their own or others' earlier predictions or assessments. Measures of earnings and information about earnings disclosed by financial reporting should, to the extent possible, be useful for those and similar uses and purposes.

48. However, accrual accounting provides measures of earnings rather than evaluations of management's performance, estimates of "earning power," predictions of earnings, assessments of risk, or confirmations or rejections of predictions or assessments. Investors, creditors, and other users of the information do their own evaluating, estimating, predicting, assessing, confirming, or rejecting. For example, procedures such as averaging or normalizing reported earnings for several periods and ignoring or averaging out the financial effects of "nonrepresentative" transactions and events are commonly used in estimating "earning power." However, both the concept of "earning power" and the techniques for estimating it are part of financial analysis and are beyond the scope of financial reporting.

Liquidity, Solvency, and Funds Flows

49. Financial reporting should provide information about how an enterprise obtains and spends cash, about its borrowing and repayment of borrowing, about its capital transactions, including cash dividends and other distributions of enterprise resources to owners, and about other factors that may affect an enterprise's liquidity or solvency. For example, although reports of an enterprise's cash receipts and cash outlays during a period are generally less useful than earnings information for measuring enterprise performance during a period and for assessing an enterprise's ability to generate favorable cash flows (paragraphs 42-46), information about cash flows or other funds flows may be useful in understanding the operations of an enterprise, evaluating its financing activities, assessing its liquidity or solvency, or interpreting earnings information provided. Information about earnings and economic resources, obligations, and owners' equity may also be useful in assessing an enterprise's liquidity or solvency.

Management Stewardship and Performance

50. Financial reporting should provide information about how management of an

enterprise has discharged its stewardship responsibility to owners (stockholders) for the use of enterprise resources entrusted to it. Management of an enterprise is periodically accountable to the owners not only for the custody and safekeeping of enterprise resources but also for their efficient and profitable use and for protecting them to the extent possible from unfavorable economic impacts of factors in the economy such as inflation or deflation and technological and social changes. To the extent that management offers securities of the enterprise to the public, it voluntarily accepts wider responsibilities for accountability to prospective investors and to the public in general. Society may also impose broad or specific responsibilities on enterprises and their managements.

51. Earnings information is commonly the focus for assessing management's stewardship or accountability. Management, owners, and others emphasize enterprise performance or profitability in describing how management has discharged its stewardship accountability. A central question for owners, managers, potential investors, the public, and government is how an enterprise and its owners are faring. Since earnings and its components for a single period are often an insufficient basis for assessing management's stewardship, owners and others may estimate "earning power" or other average they consider "representative" of long-term performance. As noted in paragraph 48, however, accrual accounting measures earnings for a period rather than "earning power" or other financial analysis concepts.

52. Financial reporting should provide information that is useful to managers and directors in making decisions in the interests of owners. Although this Statement is concerned primarily with providing information to external users, managers and directors are responsible to owners (and other investors) for enterprise performance as reflected by financial reporting and they are judged at least to some extent on the enterprise performance reported. Thus, how owners have fared during a period is of equal concern to managers and owners, and information provided should be useful to both in meeting their common goal.

53. Financial reporting, and especially financial statements, usually cannot and does not separate management performance from enterprise performance. Business enterprises are highly complex institutions, and their production and marketing processes are often long and intricate. Enterprise successes and failures are the result of the interaction of numerous factors. Management ability and performance are contributing factors, but so are events and circumstances that are often beyond the control of management, such as general economic conditions, supply and demand characteristics of enterprise inputs and outputs, price changes, and fortuitous events and circumstances. What happens to a business enterprise is usually so much a joint result of a complex interaction of many factors that neither accounting nor other statistical analysis can discern with reasonable accuracy the degree to which management, or any other factor, affected the joint result. Actions of past managements affect current periods' earnings, and actions of current management affect future periods' earnings. Financial reporting provides information about an enterprise

during a period when it was under the direction of a particular management but does not directly provide information about that management's performance. The information is therefore limited for purposes of assessing management performance apart from enterprise performance.

Management Explanations and Interpretations

54. Financial reporting should include explanations and interpretations to help users understand financial information provided. For example, the usefulness of financial information as an aid to investors, creditors, and others in forming expectations about a business enterprise may be enhanced by management's explanations of the information. Management knows more about the enterprise and its affairs than investors, creditors, or other "outsiders" and can often increase the usefulness of financial information by identifying certain transactions, other events, and circumstances that affect the enterprise and explaining their financial impact on it. In addition, dividing continuous operations into accounting periods is a convention and may have arbitrary effects. Management can aid investors, creditors, and others in using financial information by identifying arbitrary results caused by separating periods, explaining why the effect is arbitrary, and describing its effect on reported information. Moreover, financial reporting often provides information that depends on, or is affected by, management's estimates and judgment. Investors, creditors, and others are aided in evaluating estimates and judgmental information by explanations of underlying assumptions or methods used, including disclosure of significant uncertainties about principal underlying assumptions or estimates. Financial reporting may, of course, provide information in addition to that specified by financial accounting standards, regulatory rules, or custom.

THE CONCEPTUAL FRAMEWORK: A PERSPECTIVE

55. Paragraphs 40-54 focus the objectives of financial reporting by business enterprises on information about the economic resources of an enterprise, the claims to those resources, and the effects of transactions, events, and circumstances that change resources and claims to them. The paragraphs emphasize information about an enterprise's performance provided by measures of earnings and its components and also broadly describe other kinds of information that financial reporting should provide. The objectives lead to, but leave unanswered, questions such as the identity, number, and form of financial statements; elements of financial statements and their recognition, measurement, and display; information that should be provided by other means of financial reporting; and meanings and balancing or trading-off of relevance, reliability, and other criteria for evaluating and selecting accounting information (qualitative characteristics). Those matters are, as noted in paragraph 2, topics of other Statements that are expected to follow this Statement on objectives.

56. Financial statements are the basic means of communicating the information described in paragraphs 40-54 to those who use it. The elements of financial state-

ments provide "... information about the economic resources of an enterprise, the claims to those resources (obligations of the enterprise to transfer resources to other entities and owners' equity), and the effects of transactions, events, and circumstances that change resources and claims to those resources" (paragraph 40), including "... information about an enterprise's performance provided by measures of earnings and its components" (paragraph 43). Thus, the next phase of the conceptual framework project pertains to the elements of financial statements.

This Statement was adopted by the unanimous vote of the seven members of the Financial Accounting Standards Board:

Donald J. Kirk, *Chairman*
Oscar S. Gellein
John W. March
Robert A. Morgan
David Mosso
Robert T. Sprouse
Ralph E. Walters

Appendix A

BACKGROUND INFORMATION

57. The need for a conceptual framework for financial accounting and reporting, beginning with consideration of the objectives of financial reporting, is generally recognized. The Accounting Principles Board issued *APB Statement No. 4,* "Basic Concepts and Accounting Principles Underlying Financial Statements of Business Enterprises," in 1970. When the Financial Accounting Standards Board came into existence, the Study Group on the Objectives of Financial Statements was at work, and its report, "Objectives of Financial Statements," was published in October 1973 by the American Institute of Certified Public Accountants.

58. The Financial Accounting Standards Board issued a Discussion Memorandum, "Conceptual Framework for Accounting and Reporting: Consideration of the Report of the Study Group on the Objectives of Financial Statements," dated June 6, 1974 and held a public hearing on September 23 and 24, 1974 on the objectives of financial statements. The Discussion Memorandum and the hearing were based primarily on the *Report of the Study Group on the Objectives of Financial Statements.* The Board received 95 written communications responding to the Discussion Memorandum, and 20 parties presented their views orally and answered Board Members' questions at the hearing.

59. On December 2, 1976, the Board issued three documents:

Tentative Conclusions on Objectives of Financial Statements of Business Enterprises,

FASB Discussion Memorandum, "Conceptual Framework for Financial Accounting and Reporting: Elements of Financial Statements and Their Measurement," and

Scope and Implications of the Conceptual Framework Project.

The same task force, with only one membership change, provided counsel in preparing both Discussion Memoranda. Eleven persons from academe, the financial community, industry, and public accounting served on the task force while the Discussion Memoranda were written.

60. The Board considered the 12 objectives of financial statements in the Study Group Report but has not attempted to reach conclusions on some of them—for example, reporting current value and changes in current value, providing a statement of financial activities, providing financial forecasts, determining the objectives of financial statements for governmental and not-for-profit organizations, and reporting enterprise activities affecting society. Some issues about reporting current values and changes in current values were discussed in the Discussion Memorandum, "Elements of Financial Statements and Their Measurement," and the Board has a project on supplementary disclosures of the effects of changing prices on business enterprises (paragraph 61). The Board also has a project on objectives of financial reporting by organizations other than business enterprises (footnote 1). The other matters may be dealt with in later phases of the conceptual framework project.

61. The Board held public hearings (a) August 1 and 2, 1977 on the *Tentative Conclusions on Objectives of Financial Statements* and Chapters 1-5 of the Discussion Memorandum concerning definitions of the elements of financial statements and (b) January 16-18, 1978 on the remaining chapters of the Discussion Memorandum concerning capital maintenance or cost recovery, qualities of useful financial information ("qualitative characteristics"), and measurement of the elements of financial statements.

62. The Board received 283 written communications on the subject of the August 1977 hearing, of which 214 commented on the objectives and 221 commented on the elements, and 27 parties presented their views orally and answered Board Members' questions at the hearing. The Board issued an Exposure Draft of a proposed Statement of Financial Accounting Concepts on "Objectives of Financial Reporting and Elements of Financial Statements of Business Enterprises," dated December 29, 1977 and received 135 letters of comment.

63. The major difference between this Statement and the Exposure Draft is the scope of the subject matter. "Elements of financial statements of business enterprises" and the brief comments on "qualitative characteristics" (paragraphs 41-66 and 69-75, respectively, of the Exposure Draft) have been omitted to be the subjects of separate exposure drafts. Other significant changes are (a) the "Highlights" preceding the text, (b) the subheadings in the third objective (paragraphs 40-54), and (c) reorganization of the "Introduction and Background" paragraphs, including the position of "characteristics and limitations of information provided" in the forepart of the Statement.

Statement of Financial Accounting Concepts No. 2 Qualitative Characteristics of Accounting Information

STATUS

Issued: May 1980

Affects: No other pronouncements

Affected by: Paragraph 4 and footnote 2 superseded by CON 6

SUMMARY OF PRINCIPAL CONCLUSIONS

The purpose of this Statement is to examine the characteristics that make accounting information useful. Those who prepare, audit, and use financial reports, as well as the Financial Accounting Standards Board, must often select or evaluate accounting alternatives. The characteristics or qualities of information discussed in this Statement are the ingredients that make information useful and are the qualities to be sought when accounting choices are made.

All financial reporting is concerned in varying degrees with decision making (though decision makers also use information obtained from other sources). The need for information on which to base investment, credit, and similar decisions underlies the objectives of financial reporting. The usefulness of information must be evaluated in relation to the purposes to be served, and the objectives of financial reporting are focused on the use of accounting information in decision making.

The central role assigned to decision making leads straight to the overriding criterion by which all accounting choices must be judged. The better choice is the one that, subject to considerations of cost, produces from among the available alternatives information that is most useful for decision making.

Even objectives that are oriented more towards stewardship are concerned with decisions. Stewardship deals with the efficiency, effectiveness, and integrity of the steward. To say that stewardship reporting is an aspect of accounting's decision making role is simply to say that its purpose is to guide actions that may need to be taken in relation to the steward or in relation to the activity that is being monitored.

A Hierarchy of Accounting Qualities

The characteristics of information that make it a desirable commodity can be viewed as a hierarchy of qualities, with usefulness for decision making of most importance. Without usefulness, there would be no benefits from information to set against its costs.

User-Specific Factors

In the last analysis, each decision maker judges what accounting information is useful, and that judgment is influenced by factors such as the decisions to be made, the methods of decision making to be used, the information already possessed or obtainable from other sources, and the decision maker's capacity (alone or with professional help) to process the information. The optimal information for one user will not be optimal for another. Consequently, the Board, which must try to cater to many different users while considering the burdens placed on those who have to provide information, constantly treads a fine line between requiring disclosure of too much or too little information.

The hierarchy separates user-specific qualities, for example, understandability, from qualities inherent in information. Information cannot be useful to decision makers who cannot understand it, even though it may otherwise be relevant to a decision and be reliable. However, understandability of information is related to the characteristics of the decision maker as well as the characteristics of the information itself and, therefore, understandability cannot be evaluated in overall terms but must be judged in relation to a specific class of decision makers.

Primary Decision-Specific Qualities

Relevance and *reliability* are the two primary qualities that make accounting information useful for decision making. Subject to constraints imposed by cost and materiality, increased relevance and increased reliability are the characteristics that make information a more desirable commodity—that is, one useful in making decisions. If either of those qualities is completely missing, the information will not be useful. Though, ideally, the choice of an accounting alternative should produce information that is both more reliable and more relevant, it may be necessary to sacrifice some of one quality for a gain in another.

To be relevant, information must be timely and it must have predictive value *or* feedback value or both. To be reliable, information must have representational faithfulness and it must be verifiable and neutral. Comparability, which includes consistency, is a secondary quality that interacts with relevance and reliability to contribute to the usefulness of information. Two constraints are included in the hierarchy, both primarily quantitative in character. Information can be useful and yet be too costly to justify providing it. To be useful *and* worth providing, the benefits of information should exceed its cost. All of the qualities of information shown are subject to a materiality threshold, and that is also shown as a constraint.

Relevance

- Relevant accounting information is capable of making a difference in a decision by helping users to form predictions about the outcomes of past, present, and future events or to confirm or correct prior expectations. Information can make a difference to decisions by improving decision makers' capacities to predict or by providing feedback on earlier expectations. Usually, information does both at once, because knowledge about the outcomes of actions already taken will generally improve decision makers' abilities to predict the results of similar future actions. Without a knowledge of the past, the basis for a prediction will usually be lacking. Without an interest in the future, knowledge of the past is sterile.

- Timeliness, that is, having information available to decision makers before it loses its capacity to influence decisions, is an ancillary aspect of relevance. If information is not available when it is needed or becomes available so long after the reported events that it has no value for future action, it lacks relevance and is of little or no use. Timeliness alone cannot make information relevant, but a lack of timeliness can rob information of relevance it might otherwise have had.

Reliability

- The reliability of a measure rests on the faithfulness with which it represents what it purports to represent, coupled with an assurance for the user that it has that representational quality. To be useful, information must be reliable as well as relevant. Degrees of reliability must be recognized. It is hardly ever a question of black or white, but rather of more reliability or less. Reliability rests upon the extent to which the accounting description or measurement is verifiable and representationally faithful. Neutrality of information also interacts with those two components of reliability to affect the usefulness of the information.
- Verifiability is a quality that may be demonstrated by securing a high degree of consensus among independent measurers using the same measurement methods. Representational faithfulness, on the other hand, refers to the correspondence or agreement between the accounting numbers and the resources or events those numbers purport to represent. A high degree of correspondence, however, does not guarantee that an accounting measurement will be relevant to the user's needs if the resources or events represented by the measurement are inappropriate to the purpose at hand.
- Neutrality means that, in formulating or implementing standards, the primary concern should be the relevance and reliability of the information that results, not the effect that the new rule may have on a particular interest. A neutral choice between accounting alternatives is free from bias towards a predetermined result. The objectives of financial reporting serve many different information users who have diverse interests, and no one predetermined result is likely to suit all interests.

Comparability and Consistency

- Information about a particular enterprise gains greatly in usefulness if it can be compared with similar information about other enterprises and with similar information about the same enterprise for some other period or some other point in time. Comparability between enterprises and consistency in the application of methods over time increases the informational value of comparisons of relative economic opportunities or performance. The significance of information, especially quantitative information, depends to a great extent on the user's ability to relate it to some benchmark.

Materiality

- Materiality is a pervasive concept that relates to the qualitative characteristics, especially relevance and reliability. Materiality and relevance are both defined in terms of what influences or makes a difference to a decision maker, but the two terms can be distinguished. A decision not to disclose certain information may be made, say, because investors have no need for that kind of information (it is not relevant) or because the amounts involved are too small to make a difference (they are not material). Magnitude by itself, without regard to the nature of the item and the circumstances in which the judgment has to be made, will not generally be a sufficient basis for a materiality judgment. The Board's present position is that no general standards of materiality can be formulated to take into account all the considerations that enter into an experienced human judgment. Quantitative materiality criteria may be given by the Board in specific standards in the future, as in the past, as appropriate.

Costs and Benefits

- Each user of accounting information will uniquely perceive the relative value to be attached to each quality of that information. Ultimately, a standard-setting body has to do its best to meet the needs of society as a whole when it promulgates a standard that sacrifices one of those qualities for another; and it must also be aware constantly of the calculus of costs and benefits. In order to justify requiring a particular disclosure, the perceived benefits to be derived from that disclosure must exceed the perceived costs associated with it. However, to say anything precise about their incidence is difficult. There are costs of using information as well as of providing it; and the benefits from providing financial information accrue to preparers as well as users of that information.
- Though it is unlikely that significantly improved means of measuring benefits will become available in the foreseeable future, it seems possible that better ways of quantifying the incremental costs of regulations of all kinds may gradually be developed, and the Board will watch any such developments carefully to see whether they can be applied to financial accounting standards. The Board cannot cease to be concerned about the cost-effectiveness of its standards. To do so would be a dereliction of its duty and a disservice to its constituents.

Statement of Financial Accounting Concepts No. 2
Qualitative Characteristics of Accounting Information

STATEMENTS OF FINANCIAL ACCOUNTING CONCEPTS

This Statement of Financial Accounting Concepts is one of a series of publications in the Board's conceptual framework for financial accounting and reporting. Statements in the series are intended to set forth objectives and fundamentals that will be the basis for development of financial accounting and reporting standards. The objectives identify the goals and purposes of financial reporting. The fundamentals are the underlying concepts of financial accounting—concepts that guide the selection of transactions, events, and circumstances to be accounted for, their recognition and measurement, and the means of summarizing and communicating them to interested parties. Concepts of that type are fundamental in the sense that other concepts flow from them and repeated reference to them will be necessary in establishing, interpreting, and applying accounting and reporting standards.

The conceptual framework is a coherent system of interrelated objectives and fundamentals that is expected to lead to consistent standards and that prescribes the nature, function, and limits of financial accounting and reporting. It is expected to serve the public interest by providing structure and direction to financial accounting and reporting to facilitate the provision of evenhanded financial and related information that is useful in assisting capital and other markets to function efficiently in allocating scarce resources in the economy.

Establishment of objectives and identification of fundamental concepts will not directly solve financial accounting and reporting problems. Rather, objectives give direction, and concepts are tools for solving problems.

The Board itself is likely to be the most direct beneficiary of the guidance provided by the Statements in this series. They will guide the Board in developing accounting and reporting standards by providing the Board with a common foundation and basic reasoning on which to consider merits of alternatives.

However, knowledge of the objectives and concepts the Board will use in developing standards should also enable those who are affected by or interested in financial accounting standards to understand better the purposes, content, and characteristics of information provided by financial accounting and reporting. That knowledge is expected to enhance the usefulness of, and confidence in, financial accounting and reporting. Careful use of the concepts may also provide guidance in resolving new or emerging problems of financial accounting and reporting in the absence of applicable authoritative pronouncements.

Statements of Financial Accounting Concepts do not establish standards prescribing accounting procedures or disclosure practices for particular items or events, which are issued by the Board as Statements of Financial Accounting Standards. Rather, Statements in this series describe concepts and relations that will underlie future financial accounting standards and practices and in due course serve as a basis for evaluating existing standards and practices.*

The Board recognizes that in certain respects current generally accepted accounting principles may be inconsistent with those that may derive from the objectives and concepts set forth in Statements in this series. However, a Statement of Financial Accounting Concepts does not (a) require a change in existing generally accepted accounting principles, (b) amend, modify, or interpret Statements of Financial Accounting Standards, Interpretations of the FASB, Opinions of the Accounting Principles Board, or Bulletins of the Committee on Accounting Procedure that are in effect, or (c) justify either changing existing generally accepted accounting and reporting practices or interpreting the pronouncements listed in item (b) based on personal interpretations of the objectives and concepts in the Statements of Financial Accounting Concepts.

Since a Statement of Financial Accounting Concepts does not establish generally accepted accounting principles or standards for the disclosure of financial information outside of financial statements in published financial reports, it is not intended to invoke application of Rule 203 or 204 of the Rules of Conduct of the Code of Professional Ethics of the American Institute of Certified Public Accountants (or successor rules or arrangements of similar scope and intent).†

Like other pronouncements of the Board, a Statement of Financial Accounting Concepts may be amended, superseded, or withdrawn by appropriate action under the Board's *Rules of Procedure.*

FASB PUBLICATIONS ON CONCEPTUAL FRAMEWORK

Statements of Financial Accounting Concepts

No. 1, *Objectives of Financial Reporting by Business Enterprises* (November 1978)

Exposure Drafts Being (or Yet to Be) Considered by the Board

Elements of Financial Statements of Business Enterprises (December 28, 1979)

Objectives of Financial Reporting by Nonbusiness Organizations (March 14, 1980)

---

*Pronouncements such as APB Statement No. 4, *Basic Concepts and Accounting Principles Underlying Financial Statements of Business Enterprises,* and the Accounting Terminology Bulletins will continue to serve their intended purpose—they describe objectives and concepts underlying standards and practices existing at the time of their issuance.

†Rule 203 prohibits a member of the American Institute of Certified Public Accountants from expressing an opinion that financial statements conform with generally accepted accounting principles if those statements contain a material departure from an accounting principle promulgated by the Financial Accounting Standards Board, unless the member can demonstrate that because of unusual circumstances the financial statements otherwise would have been misleading. Rule 204 requires members of the Institute to justify departures from standards promulgated by the Financial Accounting Standards Board for the disclosure of information outside of financial statements in published financial reports.

Discussion Memorandums and Invitations to Comment Having Issues Being Considered by the Board

Reporting Earnings (July 31, 1979)

Financial Statements and Other Means of Financial Reporting (May 12, 1980)

Other Projects in Process

Accounting Recognition Criteria
Funds Flows and Liquidity

CONTENTS

	Paragraph Numbers
Summary of Principal Conclusions	
Glossary of Terms	
Introduction	1— 26
The Nature of Accounting Choices	6— 20
The Objectives of Financial Reporting	21— 26
The Central Role of Decision Making	27— 31
A Hierarchy of Accounting Qualities	32— 45
Features and Limitations of the Chart	33— 35
Decision Makers and Their Characteristics	36— 39
Understandability and Other User-Specific Qualities	40— 41
Relative Importance and Trade-Offs	42— 45
Relevance	46— 57
Feedback Value and Predictive Value as Components of Relevance	51— 55
Timeliness	56— 57
Reliability	58— 97
Representational Faithfulness	63— 80
Degrees of Representational Faithfulness	65— 71
Precision and Uncertainty	72— 76
Effects of Bias	77— 78
Completeness	79— 80
Verifiability	81— 89
Reliability and Relevance	90
Conservatism	91— 97
Neutrality	98—110
Comparability	111—122
Consistency	120—122
Materiality	123—132
Costs and Benefits	133—144
Appendix A: Background Information	145—151
Appendix B: Principal Respects in Which This Statement Differs From the Exposure Draft and Other Responses to Letters of Comment on the Exposure Draft	152—160
Appendix C: Quantitative Materiality Considerations	161—170

GLOSSARY OF TERMS

Bias

Bias in measurement is the tendency of a measure to fall more often on one side than the other of what it represents instead of being equally likely to fall on either side. Bias in accounting measures means a tendency to be consistently too high or too low.

Comparability

The quality of information that enables users to identify similarities in and differences between two sets of economic phenomena.

Completeness

The inclusion in reported information of everything material that is necessary for faithful representation of the relevant phenomena.

Conservatism

A prudent reaction to uncertainty to try to ensure that uncertainty and risks inherent in business situations are adequately considered.

Consistency

Conformity from period to period with unchanging policies and procedures.

Feedback Value

The quality of information that enables users to confirm or correct prior expectations.

Materiality

The magnitude of an omission or misstatement of accounting information that, in the light of surrounding circumstances, makes it probable that the judgment of a reasonable person relying on the information would have been changed or influenced by the omission or misstatement.

Neutrality

Absence in reported information of bias intended to attain a predetermined result or to induce a particular mode of behavior.

Predictive Value

The quality of information that helps users to increase the likelihood of correctly forecasting the outcome of past or present events.

Relevance

The capacity of information to make a difference in a decision by helping users to form predictions about the outcomes of past, present, and future events or to confirm or correct prior expectations.

Reliability

The quality of information that assures that information is reasonably free from error and bias and faithfully represents what it purports to represent.

Representational Faithfulness

Correspondence or agreement between a measure or description and the phenomenon that it purports to represent (sometimes called validity).

Timeliness

Having information available to a decision maker before it loses its capacity to influence decisions.

Understandability

The quality of information that enables users to perceive its significance.

Verifiability

The ability through consensus among measurers to ensure that information represents what it purports to represent or that the chosen method of measurement has been used without error or bias.

INTRODUCTION

1. The purpose of this Statement is to examine the characteristics of accounting information[1] that make that information useful. This Statement is one of a planned series of publications in the Board's conceptual framework project. It should be seen as a bridge between FASB Concepts Statement No. 1, *Objectives of Financial Reporting By Business Enterprises,* and other Statements to be issued covering the elements of financial statements and their recognition, measurement, and display. The Statement on objectives was concerned with the *purposes* of financial reporting. Later Statements will be concerned with questions about *how* those purposes are to be attained; and the standards that the Board has issued and will issue from time to time are also intended to attain those purposes. The Board believes that, in between the "why" of objectives and the "how" of other Statements and standards, it is helpful to share with its constituents its thinking about the characteristics that the information called for in its standards should have. It is those characteristics that distinguish more useful accounting information from less useful information.

2. Although those characteristics are expected to be stable, they are not immutable. They are affected by the economic, legal, political, and social environment in which financial reporting takes place and they may also change as new insights and new research results are obtained. Indeed, they ought to change if new knowledge shows present judgments to be outdated. If and when that happens, revised concepts Statements will need to be issued.

[1]"Accounting information," "information provided by financial reporting," and variations on those descriptions are used interchangeably in this Statement.

3. Although conventionally referred to as qualitative characteristics, some of the more important of the characteristics of accounting information that make it useful, or whose absence limit its usefulness, turn out on closer inspection to be quantitative in nature (for example, costliness) or to be partly qualitative and partly quantitative (for example, reliability and timeliness). While it will sometimes be important to keep those distinctions in mind, it will usually be convenient, and not misleading, to refer to all of the characteristics of information discussed in this Statement as "qualities" of information.

4. Although the discussion of the qualities of information and the related examples in this Statement refer primarily to business enterprises, the Board has tentatively concluded that similar qualities also apply to financial information reported by nonbusiness organizations. The Board intends to solicit views regarding its tentative conclusion.[2]

5. To maximize the usefulness of accounting information, subject to considerations of the cost of providing it, entails choices between alternative accounting methods. Those choices will be made more wisely if the ingredients that contribute to "usefulness" are better understood. The characteristics or qualities of information discussed in this Statement are, indeed, the ingredients that make information useful. They are, therefore, the qualities to be sought when accounting choices are made. They are as near as one can come to a set of criteria for making those choices.

The Nature of Accounting Choices

6. Accounting choices are made at two levels at least. At one level they are made by the Board or other agencies that have the power to require business enterprises to report in some particular way or, if exercised negatively, to prohibit a method that those agencies consider undesirable. An example of such a choice, made many years ago but still accepted as authoritative, is the pronouncement by the Committee on Accounting Procedure of the American Institute of Certified Public Accountants

[2]The Board's consideration of aspects of the conceptual framework that pertain to nonbusiness organizations began later than its consideration of aspects that pertain to business enterprises. To date, the Board has sponsored and published a research study on the objectives and basic concepts underlying financial reporting by organizations other than business enterprises: FASB Research Report, *Financial Accounting in Nonbusiness Organizations,* by Robert N. Anthony; issued a Discussion Memorandum, *Conceptual Framework for Financial Accounting and Reporting: Objectives of Financial Reporting by Nonbusiness Organizations;* held public hearings on the Discussion Memorandum; and issued an Exposure Draft, *Objectives of Financial Reporting by Nonbusiness Organizations.* At its May 7, 1980 meeting, the Board authorized the staff to proceed with the consideration of concepts and standards issues relating to nonbusiness organizations that are beyond the scope of the existing nonbusiness objectives project.

Editor's Note: Paragraph 4 and footnote 2 have been superseded by Concepts Statement 6, *Elements of Financial Statements.*

that ". . . the exclusion of all overheads from inventory costs does not constitute an accepted accounting procedure"[3] for general purpose external financial reporting.

7. Accounting choices are also made at the level of the individual enterprise. As more accounting standards are issued, the scope for individual choice inevitably becomes circumscribed. But there are now and will always be many accounting decisions to be made by reporting enterprises involving a choice between alternatives for which no standard has been promulgated or a choice between ways of implementing a standard.

8. Those who are unfamiliar with the nature of accounting are often surprised at the large number of choices that accountants are required to make. Yet choices arise at every turn. Decisions must first be made about the nature and definition of assets and liabilities, revenues and expenses, and the criteria by which they are to be recognized. Then a choice must be made of the attribute of assets to be measured—historical cost, current cost, current exit value, net realizable value, or present value of expected cash flows. If costs have to be allocated, either among time periods (for example, to compute depreciation) or among service beneficiaries (for example, industry segments), methods of allocation must be chosen. Further, choices must be made concerning the level of aggregation or disaggregation of the information to be disclosed in financial reports. Should a particular subsidiary company be consolidated or should its financial statements be presented separately? How many reportable segments should a company recognize? Choices involving aggregation arise at every point. Still other choices concern the selection of the terminal date of an enterprise's financial year, the form of descriptive captions to be used in its financial statements, the selection of matters to be commented on in notes or in supplementary information, and the wording to be used.

9. That list of choices, which is by no means comprehensive, illustrates some of the more important choices that arise in financial reporting. References throughout this Statement to alternative accounting policies, methods, or choices refer to the kinds of alternatives illustrated above.

10. If alternative accounting methods could be given points for each ingredient of usefulness in a particular situation, it would be an easy matter to add up each method's points and select the one (subject to its cost) that scored highest—so long, of course, as there were general agreement on the scoring system and how points were to be awarded. There are some who seem to harbor the hope that somewhere waiting to be discovered there is a comprehensive scoring system that can provide the universal criterion for making accounting choices. Unfortunately, neither the Board nor anyone else has such a system at the present time, and there is little probability that one will be forthcoming in the foreseeable future. Consequently, those who must choose among alternatives are forced to fall back on human judgment to evalu-

[3] Accounting Research Bulletin No. 43, *Restatement and Revision of Accounting Research Bulletins,* Chapter 4, par. 5.

ate the relative merits of competing methods. If it were not so, there would be no need for a standard-setting authority; for by means of the comprehensive scoring system, agreement on the "best" methods would easily be secured.

11. That does not mean that nothing can be done to aid human judgment. By identifying and defining the qualities that make accounting information useful, this Statement develops a number of generalizations or guidelines for making accounting choices that are intended to be useful to the Board, to its staff, to preparers of financial statements, and to all others interested in financial reporting. For the Board and its staff, the qualities of useful accounting information should provide guidance in developing accounting standards that will be consistent with the objectives of financial reporting. This Statement also provides a terminology that should promote consistency in standard setting. For preparers of financial information, the qualities of useful accounting information should provide guidance in choosing between alternative ways of representing economic events, especially in dealing with situations not yet clearly covered by standards. This Statement also should be useful to those who use information provided by financial reporting. For them, its main value will be in increasing their understanding of both the usefulness and the limitations of the financial information that is provided by business enterprises and other organizations, either directly by financial reporting or indirectly through the commentaries of financial analysts and others. That increased understanding should be conducive to better-informed decisions.

12. The need for improved communication, especially between the Board and its constituents, provides much of the rationale for the whole conceptual framework project and particularly for this Statement. Indeed, improved communication may be the principal benefit to be gained from it. It is important that the concepts used by the Board in reaching its conclusions be understood by those who must apply its standards and those who use the results, for without understanding, standards become mere arbitrary edicts. Communication will also be facilitated if there is widespread use of a common terminology and a common set of definitions. The terminology used in this Statement is already widely, though not universally, used and its general adoption could help to eliminate many misunderstandings. The definitions of the principal terms used have been brought together in the glossary on pages 33 and 34.

13. It should perhaps be emphasized here that this Statement is not a standard. Its purpose is not to make rules but to provide part of the conceptual base on which rule making can stand. Unless that distinction is understood, this Statement may be invested with more authority than a discussion of concepts has a right to carry.

14. Whether at the level of the Board or the individual preparer, the primary criterion of choice between two alternative accounting methods involves asking which method produces the better—that is, the more useful—information. If that question can be answered with reasonable assurance, it is then necessary to ask whether the value of the better information sufficiently exceeds that of the inferior information

to justify its extra cost, if any. If a satisfactory answer can again be given, the choice between the alternative methods is clear.

15. The qualities that distinguish "better" (more useful) information from "inferior" (less useful) information are primarily the qualities of relevance and reliability, with some other characteristics that those qualities imply. Subject to considerations of cost, the objective of accounting policy decisions is to produce accounting information that is relevant to the purposes to be served and is reliable. The meaning of those terms, the recognition that there are gradations of relevance and reliability, and the problems that arise if trade-offs between them are necessary all are matters discussed in later paragraphs of this Statement.

16. Accounting choices made by the Board and those made by individual statement preparers have this in common: they both aim to produce information that satisfies those criteria. Yet, though the objectives of the Board and of individual preparers are alike in that respect, the Board does not expect all its policy decisions to accord exactly with the preferences of every one of its constituents. Indeed, they clearly cannot do so, for the preferences of its constituents do not accord with each other. Left to themselves, business enterprises, even in the same industry, would probably choose to adopt different reporting methods for similar circumstances. But in return for the sacrifice of some of that freedom, there is a gain from the greater comparability and consistency that adherence to externally imposed standards brings with it. There also is a gain in credibility. The public is naturally skeptical about the reliability of financial reporting if two enterprises account differently for the same economic phenomena.

17. Throughout this Statement, readers should keep in mind the objectives of the Board in issuing accounting standards of widespread applicability and those of individual preparers who are concerned with the informational needs of a particular enterprise. Though the criteria by which information should be judged are the same whether the judgment is made by the Board or by a preparer, they cannot be expected always to produce agreement on a preferred choice of accounting method. The best accounting policies will provide information that best achieves the objectives of financial reporting. But whatever information is provided, it cannot be expected to be equally useful to all preparers and users, for the simple reason that individual needs and objectives vary. The Board strives to serve the needs of all, knowing that in doing so some individual preferences are sacrificed. Like motorists who observe traffic laws in the interest of their own and general traffic safety, so long as others do the same, in general, those who have to subordinate their individual preferences to observe common accounting standards will, in the long run, gain more than they lose.

18. The analogy between accounting standards and traffic laws merits closer examination. Traffic laws impose certain minima or maxima in regulating behavior but still permit considerable flexibility in driving habits. A speed limit leaves slow drivers to choose their speed below the maximum and does not prohibit passing by

other drivers. Even a requirement to drive on the right allows a driver to choose and to change lanes on all but very narrow roads. The point is that in most respects the traffic laws allow for considerable variations within a framework of rules. In setting accounting standards, the Board also strives to leave as much room as possible for individual choices and preferences while securing the degree of conformity necessary to attain its objectives.

19. This Statement must be seen as part of the larger conceptual framework, an important part of the foundations of which were laid with the publication of Concepts Statement 1. This Statement, with the proposed Statement on the elements of financial statements of business enterprises, is part of the second stage of the structure. With successive stages, the level of abstraction will give way to increasing specificity. The qualitative characteristics discussed in this document are formulated in rather general terms. As they are brought to bear on particular situations in subsequent pronouncements, however, those generalizations will give way to specific applications.

20. While this Statement concentrates on guidelines for making accounting choices, either by the Board or by those who provide financial information, its function is not to make those choices. Insofar as those choices lie within the Board's responsibility, some of them (for example, those relating to the attributes of assets and liabilities that should be measured and presented in financial statements) will be made in other parts of the conceptual framework project. Other choices will be made in the standards to be issued by the Board from time to time. The qualitative characteristics put forward in this Statement are intended to facilitate those choices and to aid in making them consistent with one another.

The Objectives of Financial Reporting

21. The objectives of financial reporting underlie judgments about the qualities of financial information, for only when those objectives have been established can a start be made on defining the characteristics of the information needed to attain them. In Concepts Statement 1, the Board set out the objectives of financial reporting for business enterprises that will guide it. The information covered by that Statement was not limited to the contents of financial statements. "Financial reporting," the Statement said, "includes not only financial statements but also other means of communicating information that relates, directly or indirectly, to the information provided by the accounting system—that is, information about an enterprise's resources, obligations, earnings, etc. [paragraph 7]."

22. The objectives of financial reporting are summarized in the following excerpts from the Statement:

> Financial reporting should provide information that is useful to present and potential investors and creditors and other users in making

rational investment, credit, and similar decisions. The information should be comprehensible to those who have a reasonable understanding of business and economic activities and are willing to study the information with reasonable diligence [paragraph 34].

Financial reporting should provide information to help present and potential investors and creditors and other users in assessing the amounts, timing, and uncertainty of prospective cash receipts from dividends or interest and the proceeds from the sale, redemption, or maturity of securities or loans. The prospects for those cash receipts are affected by an enterprise's ability to generate enough cash to meet its obligations when due and its other cash operating needs, to reinvest in operations, and to pay cash dividends and may also be affected by perceptions of investors and creditors generally about that ability, which affect market prices of the enterprise's securities. Thus, financial reporting should provide information to help investors, creditors, and others assess the amounts, timing, and uncertainty of prospective net cash inflows to the related enterprise [paragraph 37].

Financial reporting should provide information about the economic resources of an enterprise, the claims to those resources (obligations of the enterprise to transfer resources to other entities and owners' equity), and the effects of transactions, events, and circumstances that change resources and claims to those resources [paragraph 40].

Financial reporting should provide information about an enterprise's financial performance during a period. Investors and creditors often use information about the past to help in assessing the prospects of an enterprise. Thus, although investment and credit decisions reflect investors' and creditors' expectations about future enterprise performance, those expectations are commonly based at least partly on evaluations of past enterprise performance [paragraph 42].

The primary focus of financial reporting is information about an enterprise's performance provided by measures of earnings and its components [paragraph 43].

Financial reporting should provide information about how an enterprise obtains and spends cash, about its borrowing and repayment of borrowing, about its capital transactions, including cash dividends and other distributions of enterprise resources to owners, and about other factors that may affect an enterprise's liquidity or solvency [paragraph 49].

Financial reporting should provide information about how management of an enterprise has discharged its stewardship responsibility to owners (stockholders) for the use of enterprise resources entrusted to it [paragraph 50].

Financial reporting should provide information that is useful to managers and directors in making decisions in the interests of owners [paragraph 52].

23. The Statement on objectives makes clear (paragraph 31) that *financial reporting* means *general purpose external financial reporting by business enterprises.* General purpose financial reporting attempts to meet "the informational needs of external users who lack the authority to prescribe the financial information they want from an enterprise and therefore must use the information that management communicates to them" (paragraph 28). General purpose statements are not all purpose statements, and never can be.

24. An analogy with cartography has been used to convey some of the characteristics of financial reporting, and it may be useful here. A map represents the geographical features of the mapped area by using symbols bearing no resemblance to the actual countryside, yet they communicate a great deal of information about it. The captions and numbers in financial statements present a "picture" of a business enterprise and many of its external and internal relationships more rigorously—more informatively, in fact—than a simple description of it. There are, admittedly, important differences between geography and economic activity and, therefore, between maps and financial statements. But the similarities may, nevertheless, be illuminating.

25. A "general purpose" map that tried to be "all purpose" would be unintelligible, once information about political boundaries, communications, physical features, geological structure, climate, economic activity, ethnic groupings, and all the other things that mapmakers can map were put on it. Even on a so-called general purpose map, therefore, the cartographer has to select the data to be presented. The cartographer, in fact, has to decide to serve some purposes and neglect others. The fact is that all maps are really special purpose maps, but some are more specialized than others. And so are financial statements. Some of the criticisms of financial statements derive from a failure to understand that even a general purpose statement can be relevant to and can, therefore, serve only a limited number of its users' needs.

26. The objectives focus financial reporting on a particular kind of economic decision—committing (or continuing to commit) cash or other resources to a business enterprise with expectation of future compensation or return, usually in cash but sometimes in other goods or services. Suppliers, lenders, employees, owners, and, to a lesser extent, customers commonly make decisions of that kind, and managers continually make them about an enterprise's resources. Concepts Statement 1 uses investment and credit decisions as prototypes of the kind of decisions on which financial reporting focuses. Nevertheless, as just noted, the Board, in developing the qualities in this Statement, must be concerned with groups of users of financial information who have generally similar needs. Those qualities do not necessarily fit all users' needs equally well.

THE CENTRAL ROLE OF DECISION MAKING

27. All financial reporting is concerned in varying degrees with decision making

(though decision makers also use information obtained from other sources). The need for information on which to base investment, credit, and similar decisions underlies the objectives of financial reporting cited earlier.

28. Even objectives that are oriented more towards stewardship are concerned with decisions. The broader stewardship use of accounting, which is concerned with the efficiency, effectiveness, and integrity of the steward, helps stockholders or other financially interested parties (for example, bondholders) to evaluate the management of an enterprise. But that would be a pointless activity if there were no possibility of taking action based on the results. Management is accountable to stockholders through an elected board of directors, but stockholders are often passive and do not insist on major management changes as long as an enterprise is reasonably successful. Their appraisals of management's stewardship help them to assess prospects for their investments, and stockholders who are dissatisfied with management's stewardship of those investments commonly sell their stock in the enterprise. Bondholders are concerned with management's compliance with bond indentures and may take legal action if covenants are broken. Thus, decision making and stewardship are interrelated accounting objectives. Indeed, the stewardship role of accounting may be viewed as subordinate to and a part of the decision making role, which is virtually all encompassing.

29. That view of the stewardship use of accounting in no way diminishes its importance, nor does it elevate the predictive value of accounting information above its confirmatory value. In its stewardship use, accounting compiles records of past transactions and events and uses those records to measure performance. The measurement confirms expectations or shows how far actual achievements diverged from them. The confirmation or divergence becomes the basis for a decision—which will often be a decision to leave things alone. To say that stewardship reporting is an aspect of accounting's decision making role is simply to say that its purpose is to guide actions that *may* need to be taken in relation to the steward or in relation to the activity that is being monitored.

30. The central role assigned here to decision making leads straight to the overriding criterion by which all accounting choices must be judged. The better choice is the one that, subject to considerations of cost, produces from among the available alternatives information that is most useful for decision making.[4]

31. So broad a generalization looks self-evident. Indeed, it says no more than the Board said in Concepts Statement 1 (paragraph 9): "Financial reporting is not an end in itself but is intended to provide information that is useful in making business and economic decisions. . . ." The challenge is to define in more detail what makes accounting information useful for decision making. If there is a serious difference of opinion, it is not over the general nature of characteristics such as relevance and

[4]The divergence among individual needs was noted in paragraph 17. It needs to be considered here and throughout this Statement.

reliability, which clearly occupy important places in the hierarchy of qualities that make information useful. There may indeed be some disagreement about their relative importance. But more serious disagreement arises over the choice between two accounting methods (for example, methods of allocating costs or recognizing revenues) if the choice involves a judgment about which method will produce more relevant or more reliable results or a judgment about whether the superior relevance of the results of one method outweighs the superior reliability of the results of the other.

A HIERARCHY OF ACCOUNTING QUALITIES

32. The characteristics of information that make it a desirable commodity guide the selection of preferred accounting policies from among available alternatives. They can be viewed as a hierachy of qualities, with usefulness for decision making of most importance. Without usefulness, there would be no benefits from information to set against its costs. The hierarchy is represented in Figure 1.

Features and Limitations of the Chart

33. Before discussing the informational characteristics shown on the chart, some words of explanation are offered about what the chart attempts to convey. It is a limited device—limited, for example, by being in two dimensions only—for showing certain relationships among the qualities that make accounting information useful. The primary qualities are that accounting information shall be relevant and reliable. If either of those qualities is completely missing, the information will not be useful. Relevance and reliability can be further analyzed into a number of components. To be relevant, information must be timely and it must have predictive value *or* feedback value or both. To be reliable, information must have representational faithfulness and it must be verifiable and neutral (the meaning of these terms, like all the other terms used in the chart, will be discussed later). Comparability, including consistency, is a secondary quality that interacts with relevance and reliability to contribute to the usefulness of information. Finally, two constraints are shown on the chart, both primarily quantitative rather than qualitative in character. Information can be useful and yet be too costly to justify providing it. To be useful and worth providing, the benefits of information should exceed its cost. All of the qualities shown are subject to a materiality threshold, and that is also shown as a constraint. The requirement that information be reliable can still be met even though it may contain immaterial errors, for errors that are not material will not perceptibly diminish its usefulness. Similar considerations apply to the other characteristics of information shown on the chart.

34. An important limitation of the hierarchy is that while it does distinguish between primary and other qualities, it does not assign priorities among qualities. That limitation is a salutary one, however, for the relative weight to be given to different qualities must vary according to circumstances. The hierarchy should be seen as no more than an explanatory device, the purpose of which is to clarify certain relationships

FIGURE 1

A HIERARCHY OF ACCOUNTING QUALITIES

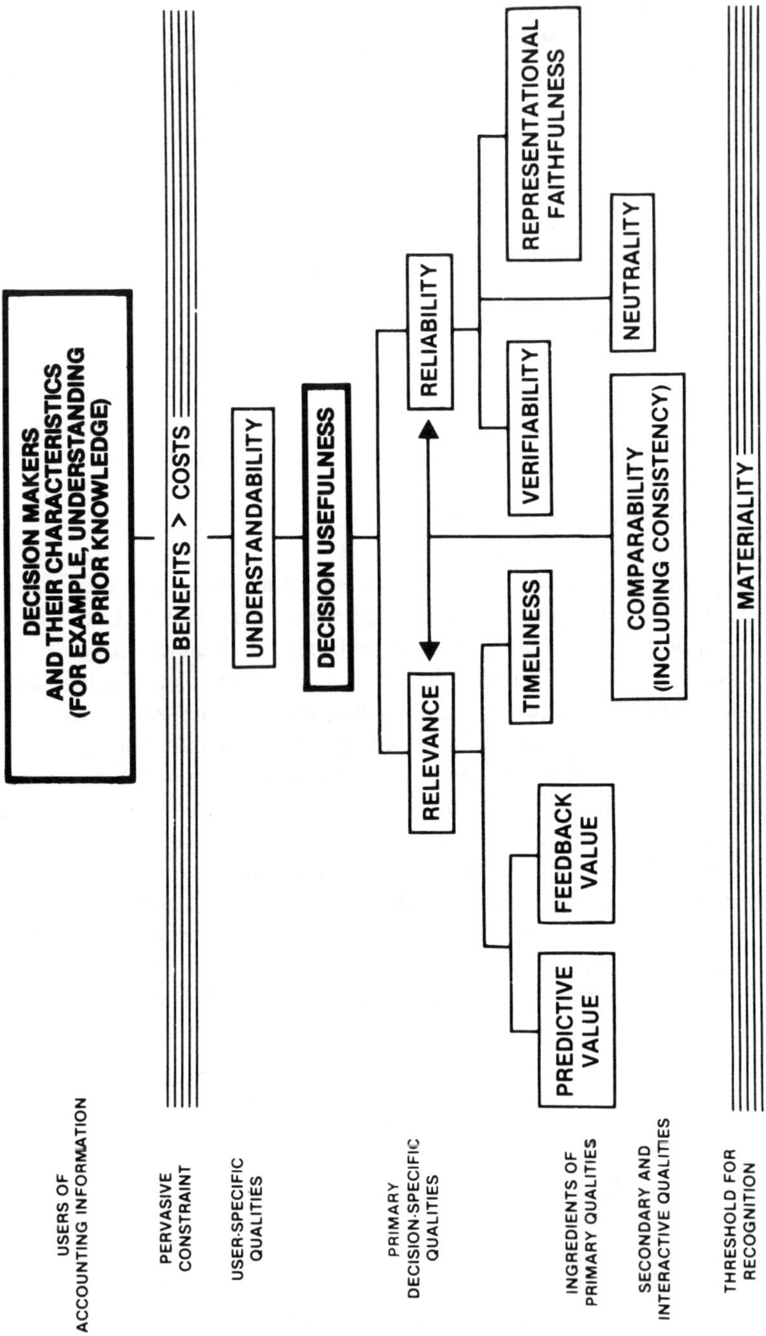

rather than to assign relative weights. To be useful, financial information must have each of the qualities shown to a minimum degree. Beyond that, the rate at which one quality can be sacrificed in return for a gain in another quality without making the information less useful overall will be different in different situations.

35. Several characteristics that some would wish to see included in the hierarchy are not shown there. Rather than confuse a discussion of its positive features by explaining at this point why certain items have been excluded, discussion of that matter has been placed in Appendix B with other responses to comment letters that have been received by the Board.

Decision Makers and Their Characteristics

36. In the last analysis, each decision maker judges what accounting information is useful, and that judgment is influenced by factors such as the decisions to be made, the methods of decision making to be used, the information already possessed or obtainable from other sources, and the decision maker's capacity (alone or with professional help) to process the information. The optimal information for one user will not be optimal for another. Consequently, the Board, which must try to cater to many different users while considering the burdens placed on those who have to provide information, constantly treads a fine line between requiring disclosure of too much information and requiring too little.

37. The better informed decision makers are, the less likely it is that any new information can add materially to what they already know. That may make the new information less useful, but it does not make it less relevant to the situation. If an item of information reaches a user and then, a little later, the user receives the same item from another source, it is not less relevant the second time, though it will have less value. For that reason, relevance has been defined in this Statement (paragraphs 46 and 47) in terms of the capacity of information to make a difference (to someone who does not already have it) rather than in terms of the difference it actually does make. The difference it actually does make may be more a function of how much is already known (a condition specific to a particular user) than of the content of the new messages themselves (decision-specific qualities of information).

38. Thus, management in general and owners of small or closely held enterprises may find at least some information provided by external financial reporting to be less useful to them than it is to stockholders of large or publicly held enterprises. The latter must rely on financial reporting for information that the former has access to as a result of their intimate relationship to their enterprise.

39. Similarly, information cannot be useful to a person who cannot understand it. However, information may be relevant to a situation even though it cannot be understood by the person who confronts the situation. Its relevance will depend on its capacity to reduce uncertainty about the situation, even though it may call for more understanding to interpret it than its prospective user can command. For example, a

hungry vegetarian traveling in a foreign country may experience difficulty in obtaining acceptable food when ordering from a menu printed in an unfamiliar language. The listing of items on the menu is relevant to the decision to be made but the traveler cannot use that information unless it is translated into another (understandable) language. Thus, the information may not be useful to a particular user even though it is relevant to the situation that the user faces. Information that cannot be understood, like information that is not available, may be relevant, but its relevance will be wasted because its capacity to make a difference cannot be utilized.

Understandability and Other User-Specific Qualities

40. The Board said in Concepts Statement 1 (paragraph 34) that information provided by financial reporting should be comprehensible to those who have a reasonable understanding of business and economic activities and are willing to study the information with reasonable diligence. The Board elaborated as follows:

> Financial information is a tool and, like most tools, cannot be of much direct help to those who are unable or unwilling to use it or who misuse it. Its use can be learned, however, and financial reporting should provide information that can be used by all—nonprofessionals as well as professionals—who are willing to learn to use it properly. Efforts may be needed to increase the understandability of financial information. Cost-benefit considerations may indicate that information understood or used by only a few should not be provided. Conversely, financial reporting should not exclude relevant information merely because it is difficult for some to understand or because some investors or creditors choose not to use it [paragraph 36].

The benefits of information may be increased by making it more understandable and, hence, useful to a wider circle of users. Understandability of information is governed by a combination of user characteristics and characteristics inherent in the information, which is why understandability and other user-specific characteristics occupy a position in the hierarchy of qualities as a link between the characteristics of users (decision makers) and decision-specific qualities of information. Other parts of the conceptual framework project that will deal with displays of financial information will have a contribution to make to this matter.

41. Understandability and similar qualities of information, for example, newness, are closely related to the characteristics of *particular* decision makers as well as *classes* of decision makers. However, the Board is concerned with qualities of information that relate to broad classes of decision makers rather than to particular decision makers. Understandability can be classified as relating to particular decision makers (does the decision maker speak that language?) or relating to classes of decision makers (is the disclosure intelligible to the audience for which it is intended?). Newness of information can be classified similarly to understandability. The Board can influence the newness of information to broad classes of decision makers, for

example, by requiring the disclosure of relevant information that was not previously available. However, the newness to a particular decision maker of generally available information depends largely on the timing of the receipt of that information by the decision maker, and that timing is subject to the effects of many variables extraneous to accounting and financial reporting. The Board establishes concepts and standards for general purpose external financial reporting by considering the needs of broad classes of decision makers and cannot base its decisions on the specific circumstances of individual decision makers.

Relative Importance and Trade-Offs

42. Although financial information must be both relevant and reliable to be useful, information may possess both characteristics to varying degrees. It may be possible to trade relevance for reliability or vice versa, though not to the point of dispensing with one of them altogether. Information may also have other characteristics shown on the chart to varying degrees, and other trade-offs between characteristics may be necessary or beneficial.

43. The question has been raised whether the relative importance to be attached to relevance and reliability should be different in financial statements and in other means of financial reporting. The issuance in September 1979 of FASB Statement No. 33, *Financial Reporting and Changing Prices,* calling for reporting by certain enterprises of supplementary information on both constant dollar and current cost bases outside of the primary financial statements, has brought into prominence the question of whether information reported outside financial statements should be allowed to be less reliable than what is reported in them.

44. Although there seems to be considerable support for the view that reliability should be the dominant quality in the information conveyed in financial statements, even at the expense of relevance, while the opposite is true of information conveyed outside the financial statements, that view has in it the seeds of danger. Like most potentially harmful generalizations, it does contain a germ of truth: almost everyone agrees that criteria for formally recognizing elements in financial statements call for a minimum level or threshold of reliability of measurement that should be higher than is usually considered necessary for disclosing information outside financial statements. But the remainder of the proposition does not follow. If it were carried to its logical conclusion and resulted in a downgrading of relevance of information in financial statements, the end would be that most really useful information provided by financial reporting would be conveyed outside the financial statements, while the audited financial statements would increasingly convey highly reliable but largely irrelevant, and thus useless, information. Those matters are germane to another part of the conceptual framework, the project on financial statements and other means of financial reporting.

45. This Statement discusses trade-offs between characteristics at several points. Those discussions apply generally to kinds of decisions and to groups of users of

accounting information but do not necessarily apply to individual users. In a particular situation, the importance attached to relevance in relation to the importance of other decision specific qualities of accounting information (for example, reliability) will be different for different information users, and their willingness to trade one quality for another will also differ. The same thing is true of other considerations such as timeliness. That fact has an important bearing on the question of preferability, for it probably puts unanimity about preferences among accounting alternatives out of reach. Even though considerable agreement exists about the qualitative characteristics that "good" accounting information should have, no consensus can be expected about their relative importance in a specific situation because different users have or perceive themselves to have different needs and, therefore, have different preferences.

RELEVANCE

46. In discussions of accounting criteria, relevance has usually been defined in the dictionary sense, as pertaining to or having a bearing on the matter in question. That broad definition is satisfactory as far as it goes—information must, of course, be logically related to a decision in order to be relevant to it. Mistaken attempts to base decisions on logically unrelated information cannot convert irrelevant information into relevant information[5] any more than ignoring relevant information makes it irrelevant. However, the meaning of relevance for financial reporting needs to be made more explicit. Specifically, it is information's capacity to "make a difference" that identifies it as relevant to a decision.

47. To be relevant to investors, creditors, and others for investment, credit, and similar decisions, accounting information must be capable of making a difference in a decision by helping users to form predictions about the outcomes of past, present, and future events or to confirm or correct expectations. "Event" is a happening of consequence to an enterprise (Exposure Draft on elements, paragraph 67), and in this context can mean, for example, the receipt of a sales order or a price change in something the enterprise buys or sells. "Outcome" is the effect or result of an event or series of events and in this context can mean, for example, that last year's profit was $X or the expectation that this year's profit will be $Y. The event in question may be a past event the outcome of which is not already known, or it may be a future event the outcome of which can only be predicted.

48. Information need not itself be a prediction of future events or outcomes to be useful in forming, confirming, or changing expectations about future events or outcomes. Information about the present status of economic resources or obligations or about an enterprise's past performance is commonly a basis for expectations (Concepts Statement 1, paragraph 42).

[5]Information theorists assert that "relevant" as an adjective qualifying "information" is redundant, for irrelevant information is mere data. This Statement does not follow that usage.

49. Information may confirm expectations or it may change them. If it confirms them, it increases the probability that the results will be as previously expected. If it changes them, it changes the perceived probabilities of the previous possible outcomes. Either way, it makes a difference to one who does not already have that information. Decisions already made need not be changed, nor need a course of action already embarked on be altered by the information. A decision to hold rather than to sell an investment is a decision, and information that supports holding can be as relevant as information that leads to a sale. Information is relevant if the degree of uncertainty about the result of a decision that has already been made is confirmed or altered by the new information; it need not alter the decision.

50. One of the more fundamental questions raised by the search for relevance in accounting concerns the choice of attribute to be measured for financial reporting purposes. Will financial statements be more relevant if they are based on historical costs, current costs, or some other attribute? The question must be left for consideration in other parts of the conceptual framework project; but because of lack of experience with information providing measures of several of those attributes and differences of opinion about their relevance and reliability, it is not surprising that agreement on the question is so difficult to obtain.

Feedback[6] Value and Predictive Value as Components of Relevance

51. Information can make a difference to decisions by improving decision makers' capacities to predict or by confirming or correcting their earlier expectations. Usually, information does both at once, because knowledge about the outcome of actions already taken will generally improve decision makers' abilities to predict the results of similar future actions. Without a knowledge of the past, the basis for a prediction will usually be lacking. Without an interest in the future, knowledge of the past is sterile.

52. The same point can be made by saying that information is relevant to a situation if it can reduce uncertainty about the situation. Information that was not known previously about a past activity clearly reduces uncertainty about its outcome, and information about past activities is usually an indispensable point of departure for attempts to foresee the consequences of related future activities. Disclosure requirements almost always have the dual purpose of helping to predict and confirming or correcting earlier predictions. The reporting of business results by segments is a good example of accounting reports whose relevance is believed to lie both in the information they convey about the past performance of segments and in their contribution to an investor's ability to predict the trend of earnings of a diversified company. Another example is to be found in interim earnings reports, which provide both feedback on past performance and a basis for prediction for anyone wishing to forecast annual earnings before the year-end.

---

[6]This inelegant term is used because no other single word has been found to comprehend both confirmation or corroboration and their opposites.

53. To say that accounting information has *predictive value* is not to say that it is itself a *prediction*. It may be useful here to draw an analogy between the financial information that analysts and others use in predicting earnings or financial position and the information that meteorologists use in forecasting weather. Meteorologists gather and chart information about actual conditions—temperatures, barometric pressures, wind velocities at various altitudes, and so on—and draw their conclusions from the relationships and patterns that they detect. Success in forecasting the weather has increased as new methods of gathering information have been developed. New kinds of information have become available, and with greater speed than was previously possible. To the simple sources of information available to our ancestors have been added satellite photographs, radar, and radiosondes to give information about the upper atmosphere. New information makes possible more sophisticated predictive models. When a meteorologist selects from among the alternative sources of information and methods of gathering information—about existing conditions, since future conditions cannot be known—those sources and methods that have the greatest predictive value can be expected to be favored. So it is with information about the existing financial state of a company and observed changes in that state from which predictions of success, failure, growth, or stagnation may be inferred. Users can be expected to favor those sources of information and analytical methods that have the greatest predictive value in achieving their specific objectives. Predictive value here means value as an *input* into a predictive process, not value directly as a prediction.

54. An important similarity and an important difference between predicting the weather and predicting financial performance may be noted. The similarity is that the meteorologist's information and the information derived from financial reporting both have to be fed into a predictive model[7] before they can throw light on the future. Financial predictions, like weather forecasts, are the joint product of a model and the data that go into it. A choice between alternative accounting methods on the basis of their predictive value can be made only if the characteristics of the model to be used are generally known. For example, the econometric models now used for economic forecasting are designed to use as data financial aggregates (among other things) as those aggregates are compiled at present. They might work less well if price-level adjusted data were used. However, it might be possible to revise the model for use with that kind of data so that even better predictions could be made. The point is that the predictive value of information cannot be assessed in the abstract. It has to be transformed into a prediction, and the nature of the transformation as well as the data used determine the outcome.

55. The important difference between meteorological and financial predictions is that only exceptionally can meteorological predictions have an effect on the weather, but business or economic decision makers' predictions often affect their subjects. For example, the use of financial models to predict business failures looks quite

[7]A model is no more than a simplified, scaled-down representation of a situation that is to be analyzed. Typically, sophisticated models are expressed in terms of mathematical equations.

successful judged in the light of hindsight by looking at the financial history of failed firms during their last declining years. But a prediction of failure can be self-fulfilling by restricting a company's access to credit. The prediction could also bring about a recovery by initiating action by managers or bankers to avert failure. Because information affects human behavior and because different people react differently to it, financial information cannot be evaluated by means of a simple tally of the correct predictions that are based on it. Nevertheless, predictive value is an important consideration in distinguishing relevant from irrelevant accounting information.

Timeliness

56. Timeliness is an ancillary aspect relevance. If information is not available when it is needed or becomes available only so long after the reported events that it has no value for future action, it lacks relevance and is of little or no use. Timeliness in the present context means having information available to decision makers before it loses its capacity to influence decisions. Timeliness alone cannot make information relevant, but a lack of timeliness can rob information of relevance it might otherwise have had.

57. Clearly, there are degrees of timeliness. In some situations, the capacity of information to influence decisions may evaporate quickly, as, for example, in a fast-moving situation such as a take-over bid or a strike, so that timeliness may have to be measured in days or perhaps hours. In other contexts, such as routine reports by an enterprise of its annual results, it may take a longer delay to diminish materially the relevance and, therefore, the usefulness of the information. But a gain in relevance that comes with increased timeliness may entail sacrifices of other desirable characteristics of information, and as a result there may be an overall gain or loss in usefulness. It may sometimes be desirable, for example, to sacrifice precision for timeliness, for an approximation produced quickly is often more useful than precise information that takes longer to get out. Of course, if, in the interest of timeliness, the reliability of the information is sacrificed to a material degree, the result may be to rob the information of much of its usefulness. What constitutes a material loss of reliability is discussed in later paragraphs. Yet, while every loss of reliability diminishes the usefulness of information, it will often be possible to approximate an accounting number to make it available more quickly without making it materially unreliable. As a result, its overall usefulness may be enhanced.

RELIABILITY

58. That information should be reliable as well as relevant is a notion that is central to accounting. It is, therefore, important to be clear about the nature of the claim that is being made for an accounting number that is described as reliable.

59. The reliability of a measure rests on the faithfulness with which it represents

what it purports to represent, coupled with an assurance for the user, which comes through verification, that it has that representational quality. Of course, degrees of reliability must be recognized. It is hardly ever a question of black or white, but rather of more reliability or less.

60. Two different meanings of reliability can be distinguished and illustrated by considering what might be meant by describing a drug as reliable. It could mean that the drug can be relied on to cure or alleviate the condition for which it was prescribed, or it could mean that a dose of the drug can be relied on to conform to the formula shown on the label. The first meaning implies that the drug is effective at doing what it is expected to do. The second meaning implies nothing about effectiveness but does imply a correspondence between what is represented on the label and what is contained in the bottle.[8]

61. Effectiveness is indeed a quality that is necessary in information, but in an accounting context it goes by another name—relevance. It is not always easy to maintain a clear distinction between relevance and reliability, as in the drug illustration, yet it is important to try to keep the two concepts apart. Given at least a minimum acceptable level of reliability, the choice of a drug will depend on its effectiveness in treating the condition for which it is prescribed.

62. Use of the term reliability in this Statement implies nothing about effectiveness. Accounting information is reliable to the extent that users can depend on it to represent the economic conditions or events that it purports to represent. As indicated in paragraph 59, reliability of accounting information stems from two characteristics that it is desirable to keep separate, representational faithfulness and verifiability. Neutrality of information also interacts with those two characteristics to affect its usefulness.

Representational Faithfulness

63. Representational faithfulness is correspondence or agreement between a measure or description and the phenomenon it purports to represent. In accounting, the phenomena to be represented are economic resources and obligations and the transactions and events that change those resources and obligations.[9]

64. Clearly, much depends on the meaning of the words "purports to represent" in the preceding paragraphs. Sometimes, but rarely, information is unreliable because

---

[8]Perhaps, more accurately, there is also a third meaning—that the drug does not have hidden undesirable side effects. The alleged undesirable economic impact of certain FASB standards is perhaps an accounting analogue to side effects of drugs, which are, in essence, costs to be considered in a cost-benefit analysis.

[9]Representational faithfulness is closely related to what behavioral scientists call "validity," as in the statement that intelligence quotients are (or are not) a valid measure of intelligence. Validity is a more convenient term than representational faithfulness, but out of its scientific context it has too broad a connotation for it to be an appropriate substitute.

of simple misrepresentation. Receivables, for example, may misrepresent large sums as collectible that, in fact, are uncollectible. Unreliability of that kind may not be easy to detect, but once detected its nature is not open to argument. More subtle is the information conveyed by an item such as "goodwill." Does a balance sheet that shows goodwill as an asset purport to represent the company as having no goodwill except what is shown? An uninformed reader may well think so, while one who is familiar with present generally accepted accounting principles will know that non-purchased goodwill is not included. The discussion of reliability in this Statement assumes a reasonably informed user (paragraphs 36-41), for example, one who understands that the information provided by financial reporting often results from approximate, rather than exact, measures involving numerous estimates, classifications, summarizations, judgments, and allocations. The following paragraphs elaborate on and illustrate the concept of representational faithfulness used in this Statement, including the considerations noted in this and the preceding paragraphs.

Degrees of Representational Faithfulness

65. The cost of acquiring assets is more often than not capable of being determined unambiguously, but that is by no means always the case. Thus, if a collection of assets is bought for a specified amount, the cost attributable to each individual item may be impossible to ascertain. The acquisition cost may also be difficult to determine if assets are acquired in exchange for assets other than cash, by issuing stock, or in transactions with related parties. If assets are converted into other assets within an enterprise, as when raw materials are converted into finished products, or buildings or equipment are constructed by an enterprise for its own use, the multiplicity of costing conventions that can be used, all within the boundaries of present generally accepted accounting principles, make it impossible to attach a unique cost to the finished asset. Thus, it may not be certain that the cost for the asset in the enterprise's records does faithfully represent its cost.

66. The problem of determining cost becomes more difficult if assets are fungible. If there have been several purchases at different prices and a number of disposals at different dates, only by the adoption of some convention (such as first-in, first-out) can a cost be attributed to the assets on hand at a particular date. Since what is shown as the assets' cost is only one of several alternatives, it is difficult to substantiate that the chosen amount does represent the economic phenomena in question.

67. In the absence of market prices for the assets in question, representational faithfulness of amounts purporting to be current costs or fair values of assets also involves the same kinds of difficulties as those already described. For example, unless there are markets for used equipment or partially processed products, the current costs or fair values of those assets can be determined only by means such as deducting estimated depreciation from current costs or fair values of similar new assets, applying price indexes to past acquisition costs, or combining the current costs of the materials, labor, and overhead used. The allocations required by those procedures inevitably cast at least some doubt on the representational faithfulness of the results.

68. As accounting concepts become more complex, assessing the faithfulness of accounting representations of economic phenomena becomes increasingly difficult, and separating relevance or effectiveness from reliability becomes much more difficult than in the drug example used earlier (paragraphs 60 and 61). Social scientists have much discussed the concept of representational faithfulness (which they call validity) in connection with educational testing, and though that field may seem remote from accounting, the difficulties that beset it in some respects bear a close resemblance to some of those encountered in accounting. If two students score 640 and 580, respectively, in a scholastic aptitude test of verbal skills, it is inferred that the first student has more verbal aptitude than the second. But does the test really measure verbal aptitude? Is it, in other words, a valid test of verbal aptitude? That is a very difficult question to answer, for what is verbal aptitude? Without a definition of the quality to be measured, the validity of the test cannot be assessed. The problem of defining intelligence and of judging whether intelligence tests validly measure it may be even more difficult because of the many different manifestations of intelligence, the problems of separating innate and acquired abilities, standardizing for differences in social conditions, and many other things.

69. The nature of the problem just described can be clarified by means of an example. A spelling test is administered orally to a group of students. The words are read aloud by the tester, and the students are required to write down the test words. Some students, though they can usually spell well, fail the test. The reason, it turns out, is that they have hearing problems. The test score purports to measure ability to spell, whereas it, in fact, is partly measuring aural acuity. The test score lacks true representational faithfulness.

70. Another example, perhaps more closely related to accounting, may serve to further highlight some possible ways in which a representation may not be faithful to the economic phenomena that it purports to represent. The Consumer Price Index for All Urban Consumers (CPI-U) is an index of price level changes affecting consumers generally and is often used to measure changes in the general purchasing power of the monetary unit itself. However, if it were used as a measure of the price change of a specific asset, a purchase of a specific consumer, or an acquisition of a specific enterprise, it would not likely provide a faithful representation. The CPI-U is a "market basket" index, based on the average price a typical consumer would pay for a selection of consumer goods. Specific price changes experienced by specific consumers will differ from the index to the extent their consumption patterns are different from the selection of goods in the index market basket if the price changes on the goods they purchase are not perfectly correlated to the changes in the index. General price indexes, such as the CPI-U, cannot acknowledge individual differences, but they may provide a reasonable measure of the loss in the general purchasing power of the monetary unit. The index must be interpreted in the context of what it was designed to do and in view of the limitations of any averaging process.

71. The discussion in the preceding paragraph illustrates some of the problems that may arise when representations of economic phenomena are used in different con-

texts than those for which they were designed. Accounting information, for example, purports to reflect the activities of a particular enterprise. However, aggregating the amounts reported by all businesses may not result in a faithful representation of total activity in the business sector, for that is not the purpose for which the accounting information was intended. Information that is representationally faithful in the context for which it was designed, therefore, may not be reliable when used in other contexts.

Precision and Uncertainty

72. Reliability does not imply certainty or precision. Indeed, any pretension to those qualities if they do not exist is a negation of reliability. Sometimes, a range within which an estimate may fall will convey information more reliably than can a single (point) estimate. In other cases, an indication of the probabilities attaching to different values of an attribute may be the best way of giving information reliably about the measure of the attribute and the uncertainty that surrounds it. Reporting accounting numbers as certain and precise if they are not is a negation of reliable reporting.

73. Different uses of information may require different degrees of reliability and, consequently, what constitutes a material loss or gain in reliability may vary according to use. An error in timekeeping of a few seconds a day will usually be acceptable to the owner of an ordinary wristwatch, whereas the same error would normally cause a chronometer to be judged unreliable. The difference is linked to use—a wristwatch is used for purposes for which accuracy within a few seconds (or perhaps a few minutes) is satisfactory; a chronometer is used for navigation, scientific work, and the like, uses for which a high degree of accuracy is required because an error of a few seconds or a fraction of a second may have large consequences. In everyday language, both the wristwatch and the chronometer are said to be reliable. By the standard of the chronometer, the wristwatch, in fact, is unreliable. Yet the watch's owner does not perceive it to be unreliable, for it is not expected to have the accuracy of a chronometer.

74. Fortunately, that is well understood by accountants. They recognize that a difference between an estimate and an accurate measurement may be material in one context and not material in another. The relationship between the concepts of reliability and materiality, including what constitutes *material* unreliability, will be discussed later in this Statement.

75. Reliability as a quality of a predictor has a somewhat different meaning from reliability as a quality of a measure. The reliability of a barometer should be judged in terms of the accuracy with which it measures air pressure and changes in air pressure. That is all that a barometer is constructed to do. Yet questions about its reliability are more likely to be couched in terms of its accuracy as a predictor of the weather, even though weather conditions in any location are the result of many factors besides air pressure in that location. Though much of the relevance of account-

ing information may derive from its value as input to a prediction model, the probability that it will lead to correct predictions does not determine its reliability as a set of measurements. The correctness of predictions depends as much on the predictive model used as on the data that go into the model. Thus, the result of a predictive process cannot be used to assess the reliability of the inputs into it any more than a run of successes by a barometer in forecasting the weather can tell us much about the accuracy with which it measures the pressure of the atmosphere.

76. The financial statements of a business enterprise can be thought of as a representation of the resources and obligations of an enterprise and the financial flows into, out of, and within the enterprise—as a model of the enterprise.[10] Like all models, it must abstract from much that goes on in a real enterprise. No model, however sophisticated, can be expected to reflect all the functions and relationships that are found within a complex organization. To do so, the model would have to be virtually a reproduction of the original. In real life, it is necessary to accept a much smaller degree of correspondence between the model and the original than that. One can be satisfied if none of the important functions and relationships are lost. Before an accounting model—either the one now used or an alternative—can be judged to represent an enterprise reliably, it must be determined that none of the important financial functions of the enterprise or its relationships have been lost or distorted. The mere fact that model works—that when it receives inputs it produces outputs—gives no assurance that it faithfully represents the original. Just as a distorting mirror reflects a warped image of the person standing in front of it or just as an inexpensive loudspeaker fails to reproduce faithfully the sounds that went into the microphone or onto the phonograph records, so a bad model gives a distorted representation of the system that it models. The question that accountants must face continually is how much distortion is acceptable. The cost of a perfect sound reproduction system puts it out of reach of most people, and perfect reliability of accounting information is equally unattainable.

Effects of Bias

77. Bias in measurement is the tendency of a measure to fall more often on one side than the other of what it represents instead of being equally likely to fall on either side. Bias in accounting measures means a tendency to be consistently too high or too low.

78. Accounting information may not represent faithfully what it purports to represent because it has one or both of two kinds of bias. The measurement method may be biased, so that the resulting measurement fails to represent what it purports to represent. Alternatively, or additionally, the measurer, through lack of skill or lack of integrity, or both, may misapply the measurement method chosen. In other words,

[10]Nothing is implied here about the possible predictive uses of the model. While it is true that models are generally used to make predictions, they need not be so used. A model is no more than a representation of certain aspects of the real world.

there may be bias, not necessarily intended, on the part of the measurer. Those two kinds of bias are further discussed in the following paragraphs and in the next section on "verifiability." Intentional bias introduced to attain a predetermined result or induce a particular mode of behavior is discussed under "neutrality" (paragraphs 98-110).

Completeness

79. Freedom from bias, both in the measurer and the measurement method, implies that nothing material is left out of the information that may be necessary to insure that it validly represents the underlying events and conditions. Reliability implies completeness of information, at least within the bounds of what is material and feasible, considering the cost. A map that is 99 percent reliable but fails to show a bridge across a river where one exists can do much harm. Completeness, however, must always be relative, for neither maps nor financial reports can show everything.

80. Completeness of information also affects its relevance. Relevance of information is adversely affected if a relevant piece of information is omitted, even if the omission does not falsify what is shown. For example, in a diversified enterprise a failure to disclose that one segment was consistently unprofitable would not, before the issuance of FASB Statement No. 14, *Accounting for Segments of a Business Enterprise,* have caused the financial reporting to be judged unreliable, but that financial reporting would have been (as it would now be) deficient in relevance. Thus, completeness, within the bounds of feasibility, is necessary to both of the primary qualities that make information useful.

Verifiability

81. The quality of verifiability contributes to the usefulness of accounting information because the purpose of verification is to provide a significant degree of assurance that accounting measures represent what they purport to represent. Verification is more successful in minimizing measurer bias than measurement bias, and thus contributes in varying degrees toward assuring that particular measures represent faithfully the economic things or events that they purport to represent. Verification contributes little or nothing toward insuring that measures used are relevant to the decisions for which the information is intended to be useful.

82. Measurer bias is a less complex concept than measurement bias. In its simplest form, it arises from intentional misrepresentation. But even honest measurers may get different results from applying the same measurement method, especially if it involves a prediction of the outcome of a future event, such as the realization of an asset. Measurer bias can be detected and eliminated by having the measurement repeated with the same result. It is, therefore, a desirable quality of an accounting measure that it should be capable of replication. The Accounting Principles Board (APB) called this characteristic verifiability, and defined it in APB Statement No. 4, *Basic Concepts and Accounting Principles Underlying Financial Statements of Busi-*

ness Enterprises: "Verifiable financial accounting information provides results that would be substantially duplicated by independent measurers using the same measurement methods" (paragraph 90).

83. The last five words of the APB's definition are significant for they imply that alternative methods may be available. Verification does not guarantee the appropriateness of the method used, much less the correctness of the resulting measure. It does carry some assurance that the measurement rule used, whatever it was, was applied carefully and without personal bias on the part of the measurer.

84. Verification implies consensus. Verifiability can be measured by looking at the dispersion of a number of independent measurements of some particular phenomenon. The more closely the measurements are likely to be clustered together, the greater the verifiability of the number used as a measure of the phenomenon.

85. Some accounting measurements are more easily verified than others. Alternative measures of cash will be closely clustered together, with a consequently high level of verifiability. There will be less unanimity about receivables (especially their net value), still less about inventories, and least about depreciable assets, for there will be disagreements about depreciation methods to be used, predictions of asset lives, and (if book values are based on historical cost) even which expenditures should be included in the investment base. More than one empirical investigation has concluded that accountants may agree more about estimates of the market values of certain depreciable assets than about their carrying values. Hence, to the extent that verification depends on consensus, it may not always be those measurement methods widely regarded as "objective" that are most verifiable.

86. The elimination of measurer bias alone from information does not insure that the information will be reliable. Even though several independent measurers may agree on a single measurement method and apply it honestly and skillfully, the result will not be reliable if the method used is such that the measure does not represent what it purports to represent. Representational faithfulness of reported measurements lies in the closeness of their correspondence with the economic transactions, events, or circumstances that they represent.

87. Two further points about verifiability and representational faithfulness need to be emphasized. First, when accountants speak of verification they may mean either that an accounting measure itself has been verified or only that the procedures used to obtain the measure have been verified. For example, the price paid to acquire a block of marketable securities or a piece of land is normally directly verifiable, while the amount of depreciation for a period is normally only indirectly verifiable by verifying the depreciation method, calculations used, and consistency of application (paragraphs 65-67). Direct verification of accounting measures tends to minimize both personal bias introduced by a measurer (measurer bias) and bias inherent in measurement methods (measurement bias). Verification of only measurement methods tends to minimize measurer bias but usually preserves any bias there may be in the selection of measurement or allocation methods.

88. Second, measurement or allocation methods are often verifiable even if the measures they produce result in a very low degree of representational faithfulness. For example, before FASB Statement No. 5, *Accounting for Contingencies,* some enterprises that were "self-insured" recorded as an expense a portion of expected future losses from fire, flood, or other casualties. If an enterprise had a large number of "self-insured" assets, expectations of future losses could be actuarially computed, and the methods of allocating expected losses to periods could be readily verified. However, since uninsured losses occurred only when a casualty damaged or destroyed a particular asset or particular assets, the representational faithfulness of the resulting allocated measures was very low. In years in which no casualties were suffered by an enterprise, the allocated expenses or losses represented nonexistent transactions or events; while in years in which assets were actually damaged or destroyed, the allocated expenses or losses may have fallen far short of representing the losses.

89. In summary, verifiability means no more than that several measurers are likely to obtain the same measure. It is primarily a means of attempting to cope with measurement problems stemming from the uncertainty that surrounds accounting measures and is more successful in coping with some measurement problems than others. Verification of accounting information does not guarantee that the information has a high degree of representational faithfulness, and a measure with a high degree of verifiability is not necessarily relevant to the decision for which it is intended to be useful.

Reliability and Relevance

90. Reliability and relevance often impinge on each other. Reliability may suffer when an accounting method is changed to gain relevance, and vice versa. Sometimes it may not be clear whether there has been a loss or gain either of relevance or of reliability. The introduction of current cost accounting will illustrate the point. Proponents of current cost accounting believe that current cost income from continuing operations is a more relevant measure of operating performance than is operating profit computed on the basis of historical costs. They also believe that if holding gains and losses that may have accrued in past periods are separately displayed, current cost income from continuing operations better portrays operating performance. The uncertainties surrounding the determination of current costs, however, are considerable, and variations among estimates of their magnitude can be expected. Because of those variations, verifiability or representational faithfulness, components of reliability, might diminish. Whether there is a net gain to users of the information obviously depends on the relative weights attached to relevance and reliability (assuming, of course, that the claims made for current cost accounting are accepted).

Conservatism

91. Nothing has yet been said about conservatism, a convention that many accountants believe to be appropriate in making accounting decisions. To quote APB Statement 4:

> Frequently, assets and liabilities are measured in a context of significant uncertainties. Historically, managers, investors, and accountants have generally preferred that possible errors in measurement be in the direction of understatement rather than overstatement of net income and net assets. This has led to the convention of conservatism . . . [paragraph 171].

92. There is a place for a convention such as conservatism—meaning prudence—in financial accounting and reporting, because business and economic activities are surrounded by uncertainty, but it needs to be applied with care. Since a preference "that possible errors in measurement be in the direction of understatement rather than overstatement of net income and net assets" introduces a bias into financial reporting, conservatism tends to conflict with significant qualitative characteristics, such as representational faithfulness, neutrality, and comparability (including consistency). To be clear about what conservatism does not mean may often be as important as to be clear about what it means.

93. Conservatism in financial reporting should no longer connote deliberate, consistent understatement of net assets and profits. The Board emphasizes that point because conservatism has long been identified with the idea that deliberate understatement is a virtue. That notion became deeply ingrained and is still in evidence despite efforts over the past 40 years to change it. The convention of conservatism, which was once commonly expressed in the admonition to "anticipate no profits but anticipate all losses," developed during a time when balance sheets were considered the primary (and often only) financial statement, and details of profits or other operating results were rarely provided outside business enterprises. To the bankers or other lenders who were the principal external users of financial statements, understatement for its own sake became widely considered to be desirable, since the greater the understatement of assets the greater the margin of safety the assets provided as security for loans or other debts.

94. Once the practice of providing information about periodic income as well as balance sheets became common, however, it also became evident that understated assets frequently led to overstated income in later periods. Perceptive accountants saw that consistent understatement was difficult to maintain over a lengthy period, and the Committee on Accounting Procedure began to say so, for example, in ARB No. 3, *Quasi-Reorganization or Corporate Readjustment—Amplification of Institute Rule No. 2 of 1934:* "Understatement as at the effective date of the readjustment of assets which are likely to be realized thereafter, though it may result in conservatism in the balance sheet, may also result in overstatement of earnings or of earned surplus

when the assets are subsequently realized. Therefore, in general, assets should be carried forward as of the date of readjustment at a fair and not unduly conservative value." The Committee also formulated the "cost or market rule" in ARB No. 29, *Inventory Pricing,* in such a way that decreases in replacement costs do not result in writing down inventory unless (a) the expected selling price also decreases or (b) costs to complete and sell inventory increase; unless those conditions are met, recognition of a loss by writing down inventory merely increases income in one or more later periods. (ARB 3 and 29 became, respectively, chapters 7A and 4 of ARB No. 43, *Restatement and Revision of Accounting Research Bulletins.*) Among the most recent admonitions on the point is that of the International Accounting Standards Committee (IASC) in International Accounting Standard No. 1, *Disclosure of Accounting Policies:* "Uncertainties inevitably surround many transactions. This should be recognized by exercising prudence in preparing financial statements. Prudence does not, however, justify the creation of secret or hidden reserves."

95. Conservatism is a prudent reaction to uncertainty to try to ensure that uncertainties and risks inherent in business situations are adequately considered. Thus, if two estimates of amounts to be received or paid in the future are about equally likely, conservatism dictates using the less optimistic estimate; however, if two amounts are not equally likely, conservatism does not necessarily dictate using the more pessimistic amount rather than the more likely one. Conservatism no longer requires deferring recognition of income beyond the time that adequate evidence of its existence becomes available or justifies recognizing losses before there is adequate evidence that they have been incurred.

96. The Board emphasizes that any attempt to understate results consistently is likely to raise questions about the reliability and the integrity of information about those results and will probably be self-defeating in the long run. That kind of reporting, however well-intentioned, is not consistent with the desirable characteristics described in this Statement. On the other hand, the Board also emphasizes that imprudent reporting, such as may be reflected, for example, in overly optimistic estimates of realization, is certainly no less inconsistent with those characteristics. Bias in estimating components of earnings, whether overly conservative or unconservative, usually influences the timing of earnings or losses rather than their aggregate amount. As a result, unjustified excesses in either direction may mislead one group of investors to the possible benefit or detriment of others.

97. The best way to avoid the injury to investors that imprudent reporting creates is to try to ensure that what is reported represents what it purports to represent. It has been pointed out in this Statement that the reliability of financial reporting may be enhanced by disclosing the nature and extent of the uncertainty surrounding events and transactions reported to stockholders and others. In assessing the prospect that as yet uncompleted transactions will be concluded successfully, a degree of skepticism is often warranted. The aim must be to put the users of financial information in the best possible position to form their own opinion of the probable outcome of the events reported. Prudent reporting based on a healthy skepticism builds confidence

in the results and, in the long run, best serves all of the divergent interests that are represented by the Board's constituents.

NEUTRALITY

98. Neutrality in accounting has a greater significance for those who set accounting standards than for those who have to apply those standards in preparing financial reports, but the concept has substantially the same meaning for the two groups, and both will maintain neutrality in the same way. Neutrality means that either in formulating or implementing standards, the primary concern should be the relevance and reliability of the information that results, not the effect that the new rule may have on a particular interest.

99. To say that information should be free from bias towards a predetermined result is not to say that standard setters or providers of information should not have a *purpose* in mind for financial reporting. Of course, information must be purposeful. But a predetermined purpose should not imply a predetermined result. For one thing, the purpose may be to serve many different information users who have diverse interests, and no one predetermined result is likely to suit them all.

100. Neutrality does not mean "without purpose," nor does it mean that accounting should be without influence on human behavior. Accounting information cannot avoid affecting behavior, nor should it. If it were otherwise, the information would be valueless—by definition, irrelevant—and the effort to produce it would be futile. It is, above all, the predetermination of a desired result, and the consequential selection of information to induce that result, that is the negation of neutrality in accounting. To be neutral, accounting information must report economic activity as faithfully as possible, without coloring the image it communicates for the purpose of influencing behavior in *some particular direction.*

101. Behavior will be influenced by financial information just as it is influenced and changed by the results of elections, college examinations, and sweepstakes. Elections, examinations, and sweepstakes are not unfair—nonneutral—merely because some people win and others lose. So it is with neutrality in accounting. The effect of "capitalization" of leases on enterprises in the leasing industry is a case in point. Recording of certain leases as assets and liabilities has been opposed by many of those enterprises on the grounds that, by making "off balance sheet" financing more difficult, it would make leasing less attractive to lessees, and that would have a detrimental effect on the business of lessors. Although it is at least debatable whether that kind of effect actually would result from lease capitalization, standard setters have not been indifferent to those fears. After carefully weighing the matter, various standard setters (including the Board) have generally concluded that those fears could not be allowed to stand in the way of what the Board and others considered to be a gain in the relevance and reliability of financial statements.

102. Some reject the notion of accounting neutrality because they think it is impossible to attain because of the "feedback effect." Information that reports on human activity itself influences that activity, so that an accountant is reporting not on some static phenomenon but on a dynamic situation that changes because of what is reported about it. But that is not an argument against neutrality in measurement. Many measurements relating to human beings—what they see when they step on a scale, what the speedometer registers when they drive a car, their performance in an athletic contest, or their academic performance, for example—have an impact on their behavior, for better or worse. No one argues that those measurements should be biased in order to influence behavior. Indeed, most people are repelled by the notion that some "big brother," whether government or private, would tamper with scales or speedometers surreptitiously to induce people to lose weight or obey speed limits or would slant the scoring of athletic events or examinations to enhance or decrease someone's chances of winning or graduating. There is no more reason to abandon neutrality in accounting measurement.

103. Another argument against the acceptance of neutrality as a necessary characteristic of accounting information is that it would inhibit the Board from working for the achievement of national goals. That view raises several issues. First, there would have to be agreement on national goals. For example, should the United States work to make energy cheap and plentiful or should it conserve natural resources for the benefit of posterity? Furthermore, governments come and go, and administrations change their political color and their policies. The Board concludes that it is not feasible to change financial accounting standards that accountants use every time governmental policy changes direction, even if it were desirable to do so. Moreover, only if accounting information is neutral can it safely be used to help guide those policies as well as to measure their results.

104. But more importantly, it is not desirable for the Board to tack with every change in the political wind, for politically motivated standards would quickly lose their credibility, and even standards that were defensible if judged against the criteria discussed in this Statement would come under suspicion because they would be tainted with guilt by association. The chairman of the SEC made the point in his statement on oil and gas accounting on August 29, 1978:

> If it becomes accepted or expected that accounting principles are determined or modified in order to secure purposes other than economic measurement—even such virtuous purposes as energy production—we assume a grave risk that confidence in the credibility of our financial information system will be undermined.[11]

105. For a standard to be neutral, it is not necessary that it treat everyone alike in all respects. A standard could require less disclosure from a small enterprise than it does

[11] Harold M. Williams, Chairman, Securities and Exchange Commission, "Accounting Practices for Oil and Gas Producers" (Washington, D.C., 1978), p. 12.

from a large one without having its neutrality impugned, if the Board were satisfied that a requirement that was cost-effective if imposed on a large enterprise would be more burdensome than it was worth if imposed on a small one. Nevertheless, in general, standards that apply differentially need to be looked at carefully to ensure that the criterion of neutrality is not being transgressed.

106. While rejecting the view that financial accounting standards should be slanted for political reasons or to favor one economic interest or another, the Board recognizes that a standard-setting authority must be alert to the economic impact of the standards that it promulgates. The consequences of those standards will usually not be easy to isolate from the effects of other economic happenings, and they will be even harder to predict with confidence when a new standard is under consideration but before it has gone into effect. Nevertheless, the Board will consider the probable economic impact of its standards as best it can and will monitor that impact as best it can after a standard goes into effect. For one thing, a markedly unexpected effect on business behavior may point to an unforeseen deficiency in a standard in the sense that it does not result in the faithful representation of economic phenomena that was intended. It would then be necessary for the standard to be revised.

107. Neutrality in accounting is an important criterion by which to judge accounting policies, for information that is not neutral loses credibility. If information can be verified and can be relied on faithfully to represent what it purports to represent—*and if there is no bias in the selection of what is reported*—it cannot be slanted to favor one set of interests over another. It may in fact favor certain interests, but only because the information points that way, much as a good examination grade favors a good student who has honestly earned it.

108. The italicized words deserve comment. It was noted earlier in this Statement that reliability implies completeness of information, at least within the bounds of what is material and feasible, considering the cost. An omission can rob information of its claim to neutrality if the omission is material and is intended to induce or inhibit some particular mode of behavior.

109. Though reliability and the absence of bias in what is to be reported bring neutrality as a by-product, the converse is not true. Information may be unreliable even though it is provided without any intention on the part of the provider to influence behavior in a particular direction. Good intentions alone do not guarantee representational faithfulness.

110. Can information that is undeniably reliable produce undesirable consequences? The answer must be another question—consequences for whom? The consequences may indeed be bad for some interests. But the dissemination of unreliable and potentially misleading information is, in the long run, bad for all interests. It may be the responsibility of other agencies to intervene to take care of special interests that they think might be injured by an accounting standard. The Board's responsibility is to the integrity of the financial reporting system, which it regards as its paramount concern.

COMPARABILITY

111. Information about an enterprise gains greatly in usefulness if it can be compared with similar information about other enterprises and with similar information about the same enterprise for some other period or some other point in time. The significance of information, especially quantitative information, depends to a great extent on the user's ability to relate it to some benchmark. The comparative use of information is often intuitive, as when told that an enterprise has sales revenue of $1,000,000 a year, one forms a judgment of its size by ranking it with other enterprises that one knows. Investing and lending decisions essentially involve evaluations of alternative opportunities, and they cannot be made rationally if comparative information is not available.

112. The difficulty in making financial comparisons among enterprises because of the use of different accounting methods has been accepted for many years as the principal reason for the development of accounting standards. Indeed, the only other possible reason for wanting accounting standards would be a belief that there was one right method among the available alternatives, and few people, if any, hold any such belief.

113. The purpose of comparison is to detect and explain similarities and differences. But, in comparing complex entities, such as human beings or business enterprises, it is useless to try to consider all similarities and differences at once, for to assess the significance of any one of them will then be impossible. Valid comparison, therefore, usually requires attention to be focused on one or two characteristics at a time. Other characteristics that are in no way correlated with those under inquiry can be ignored. Characteristics that are correlated with those under inquiry must be standardized to avoid affecting the comparison. For example, to find whether a man is overweight, one compares his weight with that of other men—not women—of the same height. That is, valid comparisons involve standardizing for gender and height because those characteristics are correlated with weight. It is not necessary to standardize for intelligence, for example, by comparing a man's weight with that of other males of similar height and intelligence because weight is not correlated with intelligence. Intelligence as a characteristic can be ignored.

114. Simple comparisons can often be made without the use of measurements expressed in units, but as the number of items to be compared increases, or if comparisons over an interval of time are desired, a unit of measure becomes indispensable. If valid comparisons are to be made over time, the unit of measurement used must be invariant. Units of money used in money measurement are not in one significant sense—their command over goods and services—invariant over time.

115. Defined in the broadest terms, comparability is the quality or state of having certain characteristics in common, and comparison is normally a quantitative assessment of the common characteristic. Clearly, valid comparison is possible only if the measurements used—the quantities or ratios—reliably represent the characteristic

that is the subject of comparison. To cite a nonaccounting example, it may be desired to compare the fertility of land in Florida and Oregon. If that were done by comparing crop yields per acre, it should be obvious that crop yield is not a reliable representation of fertility. Many other factors, such as climate and human efficiency, help to determine yields, and to use too broad a gauge to measure the characteristic of fertility invalidates the comparison.

116. While a particular datum, in some appropriate context, can be said to be relevant or reliable, it cannot be said to be comparable. Comparability is not a quality of information in the same sense as relevance and reliability are, but is rather a quality of the relationship between two or more pieces of information. Improving comparability may destroy or weaken relevance or reliability if, to secure comparability between two measures, one of them has to be obtained by a method yielding less relevant or less reliable information. Historically, extreme examples of this have been provided in some European countries in which the use of standardized charts of accounts has been made mandatory in the interest of interfirm comparability but at the expense of relevance and often reliability as well. That kind of uniformity may even adversely affect comparability of information if it conceals real differences between enterprises.

117. Generally, noncomparability is thought to arise because business enterprises do not use similar inputs, do not apply similar procedures, or do not use the same systems of classification of costs and revenues or assets and liabilities, and it is usually assumed that removal of those inconsistencies will make the results comparable. Certainly, comparability cannot be achieved without consistency of inputs and classification. For example, comparing liquidity between two enterprises by comparing their current ratios would usually not be valid if one enterprise valued its inventory on a last-in, first-out basis while the other valued inventory on first-in, first-out. The difference in practice would affect the comparison adversely to the first company, but its appearance of inferior liquidity would result from an invalid comparison, for the current value of its inventory may not have been less than that of the other company.

118. That kind of noncomparability imposes costs on users of financial statements and is best avoided, but it is relatively easy to diagnose and, with sufficient disclosure, can be rectified by a user of the information. A more difficult kind of noncomparability to deal with is the kind that results when ill-chosen or incomplete data inputs are used to generate information that fails one test of reliability—it does not truly represent what it purports to represent. If data inputs are ill-chosen or incomplete, the measures that result will not be truly comparable no matter how consistent the procedures are that are applied to them. For example, suppose it is desired to compare the performance of two investment managers. Each starts with the same portfolio, but their portfolios at the end of the year are different as a result of trades during the year. Realized gains of the two managers are equal. The ending portfolio of one shows substantial unrealized gains, the other does not. To compare their performance by comparing only realized gains implies a definition of performance that

many people would regard as incomplete and, therefore, as an unreliable representation.

119. To repeat what was said earlier, the purpose of comparison is to detect and explain similarities and differences. Comparability should not be confused with identity, and sometimes more can be learned from differences than from similarities if the differences can be explained. The ability to explain phenomena often depends on the diagnosis of the underlying causes of differences or the discovery that apparent differences are without significance. Much insight into the functioning of the capital market, for example, has been obtained from observing how market forces affect different stocks differently. Something has been learned, too, from observing that the market generally ignores apparent (cosmetic) differences among stocks that were formerly thought to be significant. Greater comparability of accounting information, which most people agree is a worthwhile aim, is not to be attained by making unlike things look alike any more than by making like things look different. The moral is that in seeking comparability accountants must not disguise real differences nor create false differences.

Consistency

120. Consistency in applying accounting methods over a span of time has always been regarded as an important quality that makes accounting numbers more useful. The standard form of an auditor's report states that the financial statements have been prepared "in conformity with generally accepted accounting principles consistently applied." The Accounting Principles Board stated in APB Opinion No. 20, *Accounting Changes,* that ". . . in the preparation of financial statements there is a presumption that an accounting principle once adopted should not be changed in accounting for events and transactions of a similar type. Consistent use of accounting principles from one accounting period to another enhances the utility of financial statements to users by facilitating analysis and understanding of comparative accounting data [paragraph 15]."

121. The same considerations apply whether comparisons involve time series data, with which discussions of consistency are mostly concerned, or cross-sectional data, which raise more general issues of comparability. Like comparability, consistency is a quality of the relationship between two accounting numbers rather than a quality of the numbers themselves in the sense that relevance and reliability are. The consistent use of accounting methods, whether from one period to another within a single firm, or within a single period across firms, is a necessary but not a sufficient condition of comparability. Consistency without genuine comparability is illustrated by time series data using units of money during periods of inflation. A 10-year summary of sales revenues covering a period when the purchasing power of the monetary unit has been declining may convey an exaggerated picture of growth unless the user of the information is accustomed to making purchasing power corrections. As before, it is the representational faithfulness of the measurements used, rather than simply

the unchanging nature of the measurement rules or the classification rules, that results in true comparability over time.

122. Consistent use of accounting principles from one accounting period to another, if pushed too far, can inhibit accounting progress. No change to a preferred accounting method can be made without sacrificing consistency, yet there is no way that accounting can develop without change. Fortunately, it is possible to make the transition from a less preferred to a more preferred method of accounting and still retain the capacity to compare the periods before and after the change if the effects of the change of method are disclosed. If a change will bring only a small improvement, the trade-off between the improvement and the loss of consistency may make it hard to judge where the advantage lies. As in all trade-offs, it is a question of costs and benefits; and the costs include the psychological cost of adopting the change. If the cost of the added disclosure that will enable the user of accounting information to compare the prechange and postchange results is less than the expected benefits from making the change, the change should be made.

MATERIALITY

123. Those who make accounting decisions and those who make judgments as auditors continually confront the need to make judgments about materiality. Materiality judgments are primarily quantitative in nature. They pose the question: Is this item large enough for users of the information to be influenced by it? However, the answer to that question will usually be affected by the nature of the item; items too small to be thought material if they result from routine transactions may be considered material if they arise in abnormal circumstances.

124. Throughout this Statement, emphasis has been placed on relevance and reliability as the primary qualitative characteristics that accounting information must have if it is to be useful. Materiality is not a primary characteristic of the same kind. In fact, the pervasive nature of materiality makes it difficult to consider the concept except as it relates to the other qualitative characteristics, especially relevance and reliability.

125. Relevance and materiality have much in common—both are defined in terms of what influences or makes a difference to an investor or other decision maker. Yet the two concepts can be distinguished. A decision not to disclose certain information may be made, say, because investors have no interest in that kind of information (it is not relevant) or because the amounts involved are too small to make a difference (they are not material). But as was noted above, magnitude by itself, without regard to the nature of the item and the circumstances in which the judgment has to be made, will not generally be a sufficient basis for a materiality judgment.

126. Materiality judgments are concerned with screens or thresholds. Is an item, an

error, or an omission large enough, considering its nature and the attendant circumstances, to pass over the threshold that separates material from immaterial items? An example of an applicant for employment who is negotiating with an employment agency will illustrate the relationship of the materiality concept to relevance and reliability. The agency has full information about a certain job for which the applicant is suited and will furnish any item of information about it. The applicant will certainly want information about the nature of the duties, the location of the job, the pay, the hours of work, and the fringe benefits. Information about vacations and job security may or may not be important enough to affect a decision concerning accepting the job. Further, the applicant may not be concerned at all with whether the office floor is carpeted or about the quality of the food in the cafeteria. All of those items are, in the broadest sense, relevant to an evaluation of the job. But some of them make no difference in a decision to accept it or not. The values placed on them by the applicant are too small for them to be material. They are not important enough to matter.

127. The employment agency example can also help to explain what is meant by a materiality threshold for reliability. Salary information accurate only to the nearest thousand dollars might not be acceptable to an applicant for an $8,000 a year job, but will almost certainly be acceptable if the job pays $100,000 a year. An error of a percentage point in the employee's rate of pension contribution would rarely make information about fringe benefits unacceptable. An error of a year in the retirement date of someone who would block the applicant's advancement might be quite material. An error of a year in the applicant's mandatory retirement date will probably be immaterial to a person 20 years old, but quite material to a 63-year-old person.

128. The more important a judgment item[12] is, the finer the screen should be that will be used to determine whether it is material. For example:

a. An accounting change in circumstances that puts an enterprise in danger of being in breach of covenant regarding its financial condition may justify a lower materiality threshold than if its position were stronger.
b. A failure to disclose separately a nonrecurrent item of revenue may be material at a lower threshold than would otherwise be the case if the revenue turns a loss into a profit or reverses the trend of earnings from a downward to an upward trend.
c. A misclassification of assets that would not be material in amount if it affected two categories of plant or equipment might be material if it changed the classification between a noncurrent and a current asset category.
d. Amounts too small to warrant disclosure or correction in normal circumstances may be considered material if they arise from abnormal or unusual transactions or events.

129. Almost always, the relative rather than the absolute size of a judgment item

[12]A judgment item is whatever has to be determined to be material or immaterial. It may be an asset or liability item, a transaction, an error, or any of a number of things.

determines whether it should be considered material in a given situation. Losses from bad debts or pilferage that could be shrugged off as routine by a large business may threaten the continued existence of a small one. An error in inventory valuation may be material in a small enterprise for which it cut earnings in half but immaterial in an enterprise for which it might make a barely perceptible ripple in the earnings. Some of the empirical investigations referred to in Appendix C throw light on the considerations that enter into materiality judgments.

130. Another factor in materiality judgments is the degree of precision that is attainable in estimating the judgment item. The amount of deviation that is considered immaterial may increase as the attainable degree of precision decreases. For example, accounts payable usually can be estimated more accurately than can contingent liabilities arising from litigation or threats of it, and a deviation considered to be material in the first case may be quite trivial in the second.

131. Some hold the view that the Board should promulgate a set of quantitative materiality guides or criteria covering a wide variety of situations that preparers could look to for authoritative support. That appears to be a minority view, however, on the basis of representations made to the Board in response to the Discussion Memorandum, *Criteria for Determining Materiality.* The predominant view is that materiality judgments can properly be made only by those who have all the facts. The Board's present position is that no general standards of materiality could be formulated to take into account all the considerations that enter into an experienced human judgment. However, that position is not intended to imply either that the Board may not in the future review that conclusion or that quantitative guidance on materiality of specific items may not appropriately be written into the Board's standards from time to time. That has been done on occasion already (for example, in the Statement on financial reporting by segments of a business enterprise), and the Board recognizes that quantitative materiality guidance is sometimes needed. Appendix C lists a number of examples of quantitative guidelines that have been applied both in the law and in the practice of accounting. However, whenever the Board or any other authoritative body imposes materiality rules, it is substituting generalized collective judgments for specific individual judgments, and there is no reason to suppose that the collective judgments are always superior. In any case, it must be borne in mind that if, to take one example, some minimum size is stipulated for recognition of a material item (for example, a segment having revenue equal to or exceeding 10 percent of combined revenues shall be recognized as a reportable segment), the rule does not prohibit the recognition of a smaller segment. Quantitative materiality guidelines generally specify minima only. They, therefore, leave room for individual judgment in at least one direction.

132. Individual judgments are required to assess materiality in the absence of authoritative criteria or to decide that minimum quantitative criteria are not appropriate in particular situations. The essence of the materiality concept is clear. The omission or misstatement of an item in a financial report is material if, in the light of surrounding circumstances, the magnitude of the item is such that it is probable that

the judgment of a reasonable person relying upon the report would have been changed or influenced by the inclusion or correction of the item.

COSTS AND BENEFITS[13]

133. Accounting information must attain some minimum level of relevance and also some minimum level of reliability if it is to be useful. Beyond those minimum levels, sometimes users may gain by sacrificing relevance for added reliability or by sacrificing reliability for added relevance; and some accounting policy changes will bring gains in both. Each user will uniquely perceive the relative value to be attached to each quality. Ultimately, a standard-setting body has to do its best to meet the needs of society as a whole when it promulgates a standard that sacrifices one of those qualities for the other; and it must also be aware constantly of the calculus of costs and benefits.

134. Unless the benefits to be derived from a commodity or service exceed the costs associated with it, it will not be sought after. When a decision to acquire a commodity is being considered, the prospective buyer will compare the costs of acquisition and maintenance with the benefits of owning the commodity. Once the purchase has been made, the owner must decide—continually, from day to day—whether the opportunity cost of ownership, the sacrifice of the sale price that cannot be realized so long as ownership continues, is less than the benefits of continued ownership. Thus, both before and after acquisition, costs and benefits must be compared, though the comparison takes a somewhat different form according to whether the acquisition has or has not been consummated.

135. Financial information is unlike other commodities in certain important respects. While, in general, it will not be desired unless its benefits exceed its costs, what makes it different from other commodities, or at least from those that are traded in the marketplace, is that whereas those other commodities are private goods, to be enjoyed only by the buyer and those with whom the buyer chooses to share them, the benefits of information cannot always be confined to those who pay for it. If the whole government and private system by which the flow of financial information is regulated could now be dismantled, if information could be traded between buyers and sellers like other commodities and could be kept from those who did not pay for it, and if consumers of information were willing to rely on their own inquiries, the balance of costs and benefits could be left to the market. But in the real world the market for information is less complete than most other markets, and a standard-setting authority must concern itself with the perceived costs and benefits of the standards it sets—costs and benefits to both users and preparers of such information, to others, like auditors, who are also concerned with it, and to anyone else in society who may be affected.

[13]This section expands on the considerations mentioned in paragraph 23 of Concepts Statement 1.

136. Most of the costs of providing financial information fall initially on the preparers, while the benefits are reaped by both preparers and users. Ultimately, the costs and benefits are diffused quite widely. The costs are mostly passed on to the users of information and to the consumers of goods and services. The benefits also are presumably passed on to consumers by assuring a steady supply of goods and services and more efficient functioning of the marketplace. But, even if the costs and benefits are not traced beyond the preparers and users of information, to say anything precise about their incidence is difficult. There are costs of using information as well as of preparing it; and much published information would be compiled for the preparer's own use even if providing it to stockholders and others were not required. The preparer enjoys other benefits also, such as improved access to capital markets, favorable impact on the enterprise's public relations, and so on.

137. The costs of providing information are of several kinds, including costs of collecting and processing the information, costs of audit if it is subject to audit, costs of disseminating it to those who must receive it, costs associated with the dangers of litigation, and in some instances costs of disclosure in the form of a loss of competitive advantages vis-a-vis trade competitors, labor unions (with a consequent effect on wage demands), or foreign enterprises. The costs to the users of information, over and above those costs that preparers pass on to them, are mainly the costs of analysis and interpretation and may include costs of rejecting information that is redundant, for the diagnosis of redundancy is not without its cost.

138. Society needs information to help allocate resources efficiently, but the benefit to any individual or company from that source is not measurable. Nor is the spur to efficiency that comes from making managers account to stockholders capable of evaluation, either at the level of the enterprise or the economy. It is impossible to imagine a highly developed economy without most of the financial information that it now generates and, for the most part, consumes; yet it is also impossible to place a value on that information.

139. From the point of view of society, the loss of competitive advantage that is said to result from some disclosure requirements is clearly in a different category from the other costs involved. Although the loss to one business enterprise may be a gain to another, the Board is aware of and concerned about the economic effects of the possible discouragement of initiative, innovation, and willingness to take risks if a reward to risk taking is denied. That is another cost that is impossible to begin to quantify.

140. The burden of the costs and the incidence of benefits fall quite unevenly throughout the economy, and it has been rightly observed that ". . . the matter of establishing disclosure requirements becomes not only a matter of judgment but also a complex balancing of many factors so that all costs and benefits receive the consideration they merit. For example, a simple rule that any information useful in making investment decisions should be disclosed fails as completely as a rule that says disclo-

sure should not be required if competitive disadvantage results."[14] The problem is to know how to accomplish that "complex balancing."

141. The Board has watched with sympathetic interest the efforts of the Cost Accounting Standards Board (CASB) to come to grips with the task of comparing the costs and benefits of its standards. The Report of the special group of consultants who were asked by the CASB to examine this matter was submitted on November 13, 1978. The conclusions were quite negative.

> Our conclusion is that no objective cost benefit calculation in aggregate quantitative terms is possible for CASB standards as a whole or for any of them individually. Reasonable people, with some experience in such matters, acting responsibly in a spirit of compromise, using such reliable information as can be gathered together, will make a "calculation," as they must if anything is to be done. But the calculation will be in ordinal rather than cardinal terms; it will be rough rather than precise; it will always be subject to revision, rather than fixed in stone. The situation is not different from that concerning the merits of many other laws, rules, regulations, and administrative decisions. Nor is our conclusion different from the conclusion reached by those concerned with the cost-benefit problem confronting the Paperwork Commission, for example.[15]

142. As the CASB's consultants point out, the reasons for that negative conclusion can be simply stated. The costs and benefits of a standard are both direct and indirect, immediate and deferred. They may be affected by a change in circumstances not foreseen when the standard was promulgated. There are wide variations in the estimates that different people make about the dollar values involved and the rate of discount to be used in reducing them to a present value. "For these reasons," the consultants conclude, "the merits of any Standard, or of the Standards as a whole, can be decided finally only by judgments that are largely subjective. They cannot be decided by scientific test."

143. Despite the difficulties, the Board does not conclude that it should turn its back on the matter, for there are some things that it can do to safeguard the cost-effectiveness of its standards. Before a decision is made to develop a standard, the Board needs to satisfy itself that the matter to be ruled on represents a significant problem and that a standard that is promulgated will not impose costs on the many for the benefit of a few. If the proposal passes that first test, a second test may subsequently be useful. There are usually alternative ways of handling an issue. Is one of them less costly and only slightly less effective? Even if absolute magnitudes cannot

[14]R. K. Mautz and William G. May, *Financial Disclosure in a Competitive Economy* (New York: Financial Executives Research Foundation, 1978), p. 6.

[15]Robert N. Anthony et al., "Report to the Cost Accounting Standards Board by a Special Group of Consultants to Consider Issues Relating to Comparing Costs with Benefits" (1978), p. 1.

be attached to costs and benefits, a comparison between alternatives may yet be possible and useful.

144. Though it is unlikely that significantly improved means of measuring benefits will become available in the foreseeable future, it seems possible that better ways of quantifying the incremental costs of regulations of all kinds may gradually be developed, and the Board will watch any such developments carefully to see whether they can be applied to financial accounting standards. Even if that hope proves to be a vain one, however, the Board cannot cease to be concerned about the cost-effectiveness of its standards. To do so would be a dereliction of its duty and a disservice to its constituents.

This Statement was adopted by the unanimous vote of the seven members of the Financial Accounting Standards Board:

Donald J. Kirk, *Chairman*
Frank E. Block
John W. March
Robert A. Morgan
David Mosso
Robert T. Sprouse
Ralph E. Walters

Appendix A

BACKGROUND INFORMATION

145. The need for a conceptual framework for financial accounting and reporting, beginning with consideration of the objectives of financial reporting, is generally recognized. The Accounting Principles Board issued APB Statement No. 4 on basic concepts and accounting principles in 1970. When the Financial Accounting Standards Board came into existence, the Study Group on the Objectives of Financial Statements was at work, and its Report, *Objectives of Financial Statements,* was published in October 1973 by the American Institute of Certified Public Accountants. A chapter of that report briefly described "certain characteristics . . . [information should possess] to satisfy users' needs"—relevance and materiality, form and substance, reliability, freedom from bias, comparability, consistency, and understandability—which the Study Group called "qualitative characteristics of reporting."

146. The Financial Accounting Standards Board issued FASB Discussion Memorandum, *Conceptual Framework for Accounting and Reporting: Consideration of the Report of the Study Group on the Objectives of Financial Statements,* dated June 6, 1974, and held a public hearing on September 23 and 24, 1974 on the objectives of financial statements. The Discussion Memorandum and the hearing were based primarily on the Report of the Study Group on the Objectives of Financial Statements. The Discussion Memorandum asked respondents to comment on the acceptability of the seven qualitative characteristics in the Report and to suggest needed modifications. The Board received 95 written communications responding to

the Discussion Memorandum, and 20 parties presented their views orally and answered Board members' questions at the hearing.

147. On December 2, 1976, the Board issued three documents:

Tentative Conclusions on Objectives of Financial Statements of Business Enterprises,

FASB Discussion Memorandum, *Conceptual Framework for Financial Accounting and Reporting: Elements of Financial Statements and Their Measurement,* and

Scope and Implications of the Conceptual Framework Project.

One chapter of the Discussion Memorandum was entitled, "Qualities of Useful Financial Information." Although it raised no specific issues, it asked respondents to explain what they meant by relevance, reliability, comparability, and other "qualitative characteristics" and to illustrate those meanings in responding to the issues about elements of financial statements and their measurement and by completing a set of matrixes designed to show trade-offs between various qualities or characteristics. The same task force, with one membership change, provided counsel in preparing both Discussion Memorandums. Eleven persons from academe, the financial community, industry, and public accounting served on the task force while the Discussion Memorandums were written.

148. The Board held public hearings (a) August 1 and 2, 1977 on the *Tentative Conclusions on Objectives of Financial Statements of Business Enterprises* and Chapters 1-5 of the Discussion Memorandum (December 1976) concerning definitions of the elements of financial statements and (b) January 16-18, 1978 on the remaining chapters of that Discussion Memorandum concerning capital maintenance or cost recovery, qualities of useful financial information ("qualitative characteristics"), and measurement of the elements of financial statements. The Board received 332 written communications on the Discussion Memorandum, of which 143 commented on the "qualitative characteristics." Twenty-seven parties presented their views orally and answered Board members' questions at the January 1978 hearing.

149. The Board issued an Exposure Draft of a proposed Statement of Financial Accounting Concepts, *Objectives of Financial Reporting and Elements of Financial Statements of Business Enterprises,* dated December 29, 1977, which included a very brief discussion of some "characteristics or qualities that make financial information useful," noting that those characteristics were to be the subject of another phase of the conceptual framework project. The Board received 135 letters of comment, of which 36 commented on the paragraphs discussing "qualitative characteristics." That discussion was not included in Concepts Statement 1.

150. The Board also issued FASB Discussion Memorandum, *Criteria for Determining Materiality,* on March 21, 1975 and held public hearings on it May 20 and 21,

1976. The Board received 96 written communications on the Discussion Memorandum, and 16 parties presented their views orally and answered Board members' questions at the hearing. The Board explored incorporating the conceptual aspects of the materiality project into the qualitative characteristics project during 1977 and 1978 and formally did so in October 1978.

151. Professor David Solomons, the Arthur Young Professor of Accounting at the Wharton School of the University of Pennsylvania, served as consultant to the Board and staff on the qualitative characteristics project.

Appendix B

PRINCIPAL RESPECTS IN WHICH THIS STATEMENT DIFFERS FROM THE EXPOSURE DRAFT AND OTHER RESPONSES TO LETTERS OF COMMENT ON THE EXPOSURE DRAFT

152. Of the changes made to the Exposure Draft that was issued on August 9, 1979, many were in response to suggestions that were made in the 89 comment letters received during the exposure period. One suggestion was that the definitions that were scattered throughout the Exposure Draft should be brought together in a glossary. That has now been done.

153. The chart that appears on page 44 now distinguishes between primary qualities, ingredients of primary qualities, and secondary qualities that make information useful. The chart also now explicitly introduces decision makers and their characteristics as factors that help to determine what information will be useful in particular situations. Those characteristics include how much knowledge decision makers already have and how well they understand the significance of new information that comes to them. That makes it possible to view relevance as a quality that information has in relation to a situation or a decision rather than as a quality that depends on the personal characteristics of the decision maker. Thus, if information that is relevant to a decision were conveyed in a language that some decision makers did not understand, it would not be useful to them because of their lack of understanding. However, understandability of information is a prerequisite to the information being useful to particular decision makers.

154. The discussion of relevance has been further clarified by recognizing more explicitly the value of information about past activities as distinct from its value for predictive purposes. Thus, predictive value and feedback value are shown as coequal ingredients of relevance. To be relevant, information must have one of them or both, and it must be timely.

155. A clearer distinction is now drawn between the degree of reliability that can be achieved in a particular situation and the perceived need for more reliability or less. In terms of the chronometer-wristwatch analogy in paragraph 73, the wristwatch is not as reliable a timekeeper as the chronometer. It does not need to be. It is the per-

ceived *need* for reliability that is different because of the different uses to which the two instruments are put. That difference does not affect the *nature* of reliability but only the degree of reliability that may be needed for particular uses.

156. The discussion of materiality has been considerably recast, with much of the detail moved into Appendix C. Though the definition of materiality is not substantially changed, its quantitative character is now given a more central position, enabling the distinction between materiality and relevance to be stated more clearly. Though both qualities are present in information only if it "can make a difference" to a decision, relevance stems from the *nature* of the information while materiality depends on the *size* of the judgment item in particular circumstances.

157. Several of those who commented on the Exposure Draft doubted that the qualitative characteristics discussed in it were "operational" in the sense that they provided clear criteria for the selection of a preferred accounting method if two or more alternatives were available. Only in a few cases were other methods of selection proposed that were claimed to be more operational, and after careful review by the Board's staff, those claims had to be rejected as being unrealistic. The Board believes that the approach to preferability choices put forward in this Statement achieves as much operationality as is feasible in the present state of knowledge.The true test will be in the contributions that the criteria discussed here can make to the formulation of future standards. Unanimous acclaim for the Board's decisions is not to be expected; but the basis for those decisions should be better understood if they can be seen to be aimed at obtaining an optimal mix (as judged by the Board) of certain clearly defined informational characteristics.

158. A number of respondents urged the Board to include additional qualitative characteristics in its "hierarchy." All of the proposed additions had already been considered and excluded because they seemed to add little value to other characteristics that were already included. The more items are added, the more the impact of each is diluted. To earn a place, therefore, something really important must be added. None of the new candidates passed that test. For example, objectivity was mentioned by several respondents. Yet, verifiability better expresses the quality that those respondents were concerned with preserving. "Objective" means having an existence independent of the observer. That does not fit accounting measurements at all well, especially measurements such as profit, depreciation and other cost allocations, earnings per share, and others of like kind. Accounting terminology will be improved if verifiability, which reflects what accountants do, replaces objectivity in the accountant's lexicon.

159. Feasibility was another candidate for inclusion in the hierarchy. That has been excluded because it adds nothing to the cost-benefit constraint. In accounting as in other fields, many things are feasible *at a cost*. But an accounting method that, though feasible, yields information that is worth less than it costs is not a good one to choose. For that reason, feasibility has not been included in the hierarchy.

160. Substance over form is an idea that also has its proponents, but it is not included because it would be redundant. The quality of reliability and, in particular, of representational faithfulness leaves no room for accounting representations that subordinate substance to form. Substance over form is, in any case, a rather vague idea that defies precise definition.

Appendix C

QUANTITATIVE MATERIALITY CONSIDERATIONS

161. Each Statement of Financial Accounting Standards issued by the Board has concluded by stating that: "The provisions of this Statement need not be applied to immaterial items." Rule 3-02 of the Securities and Exchange Commission's (SEC) Regulation S-X, "Form and Content of Financial Statements," states that if an "amount which would otherwise be required to be shown with respect to any item is not material, it need not be separately set forth."

162. Those who turn to SEC Regulation S-X for help in understanding the concept of materiality learn that a material matter is one "about which an average prudent investor ought reasonably to be informed" (Rule 1-02) and that material information is "such . . . information as is necessary to make the required statements, in the light of the circumstances under which they are made not misleading" (Rule 3-06). But those statements are not really definitions of materiality in that they provide only general guidance in distinguishing material from immaterial information.

163. The courts have stepped in to fill the gap. It is the impact of information on an investor's judgment that is at the heart of the distinction. To quote the Tenth Circuit Court of Appeals, information is material if ". . . the trading judgment of reasonable investors would not have been left untouched upon receipt of such information."[16] That is very close to the definition of materiality adopted in the *BarChris* decision, in which the judge said that a material fact was one "which if it had been correctly stated or disclosed would have deterred or tended to deter the average prudent investor from purchasing the securities in question."[17] Both statements refer to one particular kind of user of information—a prudent investor—but, of course, the essential idea that they convey is applicable to other users also.

164. Statements by the Supreme Court have given added authority to that view of materiality. In the important case of *TSC Industries Inc.* v. *Northway Inc.*,[18] a case which concerned the omission of certain facts from a proxy statement, the Court held that:

---

[16] *Mitchell* v. *Texas Gulf Sulphur Co.*, 446 F.2D 90, at 99-100 (10th Circuit, 1971).

[17] *Escott et al.* v. *BarChris Construction Corporation et al.*, 283 Fed. Supp. (District Ct. S.D. New York, 1968), p. 681.

[18] CCH *Federal Securities Law Reports* ¶95,615 (US Sup Ct. June 14, 1976).

> An omitted fact is material if there is a substantial likelihood that a reasonable shareholder would consider it important in deciding how to vote. This standard is fully consistent with the . . . general description of materiality as a requirement that "the defect have a significant *propensity* to affect the voting process." It does not require proof of a substantial likelihood that disclosure of the omitted fact would have caused the reasonable investor to change his vote. What the standard does contemplate is a showing of a substantial likelihood that, under all the circumstances, the omitted fact would have assumed actual significance in the deliberations of the reasonable shareholder. Put another way, there must be a substantial likelihood that the disclosure of the omitted fact would have been viewed by the reasonable investor as having significantly altered the "total mix" of information made available.

165. Until such time as the Supreme Court returns to this question, the *Northway* case provides the most authoritative judicial definition of what constitutes a material omitted fact. Examples, taken from earlier cases, of facts that have been held to be "material" are:[19]

1. Failure to disclose a greatly enhanced inventory value (carried on the corporation's financial statements at historical cost) and an intention to realize on it by liquidation. *Speed* v. *Transamerica Corp.*, 99 F. Supp. 808 (D. Del. 1951), *modified and aff'd.*, 235 F.2d 369 (3d Cir. 1956).
2. Failure to disclose pending negotiations to sell all of the assets of the corporation at a price per share substantially larger than that being paid to a selling shareholder. *Kardon* v. *National Gypsum Co.*, 69 F. Supp. 512 (E.D. Pa. 1946), *on the merits*, 73 F. Supp. 798 (E.D. Pa. 1947).
3. Failure to disclose the imminence of a highly profitable transaction by the corporation. *Northern Trust Co.* v. *Essaness Theatres Corp.*, 103 F. Supp. 954 (N.D. Ill. 1952).
4. Failure to disclose a readjustment of reported earnings from 85¢ per share for the first five months of the fiscal year to 12¢ per share for the first six months. *Financial Industrial Fund, Inc.* v. *McDonnell Douglas Corp.*, CCH Fed. Sec. L. Rep. ¶93,004 (D. Col. 1971).
5. Failure to disclose that investigations were pending by the SEC. *Hill York Corp.* v. *American International Franchises, Inc.*, 448 F.2d 680 (5th Cir. 1971).
6. Failure to disclose firm offers, in contrast to appraisals, greatly higher than the book value for the physical facilities of the acquired company which the acquiring company intended to liquidate as soon as possible. *Gerstle* v. *Gamble-Skogmo, Inc.*, 478 F2d 1281, 1295 (2d Cir. 1973).

[19]The following list is taken from James O. Hewitt, "Developing Concepts of Materiality and Disclosure," *The Business Lawyer*, Vol. 32 (April 1977), pp. 910 and 911. A word of caution may be in order. The extreme brevity of the citations given here inevitably causes many important aspects of these cases to be omitted.

7. Failure to disclose active negotiations by tender offeror to sell significant assets substantially below book value. *Chris Craft Industries, Inc.* v. *Piper Aircraft Corp.,* 480 F.2d 341, 367 (2d Cir. 1973).

166. The Discussion Memorandum on materiality cited some of the quantitative guides to materiality in authoritative statements issued by the SEC and other regulatory agencies and standard-setting bodies. It may be helpful to be reminded how certain specific situations have been dealt with in practice. Some of these examples of materiality are brought together again in Table 1.

Table 1

EXAMPLES OF QUANTITATIVE MATERIALITY GUIDELINES

Subject	Authority	Materiality Guidelines
Dilution of earnings per share (EPS)	APB Opinion No. 15	Reduction of EPS of less than 3% in the aggregate not material.
Separate disclosure of balance sheet items	SEC Accounting Series Release No. 41	If 10% or more of their immediate category or more than 5% of total assets.
Receivables from officers and stockholders	SEC Regulation S-X, Rule 5-04	Disclose details of receivables from any officer or principal stockholder if it equals or exceeds $20,000 or 1% of total assets.
Segmental reporting: recognition of reportable segment	Statement of Financial Accounting Standards No. 14	Revenue equals or exceeds 10% of combined revenues, etc.
Gross rental expense under leases	SEC Accounting Series Release No. 147	Disclose total rental expense, etc., if gross rents exceed 1% of consolidated revenue.
Information on present value of lease commitments under noncapitalized financing leases	SEC Accounting Series Release No. 147	Disclose if present value is 5% or more of total of long-term debt, stockholders' equity, and present value of commitments, or if impact of capitalization on income is 3% or more of average net income for most recent 3 years.

Table 1 (continued)

Subject	Authority	Materiality Guidelines
Proved oil and gas reserves	SEC Accounting Series Release No. 258	Disclose quantities of proved oil and gas reserves and historical financial data unless, for each of the two most recent years, revenues and income from oil and gas producing activities and certain oil and gas capital values do not exceed 10% of the related company totals.

167. One approach in seeking guidance about what constitutes a material item or a material error is to examine current practice empirically. One study[20] investigated the factors that entered into judgments about the materiality of an error and found that the primary factor was the ratio of the error to current income before tax. The error took on special significance if it changed the trend in income. Another study[21] examined a sample of audit reports to try to determine the factors that caused auditors to render qualified opinions when there was an accounting change. The effect on net income (as a percentage) was found to be the only significant variable, but there was little uniformity among auditors about when an accounting change was material. A much more extensive study, conducted for the Financial Executives Research Foundation[22] examined several kinds of materiality judgments. Perhaps its principal conclusion was that a "rule of thumb" of 5-10 percent of net income is widely used as a general materiality criterion.

168. A different approach looks to security prices to determine materiality norms. According to that view, "an observed association between extant security prices and reported accounting data (or changes therein) provides prima facie evidence as to the informational content of accounting numbers."[23] That means that the materiality of information released to the market can be tested by observing its impact on security prices. Of course, that can only be done after the event, whereas preparers and audi-

---

[20]Sam M. Woolsey, "Materiality Survey," *The Journal of Accountancy* (September 1973), pp. 91 and 92.

[21]Paul Frishkoff, "An Empirical Investigation of the Concept of Materiality in Accounting," *Empirical Research in Accounting: Selected Studies* (1970), pp. 116-129.

[22]James W. Pattillo, *The Concept of Materiality in Financial Reporting* (New York: Financial Executives Research Foundation, 1976).

[23]Melvin C. O'Connor and Daniel W. Collins, "Toward Establishing User-Oriented Materiality Standards," *The Journal of Accountancy* (December 1974), p. 70.

tors have to make materiality judgments before information is released to the market. Presumably they are to act in the light of market behavior observed in similar circumstances.

169. Without doubt, observations of market behavior can improve understanding of what constitutes material information. But the market's anticipation of accounting information months before it is released and the dilution of accounting influences on prices by other factors acting concurrently make price fluctuations, in the present state of knowledge, too blunt an instrument to be depended on to set materiality guidelines.

170. It is already possible to simulate some aspects of the decision making processes of auditors by constructing a model that will bring into play many of the decision variables that enter into materiality judgments.[24] Those variables would normally include the nature and size of the judgment item in question (for example, an accounting change or a contingent liability), the size of the enterprise, its financial condition and recent changes in condition, present and recent profitability, and as many as possible of the other significant factors that affect materiality judgments. Further development of such models is perhaps the most promising line of research that needs to be pursued before accountants can hope to be relieved of the onerous duty of making materiality decisions. But, until further progress has been made, that duty must continue to be discharged by the exercise of judgment taking into account as many relevant considerations as possible.

---

[24]For an example, see "Policy-Capturing on Selected Materiality Judgments," by James R. Boatsman and Jack C. Robertson (*Accounting Review,* April 1974, pp. 342-352).

Statement of Financial Accounting Concepts No. 3 Elements of Financial Statements of Business Enterprises

STATUS

Issued: December 1980

Affects: No other pronouncements

Affected by: Superseded by CON 6

Concepts No. 6 replaces Concepts No. 3 expanding its scope to encompass not-for-profit organizations. Below is a cross-reference list showing where paragraphs in Concepts No. 3 may be found in Concepts No. 6.

	Concepts Statements No.3	Concepts Statements No.6
	Paragraph Numbers	Paragraph Numbers
Introduction	1– 17	1– 23
Scope and Content of Statement	1– 8	1– 8
Other Possible Elements of Financial Statements	3– 4	3– 4
Elements and Financial Representations	5– 7	5– 7
Other Scope and Content Matters	8	8
Objectives, Qualitative Characteristics, and Elements	9– 13	9– 19
Interrelation of Elements—Articulation	14– 15	20– 21
Definition, Recognition, Measurement, and Display	16– 17	22– 23
Definitions of Elements	18– 89	24–133
Assets	19– 27	25– 34
Characteristics of Assets	20– 24	26– 31
Transactions and Events That Change Assets	25– 26	32– 33
Valuation Accounts	27	34
Liabilities	28– 36	35– 43
Characteristics of Liabilities	29– 33	36– 40
Transactions and Events That Change Liabilities	34– 35	41– 42
Valuation Accounts	36	43
Effects of Uncertainty	37– 42	44– 48
Note on Uncertainty and Certain Recognition Matters	42	deleted
Equity	43– 51	49– 65
Characteristics of Equity of Business Enterprises	44– 47	60– 63

	Concepts Statements No.3 Paragraph Numbers	Concepts Statements No.6 Paragraph Numbers
Equity and Liabilities	48– 49	54– 59
Transactions and Events That Change Equity	50– 51	64– 65
Investments by and Distributions to Owners	52– 55	66– 69
Characteristics of Investments by and Distributions to Owners	54– 55	68– 69
Comprehensive Income of Business Enterprises	56– 62	70– 77
Concepts of Capital Maintenance	57– 58	71– 72
Characteristics, Sources, and Components of Comprehensive Income	59– 62	73– 77
Revenues	63– 64	78– 79
Characteristics of Revenues	64	79
Expenses	65– 66	80– 81
Characteristics of Expenses	66	81
Gains and Losses	67– 73	82– 89
Characteristics of Gains and Losses	69– 71	84– 86
Revenues, Expenses, Gains, and Losses	72– 73	87– 89
Accrual Accounting and Related Concepts	74– 89	134–152
Transactions, Events, and Circumstances	75– 78	135–138
Accrual Accounting	79– 80	139–140
Accrual and Deferral (Including Allocation and Amortization)	81– 82	141–142
Realization and Recognition	83	143
Recognition, Matching, and Allocation	84– 89	144–152
Appendix A: Background Information	90– 95	153–163
Appendix B: Characteristics of Assets, Liabilities, and Equity or Net Assets and of Changes in Them	96–180	164–255
Purpose and Summary of Appendix	96–102	164–170
Characteristics of Assets	103–123	171–191
Future Economic Benefits	104–114	172–182
Assets and Costs	110–114	178–182
Control by a Particular Entity	115–121	183–189
Control and Legal Rights	118–119	186–187
Noncontrolled Benefits	120–121	188–189
Occurrence of a Past Transaction or Event	122–123	190–191
Characteristics of Liabilities	124–143	192–211
Required Future Sacrifice of Assets	125–130	193–198
Liabilities and Proceeds	130	198
Obligation of a Particular Entity	131–137	199–205
Occurrence of a Past Transaction or Event	138–143	206–211

	Concepts Statements No.3 Paragraph Numbers	Concepts Statements No.6 Paragraph Numbers
Characteristics of Equity of Business Enterprises	144–146	212–214
Residual Interest	145	213
Invested and Earned Equity	146	214
Characteristics of Comprehensive Income of Business Enterprises and Its Components	147–152	215–220
Interest in Information about Sources of Comprehensive Income	151–152	219–220
Examples to Illustrate Concepts	153–180	229–255
Deferred Gross Profit on Installment Sales	156–158	232–234
Debt Discount, Premium, and Issue Cost	159–162	235–239
Deferred Income Tax Credits	163–165	240–242
Deferred Investment Tax Credits	166–168	243–245
Deferred Costs of Assets	169–173	246–250
Estimated Loss on Purchase Commitments	174–176	251–253
Other Losses Incurred	177–178	deleted
Minority Interests and Stock Purchase Warrants	179	254
Examples Do Not Govern Practice	180	255

(The next page is 144.)

Statement of Financial Accounting Concepts No. 4 Objectives of Financial Reporting by Nonbusiness Organizations

STATUS

Issued: December 1980

Affects: No other pronouncements

Affected by: No other pronouncements

HIGHLIGHTS

[*Best understood in context of full Statement*]

- This Statement establishes the objectives of general purpose external financial reporting by nonbusiness organizations.

  —Based on its review of those objectives and the objectives set forth in FASB Concepts Statement No. 1, *Objectives of Financial Reporting by Business Enterprises,* the Board has concluded that it is not necessary to develop an independent conceptual framework for any particular category of entities.

  —The two sets of objectives will serve as the foundation of an integrated conceptual framework for financial accounting and reporting that, when completed, will have relevance to all entities while providing appropriate consideration of any different reporting objectives and concepts that may apply to only certain types of entities.

  —Pending resolution of the appropriate structure for setting financial accounting and reporting standards for state and local governmental units, the Board has deferred a final decision on whether the objectives in this Statement should apply to general purpose external financial reporting of those units. On the basis of its study to date, the Board is aware of no persuasive evidence that the objectives in this Statement are inappropriate for that type of financial reporting by state and local governmental units.

  —Based on its study, the Board believes that the objectives of general purpose external financial reporting for government-sponsored entities (for example, hospitals, universities, or utilities) engaged in activities that are not unique to government should be similar to those of business enterprises or other nonbusiness organizations engaged in similar activities.

- This Statement focuses on organizations that have predominantly nonbusiness characteristics that heavily influence the operations of the organization.

  —The major distinguishing characteristics of nonbusiness organizations include: (a) receipts of significant amounts of resources from resource providers who do not expect to receive either repayment or economic benefits proportionate to resources provided, (b) operating purposes that are primarily other than to provide goods or services at a profit or profit equivalent, and (c) absence of defined ownership interests that can be sold, transferred, or redeemed, or that convey entitlement to a share of a residual distribution of resources in the event of liquidation of the organization.

  —These characteristics result in certain types of transactions that are infrequent in business enterprises, such as contributions and grants, and in the absence of transactions with owners.

  —The line between nonbusiness organizations and business enterprises is not always sharp since the incidence and relative importance of those characteristics in any organization are different. This suggests that, for purposes of developing financial reporting objectives, a spectrum of organizations exists ranging from those with clearly dominant nonbusiness characteristics to those with wholly business characteristics.

  —Examples of organizations that clearly fall outside the focus of this Statement include all investor-owned enterprises and other types of organizations, such as mutual insurance companies and other mutual cooperative entities that provide dividends, lower costs, or other economic benefits directly and proportionately to their owners, members, or participants.

  —Examples of organizations that clearly fall within the focus of this Statement include most human service organizations, churches, foundations, and some other organizations, such as those private nonprofit hospitals and nonprofit schools that receive a significant portion of their financial resources from sources other than the sale of goods and services.

  —Borderline cases may exist where organizations possess some of the distinguishing characteristics but not others. Examples are those private nonprofit hospitals and nonprofit schools that may receive relatively small amounts of contributions and grants but finance their capital needs largely from the proceeds of debt issues and their operating needs largely from service charges. As a result, the objectives of Concepts Statement 1 may be more appropriate for those organizations.

- The objectives in this Statement stem from the common interests of those who provide resources to nonbusiness organizations in the services those organizations provide and their continuing ability to provide services.

- Nonbusiness organizations generally have no single indicator of performance comparable to a business enterprise's profit. Thus, other indicators of performance usually are needed.

- The performance of nonbusiness organizations generally is not subject to the test of direct competition in markets to the extent that business enterprises are.

  —Other kinds of controls introduced to compensate for the lesser influence of markets are a major characteristic of their operations and affect the objectives of their financial reporting. Controls, such as formal budgets and donor restrictions on the use of resources, give managers a special responsibility to ensure compliance. Information about departures from those mandates is important in assessing how well managers have discharged their stewardship responsibilities.

- The objectives in this Statement apply to general purpose external financial reporting by nonbusiness organizations.

  —The objectives stem primarily from the needs of external users who generally cannot prescribe the information they want from an organization.

  —In addition to information provided by general purpose external financial reporting, managers and, to some extent, governing bodies need a great deal of internal accounting information to carry out their responsibilities in planning and controlling activities. That information and information directed at meeting the specialized needs of users having the power to obtain the information they need are beyond the scope of this Statement.

- The objectives of financial reporting are affected by the economic, legal, political, and social environment in which financial reporting takes place.

  —The operating environments of nonbusiness organizations and business enterprises are similar in many ways. Both nonbusiness organizations and business enterprises produce and distribute goods and services and use scarce resources in doing so.

  —Differences between nonbusiness organizations and business enterprises arise in the ways they obtain resources. Noneconomic reasons are commonly factors in decisions to provide resources to particular nonbusiness organizations.

- The objectives also are affected by the characteristics and limitations of the kind of information that financial reporting can provide.

  —The information provided by financial reporting is primarily financial in nature: It is generally quantified and expressed in units of money. However, quantified information expressed in terms other than units of money and nonquantified information may be needed to understand the significance of information expressed in units of money or to help in assessing the performance of a nonbusiness organization.

—The information provided by financial reporting pertains to individual reporting entities, often results from approximate rather than exact measures, largely reflects the effects of transactions and events that have already happened, is but one source of information needed by those who make decisions about nonbusiness organizations, and is provided and used at a cost.

- The objectives state that:

—Financial reporting by nonbusiness organizations should provide information that is useful to present and potential resource providers and other users in making rational decisions about the allocation of resources to those organizations.

—Financial reporting should provide information to help present and potential resource providers and other users in assessing the services that a nonbusiness organization provides and its ability to continue to provide those services.

—Financial reporting should provide information that is useful to present and potential resource providers and other users in assessing how managers of a nonbusiness organization have discharged their stewardship responsibilities and about other aspects of their performance.

—Financial reporting should provide information about the economic resources, obligations, and net resources of an organization, and the effects of transactions, events, and circumstances that change resources and interests in those resources.

—Financial reporting should provide information about the performance of an organization during a period. Periodic measurement of the changes in the amount and nature of the net resources of a nonbusiness organization and information about the service efforts and accomplishments of an organization together represent the information most useful in assessing its performance.

—Financial reporting should provide information about how an organization obtains and spends cash or other liquid resources, about its borrowing and repayment of borrowing, and about other factors that may affect an organization's liquidity.

—Financial reporting should include explanations and interpretations to help users understand financial information provided.

- Background information relating to the development of this Statement is included in paragraphs 57-66. Paragraph 67 contains a comparison of the objectives in this Statement to those in Concepts Statement 1.

Statement of Financial Accounting Concepts No. 4
Objectives of Financial Reporting by Nonbusiness Organizations

STATEMENTS OF FINANCIAL ACCOUNTING CONCEPTS

This Statement of Financial Accounting Concepts is one of a series of publications in the Board's conceptual framework for financial accounting and reporting. Statements in the series are intended to set forth objectives and fundamentals that will be the basis for development of financial accounting and reporting standards. The objectives identify the goals and purposes of financial reporting. The fundamentals are the underlying concepts of financial accounting—concepts that guide the selection of transactions, events, and circumstances to be accounted for; their recognition and measurement; and the means of summarizing and communicating them to interested parties. Concepts of that type are fundamental in the sense that other concepts flow from them and repeated reference to them will be necessary in establishing, interpreting, and applying accounting and reporting standards.

The conceptual framework is a coherent system of interrelated objectives and fundamentals that is expected to lead to consistent standards and that prescribes the nature, function, and limits of financial accounting and reporting. It is expected to serve the public interest by providing structure and direction to financial accounting and reporting to facilitate the provision of evenhanded financial and related information that helps promote the efficient allocation of scarce resources in the economy and society, including assisting capital and other markets to function efficiently.

Establishment of objectives and identification of fundamental concepts will not directly solve financial accounting and reporting problems. Rather, objectives give direction and concepts are tools for solving problems.

The Board itself is likely to be the most direct beneficiary of the guidance provided by the Statements in this series. They will guide the Board in developing accounting and reporting standards by providing the Board with a common foundation and basic reasoning on which to consider merits of alternatives.

However, knowledge of the objectives and concepts the Board will use in developing standards also should enable those who are affected by or interested in financial accounting standards to understand better the purposes, content, and characteristics of information provided by financial accounting and reporting. That knowledge is expected to enhance the usefulness of, and confidence in, financial accounting and reporting. The concepts also may provide some guidance in analyzing new or emerging problems of financial accounting and reporting in the absence of applicable authoritative pronouncements.

Statements of Financial Accounting Concepts do not establish standards prescribing accounting procedures or disclosure practices for particular items or events, which are issued by the Board as Statements of Financial Accounting Standards. Rather, Statements in this series describe concepts and relations that will underlie

future financial accounting standards and practices and in due course serve as a basis for evaluating existing standards and practices.*

The Board recognizes that in certain respects current generally accepted accounting principles may be inconsistent with those that may derive from the objectives and concepts set forth in Statements in this series. However, a Statement of Financial Accounting Concepts does not (a) require a change in existing generally accepted accounting principles; (b) amend, modify, or interpret Statements of Financial Accounting Standards, Interpretations of the FASB, Opinions of the Accounting Principles Board, or Bulletins of the Committee on Accounting Procedure that are in effect; or (c) justify either changing existing generally accepted accounting and reporting practices or interpreting the pronouncements listed in item (b) based on personal interpretations of the objectives and concepts in the Statements of Financial Accounting Concepts.

Since a Statement of Financial Accounting Concepts does not establish generally accepted accounting principles or standards for the disclosure of financial information outside of financial statements in published financial reports, it is not intended to invoke application of Rule 203 or 204 of the Rules of Conduct of the Code of Professional Ethics of the American Institute of Certified Public Accountants (or successor rules or arrangements of similar scope and intent).†

Like other pronouncements of the Board, a Statement of Financial Accounting Concepts may be amended, superseded, or withdrawn by appropriate action under the Board's *Rules of Procedure.*

---

*Generally accepted accounting principles for nonbusiness organizations are primarily set forth in publications of the American Institute of Certified Public Accountants (AICPA) and other bodies, such as the National Council on Governmental Accounting (NCGA). The Board has agreed to exercise responsibility, except as noted below, for all the specialized accounting and reporting principles and practices in AICPA Statements of Position and Guides that are neither superseded by nor contained in Accounting Research Bulletins, Accounting Principles Board Opinions, FASB Statements, and FASB Interpretations. The Board deferred similar action with regard to those specialized accounting and reporting principles and practices contained in the AICPA Industry Audit Guide, *Audits of State and Local Governmental Units,* and the three Statements of Position (75-3, *Accruals of Revenues and Expenditures by State and Local Governmental Units;* 77-2, *Accounting for Interfund Transfers of State and Local Governmental Units;* and 80-2, *Accounting and Financial Reporting by Governmental Units*) that supplement that Guide. In so doing, the Board noted that at the present time the accounting and reporting by such governmental units is addressed by the AICPA and the NCGA. The Board also noted that discussions are continuing among interested parties, including the AICPA, the Financial Accounting Foundation (FAF), and NCGA, as to what the appropriate structure for accounting standard setting for such governmental units should be. Until the matter is resolved, the FASB proposes no changes with respect to its involvement with pronouncements in that area (paragraphs 3-5).

†Rule 203 prohibits a member of the American Institute of Certified Public Accountants from expressing an opinion that financial statements conform with generally accepted accounting principles if those statements contain a material departure from an accounting principle promulgated by the Financial Accounting Standards Board, unless the member can demonstrate that because of unusual circumstances the financial statements otherwise would have been misleading. Rule 204 requires members of the Institute to justify departures from standards promulgated by the Financial Accounting Standards Board for the disclosure of information outside of financial statements in published financial reports.

FASB PUBLICATIONS ON CONCEPTUAL FRAMEWORK

Statements of Financial Accounting Concepts

No.1, *Objectives of Financial Reporting by Business Enterprises* (November 1978)

No. 2, *Qualitative Characteristics of Accounting Information* (May 1980)

No. 3, *Elements of Financial Statements of Business Enterprises* (December 1980)

Discussion Memorandums and Invitations to Comment Having Issues Being (or Yet to Be) Considered by the Board

Elements of Financial Statements and Their Measurement (December 2, 1976)

Reporting Earnings (July 31, 1979)

Financial Statements and Other Means of Financial Reporting (May 12, 1980)

Reporting Funds Flows, Liquidity, and Financial Flexibility (December 15, 1980)

Other Projects in Process

Accounting Recognition Criteria

CONTENTS

	Paragraph Numbers
Highlights	
Introduction and Background	1—32
Scope	1— 9
General	1— 2
State and Local Governmental Units	3— 5
Distinguishing Characteristics of Nonbusiness Organizations	6— 9
General Purpose External Financial Reporting	10—12
Environmental Context of Objectives	13—22
Characteristics and Limitations of Information Provided by Financial Reporting	23—28
Types of Users and Their Interests	29—32
Objectives of Financial Reporting	33—55
Information Useful in Making Resource Allocation Decisions	35—37
Information Useful in Assessing Services and Ability to Provide Services	38—39
Information Useful in Assessing Management Stewardship and Performance	40—42
Information about Economic Resources, Obligations, Net Resources, and Changes in Them	43—54
Economic Resources, Obligations, and Net Resources	44—46
Organization Performance	47—53
Nature of and Relation between Inflows and Outflows	48—50
Service Efforts and Accomplishments	51—53
Liquidity	54
Managers' Explanations and Interpretations	55
The Nonbusiness Objectives Project—A Perspective	56
Appendix A: Background Information	57—66
Brief History of FASB Nonbusiness Objectives Project	57—64
State and Local Governmental Units	65—66
Appendix B: Comparison of Objectives in This Statement to Those in Concepts Statement 1	67

INTRODUCTION AND BACKGROUND

Scope

General

1. This Statement establishes the objectives of general purpose external financial reporting by nonbusiness organizations. Those objectives, together with the objectives set forth in FASB Concepts Statement No. 1, *Objectives of Financial Reporting by Business Enterprises,* will serve as the foundation of the conceptual framework the Board is developing for financial accounting and reporting. Based on its review of the similarities and differences between those two sets of objectives, the Board has concluded that it is not necessary to develop an independent conceptual framework for any particular category of entities (e.g., nonbusiness organizations or business enterprises). Rather, its goal is to develop an integrated conceptual framework that has relevance to all entities and that provides appropriate consideration of any different reporting objectives and concepts that may apply to only certain types of entities. Consideration of the differences between the objectives of financial reporting set forth in this Statement and those in Concepts Statement 1 will be most useful in helping to identify those areas that may require unique treatment. Appendix A to this Statement provides background information. Appendix B compares the objectives of this Statement and Concepts Statement 1, noting the many areas of similarity and the few, but important, areas of difference (paragraph 9).

2. This Statement uses terminology that has been chosen carefully to avoid prejudging issues that may be subjects of other conceptual framework projects. For example, it uses the terms *resource inflows* and *outflows* rather than *revenues, expenses,* and *expenditures.* The reasons for the Board's conclusions are included in the text rather than in a separate appendix.

State and Local Governmental Units

3. From its outset, the project leading to this Statement has included governmental units in its scope, and the Exposure Draft included governmental examples. On the basis of its study to date, the Board is aware of no persuasive evidence that the objectives in this Statement are inappropriate for general purpose external financial reports of governmental units. Nonetheless, the appropriate structure for setting financial accounting and reporting standards for state and local governmental units continues to be discussed.[1] Pending resolution of that issue, the Board has deferred a final decision on whether the objectives set forth in this Statement should apply to general purpose external financial reporting by state and local governmental units.

[1]The Board recognizes that standard setting for the federal government is not in question. Although the Board sees no conceptual reasons why the objectives in this Statement could not be applied to general purpose external financial reporting by the federal government, the Board acknowledges that determination is the responsibility of others.

4. If the responsibility for standard setting was ultimately given to the Financial Accounting Standards Board, the Board would expect to consider the findings of research in process by the National Council on Governmental Accounting (NCGA), the Council of State Governments (CSG) (paragraphs 65 and 66), and other intervening research. Before reaching a decision, it would also solicit additional views regarding the applicability of the conclusions in this Statement to general purpose external financial reporting of state and local governmental units.

5. Based on its study, the Board believes that the objectives of general purpose external financial reporting for government-sponsored entities (for example, hospitals, universities, or utilities) engaged in activities that are not unique to government should be similar to those of business enterprises or other nonbusiness organizations engaged in similar activities. Accordingly, examples of such government-sponsored organizations and activities are included in the sections of this Statement that discuss the environment in which nonbusiness organizations operate and the users of their financial reports.

Distinguishing Characteristics of Nonbusiness Organizations

6. The major distinguishing characteristics of nonbusiness organizations include:

a. Receipts of significant amounts of resources from resource providers who do not expect to receive either repayment or economic benefits proportionate to resources provided
b. Operating purposes that are other than to provide goods or services at a profit or profit equivalent
c. Absence of defined ownership interests that can be sold, transferred, or redeemed, or that convey entitlement to a share of a residual distribution of resources in the event of liquidation of the organization.

These characteristics result in certain types of transactions that are largely, although not entirely, absent in business enterprises, such as contributions and grants,[2] and to the absence of transactions with owners, such as issuing and redeeming stock and paying dividends. Because the authoritative accounting literature has largely focused on problems commonly encountered in business enterprises, it has not dealt comprehensively with these unique areas in nonbusiness organizations.

7. This Statement focuses on organizations that have predominantly nonbusiness characteristics that heavily influence the operations of the organization. The line

[2]These types of transactions are classified in APB Statement No. 4, *Basic Concepts and Accounting Principles Underlying Financial Statements of Business Enterprises,* as nonreciprocal transfers. Nonreciprocal transfers are therein defined as "transfers in one direction of resources or obligations, either from the enterprise to other entities or from other entities to the enterprise" (paragraphs 62 and 182). Two types of such transfers noted are: (a) transfers between the enterprise and its owners and (b) transfers between the enterprise and entities other than owners. Transactions of the second type frequently are found in nonbusiness organizations.

between nonbusiness organizations and business enterprises is not always sharp since the incidence and relative importance of those characteristics in any organization are different. This suggests that, for purposes of developing financial reporting objectives, a spectrum of organizations exists ranging from those with clearly dominant nonbusiness characteristics to those with wholly business characteristics. Examples of organizations that clearly fall outside the focus of this Statement include all investor-owned enterprises and other types of organizations, such as mutual insurance companies and other mutual cooperative entities that provide dividends, lower costs, or other economic benefits directly and proportionately to their owners, members, or participants. The objectives of financial reporting set forth in Concepts Statement 1 are appropriate for those types of organizations. Examples of organizations that clearly fall within the focus of this Statement include most human service organizations, churches, foundations, and some other organizations, such as those private nonprofit hospitals and nonprofit schools that receive a significant portion of their financial resources from sources other than the sale of goods and services.[3] As happens with any distinction, there will be borderline cases. This will be true especially for organizations that possess some of the distinguishing characteristics of nonbusiness organizations but not others.

8. Some organizations have no ownership interests but are essentially self-sustaining from fees they charge for goods and services. Examples are those private nonprofit hospitals and nonprofit schools that may receive relatively small amounts of contributions and grants but finance their capital needs largely from the proceeds of debt issues and their operating needs largely from service charges rather than from private philanthropy or governmental grants. As a result, assessment of amounts, timing, and uncertainty of cash flows becomes the dominant interest of their creditors and other resource providers and profitability becomes an important indicator of performance. Consequently, the objectives of Concepts Statement 1 may be more appropriate for those organizations.[4]

9. The objectives in this Statement stem from the common interests of those who provide resources to nonbusiness organizations in the services those organizations provide and their continuing ability to provide services. In contrast, the objectives of financial reporting of Concepts Statement 1 stem from the interests of resource pro-

[3]The FASB Research Report, *Financial Accounting in Nonbusiness Organizations,* distinguishes two types of nonprofit organizations based "on a difference in the source of the financial resources" (page 161). A Type A nonprofit organization is therein defined as "a nonprofit organization whose financial resources are obtained, entirely, or almost entirely, from revenues from the sale of goods and services" (page 162). A Type B nonprofit organization, in contrast, is defined as "a nonprofit organization that obtains a significant amount of financial resources from sources other than the sale of goods and services" (page 162). The Type B category corresponds to the type of organizations that clearly falls within the focus of this Statement.

[4]The organizations described in this paragraph correspond to the Type A category described in the preceding footnote. To the extent, however, that Type A organizations have the unique transactions described in paragraph 6, they naturally will be impacted by standards promulgated by the Board in those areas.

viders in the prospects of receiving cash as a return of and return on their investment.[5] Despite different interests, resource providers of all entities look to information about economic resources, obligations, net resources, and changes in them for information that is useful in assessing their interests. All such resource providers focus on indicators of organization performance and information about management stewardship. Nonbusiness organizations generally have no single indicator of performance comparable to a business enterprise's profit. Thus, other indicators of performance are usually needed. This Statement sets forth two performance indicators for nonbusiness organizations: information about the nature of and relation between inflows and outflows of resources and information about service efforts and accomplishments. Moreover, the performance of nonbusiness organizations generally is not subject to the test of direct competition in markets to the extent that business enterprises are. Other kinds of controls introduced to compensate for the lesser influence of markets are a major characteristic of their operations and affect the objectives of their financial reporting. Controls, such as formal budgets and donor restrictions on the use of resources, give managers a special responsibility to ensure compliance. Information about departures from those mandates that may impinge upon an organization's financial performance or its ability to provide a satisfactory level of services is important in assessing how well managers have discharged their stewardship responsibilities. Paragraphs 13-22 compare the environments of nonbusiness organizations and business enterprises and provide a basis for the similarities and differences noted in this section and elsewhere in this Statement.

General Purpose External Financial Reporting

10. The objectives in this Statement apply to general purpose external financial reporting by nonbusiness organizations. The aim of that type of financial reporting is limited. It does not attempt to meet all informational needs of those interested in nonbusiness organizations nor to furnish all the types of information that financial reporting can provide. For example, although managers and governing bodies of nonbusiness organizations are interested in the information provided by general purpose external financial reporting, they also need additional information to help them carry out their planning, controlling, and other stewardship responsibilities (paragraph 32). Nor is general purpose external financial reporting intended to meet specialized needs of regulatory bodies, some donors or grantors, or others having the authority to obtain the information they need (paragraph 31). Rather, general purpose external financial reporting focuses on providing information to meet the common interests of external users who generally cannot prescribe the information they want from an organization. Those users must use the information that is communi-

[5]Creditors of nonbusiness organizations are also interested in receiving cash. Because of the differences in environment (principally the motivations of other resource providers) and different indicators of the performance of a nonbusiness organization, creditors also look to information useful in assessing the services that type of organization provides and its ability to continue to provide services to satisfy their basic interest in the prospect for cash flows.

cated to them by the organization. The most obvious and important users fitting that description in the nonbusiness environment are resource providers, such as members, taxpayers, contributors, and creditors (paragraph 36).

11. The objectives in this Statement are not restricted to information communicated by financial statements. Financial reporting includes not only financial statements but also other means of communicating information that relates, directly or indirectly, to the information provided by the accounting system, that is, information about an organization's resources and obligations.[6]

12. For convenience, *financial reporting* is used in place of *general purpose external financial reporting by nonbusiness organizations* in the remainder of this Statement.

Environmental Context of Objectives

13. Financial reporting is not an end in itself but is intended to provide information that is useful in making economic decisions—for making reasoned choices among alternative uses of scarce resources.[7] Thus, the objectives in this Statement stem largely from the needs of those for whom the information is intended. Those needs depend significantly on the activities of nonbusiness organizations and the decisions that users of the information make about them. Accordingly, the objectives in this Statement are affected by the economic, legal, political, and social environment within which those organizations function in the United States. The objectives are also affected by the characteristics and limitations of the information that financial reporting can provide (paragraphs 23-28).

14. The operating environments of nonbusiness organizations and business enterprises are similar in many ways. Both nonbusiness organizations and business enterprises produce and distribute goods or services and use scarce resources in doing so. They sometimes provide essentially the same goods or services. For example, both municipal transportation systems significantly subsidized by general tax revenues and private bus lines may carry passengers within a large city, and both private nonprofit organizations supported by significant philanthropy and investor-owned enterprises may operate theatrical, dance, and musical organizations.[8] Both non-

[6]Distinctions between financial reporting and financial statements are discussed at more length in Concepts Statement 1 (paragraphs 5-8), and are the subject of another phase of the Board's conceptual framework project.

[7]Economic decisions about nonbusiness organizations may take different forms depending on the factors that are evident in the resource allocation process affecting an organization. For example, if an element of compulsion is present as it is with members paying dues or taxpayers paying taxes, this Statement describes processes, such as approval of budgets, elections, referendums, and involvement in legislative processes, through which resource providers decide or influence decisions about matters that affect the amount and use of resources allocated to organizations. A member may discontinue membership or a taxpayer may choose to locate in one governmental jurisdiction rather than another as a result of assessment of their respective policies. That kind of action also represents, in part, the result of an economic decision.

[8]Other nonprofit organizations (paragraph 8) lacking all the distinguishing characteristics of nonbusiness organizations also may provide the services described in this sentence.

business organizations and business enterprises obtain resources from external sources and are accountable to those who provide resources or their representatives. Both are integral parts of the national economy and interrelate directly or indirectly with other organizations. Both own or control supplies of resources, some of which are used in current operations and some of which are held for use in future periods. Both incur obligations. Some nonbusiness organizations, as well as business enterprises, incur and pay taxes, and both are subject to governmental laws and regulations. Both must be financially viable: To achieve their operating objectives, they must, *in the long run,* receive at least as many resources as they need to provide goods and services at levels satisfactory to resource providers and other constituents.[9] Both generally obtain resources from the same pool of resource providers, and the resources available for use by all organizations are limited.

15. Differences between nonbusiness organizations and business enterprises arise principally in the ways they obtain resources. The following descriptions begin with areas of greatest similarity between nonbusiness organizations and business enterprises and end with the areas of greatest difference.

16. Both nonbusiness organizations and business enterprises obtain resources in exchange transactions in markets. Both obtain labor, materials, and facilities or their use by paying for them or agreeing to pay for them in the future.[10] Both may borrow funds through bank loans, mortgages, or other direct loans or through issuing debt securities to creditors who commonly may evaluate and compare the risks and returns of securities of both nonbusiness organizations and business enterprises.

17. Both nonbusiness organizations and business enterprises may obtain resources by charging a price or fee for goods or services they provide, but the purpose of sales of goods or services is different. Some nonbusiness organizations may sell goods or services at prices that equal or exceed costs, but many nonbusiness organizations commonly provide goods or services at prices less than costs. Nonbusiness organizations also commonly provide goods or services free of charge. Moreover, those that charge prices sufficient to cover costs often use resources from those sales to subsidize other activities within the organization. For example, the football or basketball program at a college or university may finance both intercollegiate and intramural athletic programs. Although sales of goods or services may be important sources of financing for some nonbusiness organizations, nonbusiness organizations generally are not expected to and do not need to cover all costs, and perhaps earn profits, by sales because they rely significantly on other continuing sources of financing (paragraph 18). For example, some nonbusiness organizations have the power to assess dues, taxes, or other compulsory contributions, and others depend significantly on

[9]Some nonbusiness organizations are established for short-term purposes and are not intended to survive after completing their operating objectives, such as an organization established to erect a memorial.

[10]Nonbusiness organizations also may receive significant donations of labor, materials, and facilities or their use from resource providers.

voluntary contributions. In contrast, business enterprises attempt to sell goods or services at prices that enable them to repay or compensate all resource providers, including owners and others who expect a monetary return for providing resources. Profit is the basis for compensating owners and others for providing resources, and expectations of profit are necessary to attract resources. Moreover, unprofitable business enterprises find it increasingly difficult to borrow or otherwise obtain resources. Sales of goods or services are not only significant sources of resources for business enterprises but also underlie their ability to obtain resources from other sources.

18. Members, contributors, taxpayers, and others who provide resources to nonbusiness organizations do so for reasons different from those of owners of business enterprises. All nonbusiness organizations obtain significant resources from resource providers who either expect no economic benefits or expect benefits received not to be proportionate to the resources provided. Those resources are often provided for charitable, humanitarian, religious, or other noneconomic reasons.[11] As a result, those who provide resources to a nonbusiness organization and those who benefit from the goods or services it provides may be different individuals or groups. Owners of business enterprises, in contrast, generally expect returns through dividends or price appreciation of their securities commensurate with the perceived risk.

19. As the preceding paragraphs indicate, noneconomic reasons are commonly factors in decisions to provide resources to particular nonbusiness organizations. For example, contributors[12] to philanthropic organizations, such as charities, and to some membership organizations, such as churches, generally seek no direct economic benefits. Rather, their reasons for voluntarily providing resources relate to their interests in furthering the purpose and goals of the organization. The goals may involve a wide range of endeavors including those of a charitable, cultural, educational, economic, religious, scientific, social, or political nature. Some kinds of membership organizations, such as professional and trade associations, assess membership dues. Persons joining these organizations often seek noneconomic benefits, such as recognition or prestige, in addition to direct service benefits.

20. Nonbusiness organizations and business enterprises have different degrees of involvement with markets. Most transactions of business enterprises with other enti-

[11]Contributors to nonbusiness organizations often provide resources, such as property, materials, and uncompensated volunteer labor, in addition to financial resources. In many nonbusiness organizations, such as charities and youth groups, these donated materials and services are significant factors in the organization's operations. In other nonbusiness organizations, especially those operated by religious bodies, services contributed by personnel at far less than their market value are equally significant. Such donated or contributed services and materials are rarely found in business enterprises.

[12]Contributors include donors and prospective donors, grantors and prospective grantors, and federated fund-raising organizations that solicit contributions and then redistribute those contributions to nonbusiness organizations after deducting fund raising and other costs.

ties involve exchange prices in active markets; that market mechanism provides a measure of the utility and satisfaction of goods and services businesses buy and sell and of the overall performance of those enterprises. Nonbusiness organizations also borrow money and buy goods and services in markets and may or may not sell goods or services in markets. However, market transactions play a more limited role in the resource allocation process of nonbusiness organizations because those organizations do not finance their operations through equity markets and they commonly receive resources and provide goods or services in other than market transactions. Since market controls exist to a lesser degree for nonbusiness organizations than for business enterprises, other kinds of controls are introduced to compensate for their absence.

21. Resource providers or governing bodies may restrict or mandate the ways a nonbusiness organization may spend the resources provided. Spending mandates generally take one of two forms: specific budgetary appropriations or direct restrictions by donors or grantors. For example, a budgetary appropriation may limit the amount that a church may spend for its educational program or that a governmental unit may spend to subsidize its public transportation system, a donor or grantor may specify that a gift to a museum must be used to construct a new wing, or an agency of the federal government may specify that its grant to a university must be used for medical research. Those mandates give managers of nonbusiness organizations a special responsibility to ensure compliance. Although spending mandates also may exist in business enterprises, they are less common. Their effects on the conduct and control of the activities of business enterprises are less pervasive than in nonbusiness organizations.

22. Budgets are particularly significant in the nonbusiness environment. Both business and nonbusiness organizations use budgets to allocate and control uses of resources. However, in nonbusiness organizations for which providing resources is compulsory (for example, many membership organizations and governmental units), budgets are significant factors not only in allocating resources within an organization but also in obtaining resources. For example, budgets in membership organizations and governmental units are often pivotal in establishing the level of dues, taxes, or fees to be imposed; the level of services to be provided; and the desired relation between the two. Members and taxpayers may have the opportunity, either by direct vote or through elected representatives, to participate in developing and approving budgets. Elections and referendums also offer opportunities to change policies and the amounts and uses of resources provided. In other kinds of nonbusiness organizations, budgets may be important to voluntary donors in deciding whether to provide resources to nonbusiness organizations and in establishing the level of their giving.

Characteristics and Limitations of Information Provided by Financial Reporting

23. The objectives of financial reporting by nonbusiness organizations are affected not only by the environment in which financial reporting takes place but also by the

characteristics and limitations of the kind of information that financial reporting, and particularly financial statements, can provide. The information provided by financial reporting is primarily financial in nature: It is generally quantified and expressed in terms of units of money. Information that is to be incorporated formally in financial statements must be quantifiable in terms of units of money. Other information can be disclosed in financial statements (including notes) or by other means, but financial statements involve adding, subtracting, multiplying, and dividing numbers that depict economic things and events and require a common denominator. Quantified information expressed in terms other than units of money (such as number of employees or units of services or products provided) and nonquantified information (such as descriptions of operations or explanations of policies) that are reported normally relate to or underlie the financial information. Information that is not expressed in terms of units of money may be needed to understand the significance of information expressed in terms of units of money or to help in assessing the performance of a nonbusiness organization (paragraphs 47-53). Financial reporting by nonbusiness organizations, however, is limited in its ability to provide direct measures of the quality of goods and services provided in the absence of market-determined exchange prices or the degree to which they satisfy the needs of service beneficiaries and other consumers.

24. The information provided by financial reporting pertains to individual nonbusiness reporting entities. This Statement, however, does not include criteria for determining the appropriate reporting entity for purposes of financial reporting by nonbusiness organizations. That matter will need to be addressed by other projects.[13]

25. The information provided by financial reporting often results from approximate, rather than exact, measures. The measures commonly involve numerous estimates, classifications, summarizations, judgments, and allocations. Thus, despite the aura of precision that may seem to surround financial reporting in general and financial statements in particular, with few exceptions the measures are approximations which may be based on rules and conventions rather than exact amounts.

26. The information provided by financial reporting largely reflects the effects of transactions and events that have already happened. Governing bodies and managers may use budgets to communicate information about plans or projections, but most of the information provided by financial reporting is historical, including comparisons of actual results with previously approved budgets. The acquisition price of land and the current market price of a marketable equity security are other examples of historical data included in financial reports. No future amounts or events are involved. Estimates resting on expectations of the future are often needed in financial reporting, but their major use, especially of those formally incorporated in financial statements, is to measure financial effects of past transactions or events or the present status of an asset or liability.

[13]A discussion of the reporting entity issue can be found in the FASB Research Report on financial accounting in nonbusiness organizations, pages 18-21.

27. Financial reporting is but one source of information needed by those who make economic decisions about nonbusiness organizations. They need to combine information provided by financial reporting with relevant social, economic, and political information from other sources.

28. The information provided by financial reporting involves a cost to provide and use. The cost includes not only the resources directly expended to provide the information but also may include adverse effects on an organization from disclosing it. For example, comments about a pending lawsuit may jeopardize a successful defense. The collective time needed to understand and use information is also a cost. Generally, the benefits of information provided should be expected to at least equal the cost involved.[14] However, the benefits and costs usually are difficult to measure. Different persons will honestly disagree about whether the benefits of the information justify its cost.

Types of Users and Their Interests

29. Many people base economic decisions on their relationships to and knowledge about nonbusiness organizations and, thus, are interested in the information provided by financial reporting. Among present and potential users are members, taxpayers, contributors, grantors, lenders, suppliers, creditors, employees, managers, directors and trustees, service beneficiaries, financial analysts and advisors, brokers, underwriters, lawyers, economists, taxing authorities, regulatory authorities, legislators, the financial press and reporting agencies, labor unions, trade associations, researchers, teachers, and students. The following groups are especially interested in information provided by the financial reporting of a nonbusiness organization:

a. *Resource providers.* Resource providers include those who are directly compensated for providing resources—lenders, suppliers, and employees (paragraph 16)—and those who are not directly and proportionately compensated—members, contributors, and taxpayers (paragraph 18).[15]
b. *Constituents.* Constituents are those who use and benefit from the services rendered by the organization. In some nonbusiness organizations, constituents include resource providers (for example, members who pay dues or taxpayers), and distinguishing constituents from resource providers may serve no function. However, resource providers and service beneficiaries are largely different groups or individuals in some organizations. The degree to which service beneficiaries are a distinctive part of a constituency depends largely on the extent of

[14]Paragraphs 133-144 of FASB Concepts Statement No. 2, *Qualitative Characteristics of Accounting Information,* expand on the cost/benefit considerations discussed in this paragraph. The Board intends to solicit views regarding its tentative conclusion that the qualities of information set forth in Concepts Statement 2 also apply to accounting information of nonbusiness organizations.

[15]Taxpayers provide resources to nonbusiness organizations both directly and indirectly. They pay taxes to all levels of government. Governments (especially federal and state), in turn, provide funding to other levels of government, government-sponsored entities, and private nonbusiness organizations.

separation between those providing the resources and those using and receiving the service benefits.

c. *Governing and oversight bodies.* Governing and oversight bodies are those responsible for setting policies and for overseeing and appraising managers of nonbusiness organizations. Governing bodies include boards of trustees, boards of overseers or regents, legislatures, councils, and other bodies with similar responsibilities. Oversight bodies also are responsible for reviewing the organization's conformance with various laws, restrictions, guidelines, or other items of a similar nature. Oversight bodies include national headquarters of organizations with local chapters, accrediting agencies, agencies acting on behalf of contributors and constituents, oversight committees of legislatures, and governmental regulatory agencies. In some nonbusiness organizations, governing bodies commonly are elected representatives of a constituency that is largely comprised of resource providers. In other nonbusiness organizations, governing bodies may be self-perpetuating through election of their successors.

d. *Managers.* Managers of an organization are responsible for carrying out the policy mandates of governing bodies and managing the day-to-day operations of an organization. Managers include certain elected officials; managing executives appointed by elected governing bodies, such as school superintendents, agency heads, and executive directors; and staff, such as fund-raising and program directors.

30. Present and potential users of the information provided by financial reporting by a particular nonbusiness organization share a common interest in information about the services provided by the nonbusiness organization, its efficiency and effectiveness in providing those services, and its ability to continue to provide those services. Resource providers, such as members and contributors, may be interested in that information as a basis for assessing how well the organization has met its objectives and whether to continue support. Taxpayers may need similar information to help them assess whether governmental units and government-sponsored entities have achieved their operating objectives. In addition, they may want to know how the services provided by the governmental unit or government-sponsored entity are likely to affect the amount of taxes and fees they will be required to pay. Resource providers, such as lenders, suppliers, and employees, view a nonbusiness organization as a source of payment for the cash, goods, or services they supply. Their interest stems from concern about the organization's ability to generate cash flows for timely payment of the organization's obligations to them. Governing and oversight bodies also use information about services rendered to help them evaluate whether managers have carried out their policy mandates and to change or formulate new policies for the organization. That information also is important to managers in evaluating the accomplishment of the responsibilities for which they are accountable to governing bodies, resource providers, and other constituents. Constituents, including recipients and beneficiaries of services who as a group are distinct from resource providers, share a direct interest in similar information.

31. Some users have specialized needs but also have the power to obtain the infor-

mation they need. For example, donors and grantors who restrict the use of resources they provide often stipulate that they be apprised periodically of the organization's compliance with the terms and conditions of the gift or grant. Creditors also may be able to stipulate that certain specialized types of information be provided. Special-purpose reports directed at those kinds of needs are beyond the scope of this Statement.

32. Managers and, to some extent, governing bodies commonly are described as "internal users." In addition to the information provided by financial reporting, they need a great deal of internal accounting information to carry out their responsibilities in planning and controlling activities. Much of that information relates to particular decisions or to managers' exercise of their stewardship responsibility to ensure that resources are used for their intended purposes. For example, governing bodies and managers need information to evaluate properly the competing requests for funding of capital projects. They also need information to assist them in complying or overseeing compliance with spending mandates established by budgetary appropriations or donor or grantor restrictions. They need to know how much of a budgetary appropriation or restricted grant is unspent or uncommitted. They need to know that restricted resources were expended or committed in compliance with related mandates. Generally, both the number of spending mandates and the detail about them required to meet the informational needs of managers are so great that the usefulness of general purpose external financial reports would be reduced significantly if they reported the status of compliance with each mandate (paragraph 41). Since the type of reporting described in this paragraph needs to be tailored to meet the specialized needs of managers and governing bodies of particular organizations, it is beyond the scope of this Statement.

OBJECTIVES OF FINANCIAL REPORTING

33. The following objectives of financial reporting flow from the preceding paragraphs and proceed from the general to the specific. The objectives begin with a broad focus on information that is useful to resource providers and other users in making rational decisions about allocating resources to nonbusiness organizations. The focus is then narrowed to the needs of resource providers and other users for information about the services an organization provides and its ability to continue to provide those services. That directs their attention to information about the organization's performance and how its managers have discharged their stewardship responsibility. Finally, the objectives focus on the types of information financial reporting can provide to meet those needs. The reasons for focusing the objectives of financial reporting on decisions generally made by resource providers are given in paragraph 36. That focus and wording do not mean that the objectives apply to only resource providers. On the contrary, information that satisfies the objectives should be useful to all who are interested in a nonbusiness organization's present and future capacity to render service and achieve its operating goals.

34. The objectives are those of financial reporting rather than goals for resource providers or others who use the information or for the economy or society as a whole. The role of financial reporting in the economy and society is to provide information that is useful in making decisions about allocating scarce resources, not to determine what those decisions should be. For example, information that tries to indicate that a relatively inefficient user of resources is efficient or information that is directed toward a particular goal, such as encouraging the reallocation of resources in favor of certain programs or activities of nonbusiness organizations, is likely to fail to serve the broader objectives that financial reporting is intended to serve. The role of financial reporting requires it to provide neutral information.

Information Useful in Making Resource Allocation Decisions

35. Financial reporting by nonbusiness organizations should provide information that is useful to present and potential resource providers and other users in making rational decisions about the allocation of resources to those organizations. The information should be comprehensible to those who have a reasonable understanding of an organization's activities and are willing to study the information with reasonable diligence.

36. Resource providers are important users of information provided by financial reporting who generally cannot prescribe the information they want. Their decisions significantly affect both nonbusiness organizations and the allocation of resources in society generally. In addition, information provided to meet the needs of present and potential resource providers is likely to be useful to others who are interested in essentially the same aspects of nonbusiness organizations as resource providers.

37. The potential users listed in paragraph 29 understand, to varying degrees, the environment within which a nonbusiness organization operates, the nature of its activities, and related matters. Their understanding of information provided by financial reporting and the extent to which they use and rely on it also varies greatly. Financial reporting information is a tool and, like most tools, cannot be of much direct help to those who are unable or unwilling to use it or who misuse it. Its use can be learned, however, and financial reporting should provide information that can be used by all who are willing to learn to use it properly. Efforts may be needed to increase the understandability of information provided by financial reporting. Cost/benefit considerations may indicate that information understood or used by only a few should not be provided.[16] Conversely, financial reporting should not exclude relevant information merely because it is difficult for some to understand or because some choose not to use it.

Information Useful in Assessing Services and Ability to Provide Services

38. Financial reporting should provide information to help present and potential

[16]See footnote 14.

resource providers and other users in assessing the services[17] that a nonbusiness organization provides and its ability to continue to provide those services.[18] They are interested in that information because the services are the end for which the resources are provided. The relation of the services provided to the resources used to provide them helps resource providers and others assess the extent to which the organization is successful in carrying out its service objectives.

39. Resources are the lifeblood of an organization in the sense that it uses resources to provide services. A nonbusiness organization cannot, in the long run, continue to achieve its operating objectives unless the resources made available to it at least equal the resources needed to provide services at levels satisfactory to resource providers and other constituents. Although decisions of potential and present resource providers to provide or continue to provide resources involve expectations about future services of an organization, those expectations commonly are based at least partly on evaluations of past performance. Thus, resource providers tend to direct their interest to information about the organization's resources and how it acquires and uses resources. The focus of that interest is information about the organization's performance and how its managers have discharged their stewardship responsibility during a period.

Information Useful in Assessing Management Stewardship and Performance

40. Financial reporting should provide information that is useful to present and potential resource providers and other users in assessing how managers of a nonbusiness organization have discharged their stewardship responsibilities and about other aspects of their performance. Managers of an organization are accountable to resource providers and others, not only for the custody and safekeeping of organization resources, but also for their efficient and effective use. Those who provide resources to nonbusiness organizations do not have a profit indicator to guide their resource allocation decisions and may not have an immediate choice about the amounts of their contributions. They must look to managers to represent their interests and to make operating cost/benefit judgments that achieve the objectives of the organizations with minimum use of resources. Managers also are accountable for compliance with statutory, contractual, or other limitations.

41. Information about an organization's performance (paragraphs 47-53) should be the focus for assessing the stewardship or accountability of managers of a nonbusiness organization. Users also need assurance that managers have exercised their special responsibilities to ensure that an organization uses resources in the manner

[17]The term *services* in this context encompasses the goods as well as the services a nonbusiness organization may provide.

[18]An organization's ability to continue to provide services ultimately depends on its ability to obtain resources from resource providers. The ability to obtain sufficient resources normally is not discussed in general purpose external financial reports unless that ability is in doubt. Paragraphs 43-55 discuss the type of information financial reporting can provide to meet the objective in paragraph 38.

specifically designated by resource providers. General purpose external financial reporting can best meet that need by disclosing failures to comply with spending mandates that may impinge on an organization's financial performance or on its ability to continue to provide a satisfactory level of services.

42. Financial reporting is limited in its ability to distinguish the performance of managers from that of the organization itself. Nonbusiness organizations are often highly complex institutions, and the processes by which they acquire resources and render services often are long and intricate. Organizational successes and failures are the result of numerous factors. The ability and performance of managers are contributing factors, as are events and circumstances that often are beyond the control of managers. It is usually not possible to determine the degree to which managers, or any other specific factors, have affected the result. Actions of past managers affect current periods' performance, and actions of present managers affect future periods' performance.

Information about Economic Resources, Obligations, Net Resources, and Changes in Them

43. Financial reporting should provide information about the economic resources, obligations, and net resources of an organization and the effects of transactions, events, and circumstances that change resources and interests in those resources.[19] That type of information is useful in achieving each of the above objectives.

Economic Resources, Obligations, and Net Resources

44. Financial reporting should provide information about an organization's economic resources, obligations, and net resources. That information helps resource providers and others identify the organization's financial strengths and weaknesses, evaluate information about the organization's performance during a period (paragraphs 47-53), and assess its ability to continue to render services.

45. Information about an organization's economic resources, obligations, and net resources also provides direct indications of the cash flow potential of some resources and of the cash needed to satisfy many, if not most, obligations. The assessment of cash flow potential is important because it relates directly to the organization's ability to provide the goods and services for which it exists.

46. Resources provided to nonbusiness organizations often are restricted by pro-

---

[19]In FASB Concepts Statement No. 3, *Elements of Financial Statements of Business Enterprises,* the Board has attempted to define many elements (for example, assets and liabilities) in a way that they could apply to all types of entities. In the near future, the Board expects to consider and solicit views about which, if any, of the definitions are inappropriate or may require modification for nonbusiness organizations and whether other elements are needed for financial statements of nonbusiness organizations.

viders as to time and for particular purposes (paragraph 21). Accordingly, information about restrictions on the use of resources is important for assessing the types and levels of services an organization is able to provide. That information is also important to creditors in assessing their prospects for receiving cash.[20]

Organization Performance

47. Financial reporting should provide information about the performance of an organization during a period. Periodic measurement of the changes in the amount and nature of the net resources of a nonbusiness organization and information about the service efforts and accomplishments of an organization together represent the information most useful in assessing its performance.

Nature of and Relation between Inflows and Outflows

48. Financial reporting should provide information about the amounts and kinds of inflows and outflows of resources during a period. It should distinguish resource flows that change net resources, such as inflows of fees or contributions and outflows for wages and salaries, from those that do not change net resources, such as borrowings or purchases of buildings. It also should identify inflows and outflows of restricted resources.

49. Financial reporting should provide information about the relation between inflows and outflows of resources during a period. Those who provide resources to a nonbusiness organization and others want to know how and why net resources changed during a period. To meet that need, financial reporting must distinguish between resource flows that are related to operations and those that are not.[21] In this way, financial reporting may provide information that is useful in assessing whether the activities of a nonbusiness organization during a particular period have drawn upon, or have contributed to, past or future periods. Thus, it should show the relation of resources used in operations of a period to resource inflows available to finance those operations. Similarly, it should provide information about changes in resources that are not related to operations. For example, resource providers to colleges or universities need information about changes in an organization's endowment and plant to understand more fully the changes in its net resources during a period.

[20]Issues that affect how, if at all, restricted resources are displayed in financial statements, for example, by using multi-column presentations or disclosure in the notes, are outside the scope of this Statement and may be the subject of future Board projects.

[21]Resource flows that are not related to operations have been described in various ways, for example, as "nonexpendable," "capital," or "restricted" flows. The Board's endorsement of distinguishing these types of flows is not intended to prejudge future determinations of (a) the criteria that should be used in making this distinction and (b) how and in what financial statements different types of flows might be displayed.

50. The information described in paragraphs 47-49 measured by accrual accounting generally provides a better indication of an organization's performance than does information about cash receipts and payments.[22] Accrual accounting attempts to record the financial effects of transactions, events, and circumstances that have cash consequences for an organization in the periods in which those transactions, events, and circumstances occur rather than in only the periods in which cash is received or paid by the organization. Accrual accounting is concerned with the process by which cash is obtained and used, not with just the beginning and end of that process. It recognizes that the acquisition of resources needed to provide services and the rendering of services by an organization during a period often do not coincide with the cash receipts and payments of the period.[23]

Service efforts and accomplishments

51. Information about an organization's service efforts and accomplishments is useful to resource providers and others in assessing the performance of a nonbusiness organization and in making resource allocation decisions, particularly because:

a. The accomplishments of nonbusiness organizations generally cannot be measured in terms of sales, profit, or return on investment.
b. Resource providers often are not in a position to have direct knowledge of the goods or services provided when they also are not users or beneficiaries of those goods and services.

52. Financial reporting should provide information about the service efforts of a nonbusiness organization. Information about service efforts should focus on how the organization's resources (inputs such as money, personnel, and materials) are used in providing different programs or services. Techniques for measuring the costs of significant programs or services are well developed and this information normally should be included in financial statements.

53. Ideally, financial reporting also should provide information about the service accomplishments of a nonbusiness organization. Information about service accomplishments in terms of goods or services produced (outputs) and of program

[22]In some relatively small organizations, the benefits of the better information obtained from accrual accounting may not justify the costs of obtaining that information (footnote 14).

[23]Accrual accounting is concerned with the timing of recognizing transactions, events, and circumstances that have financial effects on an organization. This paragraph is not intended to prejudge specific recognition and measurement issues involved in applying accrual accounting in the nonbusiness area. For example, whether certain inflows of financial resources, such as taxes, grants, and contributions, should be recognized in the period when a claim arises, when they are received, when they are appropriated for use, when they are used, or when other events occur, is beyond the scope of this Statement.

results[24] may enhance significantly the value of information provided about service efforts. However, the ability to measure service accomplishments, particularly program results, is generally undeveloped. At present, such measures may not satisfy the qualitative characteristics of accounting information identified in Concepts Statement 2. Research should be conducted to determine if measures of service accomplishments with the requisite characteristics of relevance, reliability, comparability, verifiability, and neutrality can be developed. If such measures are developed, they should be included in financial reports. In the absence of measures suitable for financial reporting, information about service accomplishments may be furnished by managers' explanations and sources other than financial reporting.

Liquidity

54. Financial reporting should provide information about how an organization obtains and spends cash or other liquid resources, about its borrowing and repayment of borrowing, and about other factors that may affect its liquidity. Information about those resource flows may be useful in understanding the operations of an enterprise, evaluating its financing activities, assessing its liquidity, or interpreting performance information provided. Information about performance and economic resources, obligations, and net resources also may be useful in assessing an enterprise's liquidity.

Managers' Explanations and Interpretations

55. Financial reporting should include explanations and interpretations to help users understand financial information provided. For example, the usefulness of financial information to resource providers and others may be enhanced by managers' explanations of the information. Since managers usually know more about the organization and its affairs than do resource providers or others outside the organization, they often can increase the usefulness of information provided by financial reporting by identifying certain transactions, events, and circumstances that affect the organization and by explaining their financial impact.[25] In addition, dividing continuous operations into accounting periods is a convention and may have arbitrary effects. Managers can enhance the usefulness of information contained in financial reports by identifying arbitrary results caused by allocations between periods and by describing the effects of those allocations on reported information. Moreover, financial reporting often provides information that depends on, or is affected by, managers' estimates and judgments. Users are aided in evaluating esti-

[24]Service accomplishments generally may be viewed as the results of service efforts. The FASB Research Report, *Reporting of Service Efforts and Accomplishments,* distinguishes two possible measures of accomplishments, outputs and results. "*Outputs* usually are observable directly as a result of service delivery; they describe goods and services provided by service delivery but do not measure impact upon clients or problems. . . . *Results* . . . represent impact upon clients or problem situations" (page 7). In discussing this latter measure, this Statement uses the term *program results.*

[25]These discussions may include information about service efforts and accomplishments as described in paragraphs 51-53.

mates and judgments by explanations of underlying assumptions and methods used, including disclosure of significant uncertainties about principal underlying assumptions or estimates.

THE NONBUSINESS OBJECTIVES PROJECT—A PERSPECTIVE

56. Paragraphs 43-54 focus on information that assists resource providers and other users in assessing an organization's financial viability, its performance, and how the organization's managers have discharged their stewardship responsibilities. Those paragraphs emphasize information about an organization's economic resources, obligations, and net resources and its performance during a period. The objectives lead to, but leave unanswered, questions such as the identity, number, and form of financial statements; elements of financial statements and their recognition, measurement, and display; and criteria for determining the reporting entity. The Board's approach to resolving those questions will be to integrate consideration of nonbusiness organizations into its series of conceptual framework projects. That integration may involve initiating new projects to deal with issues that may be more prevalent in or unique to nonbusiness organizations.

This Statement was adopted by the unanimous vote of the seven members of the Financial Accounting Standards Board:

Donald J. Kirk, *Chairman*
Frank E. Block
John W. March
Robert A. Morgan
David Mosso
Robert T. Sprouse
Ralph E. Walters

Appendix A

BACKGROUND INFORMATION

Brief History of FASB Nonbusiness Objectives Project

57. The Board's project on objectives of financial reporting by nonbusiness organizations is related to and part of its effort to develop a conceptual framework for financial reporting. The Board began its work on a conceptual framework in 1973 and used as a point of departure the Report of the Study Group on the Objectives of Financial Statements, *Objectives of Financial Statements* (Trueblood Report), published by the American Institute of Certified Public Accountants in October 1973. That report included governmental and not-for-profit organizations in its scope.

58. As more fully discussed in paragraphs 57-62 of Concepts Statement 1, the Board initially considered the 12 objectives of financial statements in the Trueblood Report but decided to concentrate its initial efforts on formulating objectives of financial

reporting by business enterprises. Initially, therefore, the Board did not attempt to reach conclusions on the objectives of financial reporting for governmental and not-for-profit organizations.

59. The need to consider the objectives of general purpose external financial reporting by nonbusiness organizations generally is recognized. An increasing number of public officials and private citizens are questioning the relevance and reliability of financial accounting and reporting by nonbusiness organizations. That concern has been reflected in legislative initiatives and well-publicized allegations of serious deficiencies in the financial reporting of various types of nonbusiness organizations.

60. In response to those concerns, the Board, in August 1977, engaged Professor Robert N. Anthony of the Harvard Business School to prepare a research report aimed at identifying the objectives of financial reporting by organizations other than business enterprises. A 53-member advisory group was appointed to assist in that effort. When the Board began consideration of objectives of financial reporting by nonbusiness organizations in August 1977, significant progress already had been made on the objectives of financial reporting by business enterprises. Rather than delay progress on that project to include nonbusiness organizations in its scope, and to explore thoroughly the issues in the nonbusiness area, the Board proceeded with two separate objectives projects. The Board issued Concepts Statement 1 in November 1978. Paragraph 1 of Concepts Statement 1 states:

> This Statement establishes the objectives of general purpose external financial reporting by business enterprises. Its concentration on business enterprises is not intended to imply that the Board has concluded that the uses and objectives of financial reporting by other kinds of entities are, or should be, the same as or different from those of business enterprises. Those and related matters, including whether and, if so, how business enterprises and other organizations should be distinguished for the purpose of establishing objectives of and basic concepts underlying financial reporting, are issues in another phase of the Board's conceptual framework project.

61. In May 1978, the Board published the FASB Research Report, *Financial Accounting in Nonbusiness Organizations,* prepared by Professor Anthony. The Board added the nonbusiness objectives project to its technical agenda on May 11, 1978 and directed the staff to prepare a Discussion Memorandum to solicit public comment. The Discussion Memorandum was issued on June 15, 1978. It focused on specific issues discussed in the Research Report and identified those on which the Board sought comments.

62. The Board held public hearings in Washington, D.C. on October 12 and 13, 1978; in San Francisco on October 19 and 20, 1978; and in Chicago on November 3, 1978. The Board received 87 written responses to the Discussion Memorandum, and 48 oral presentations were made at the public hearings.

63. The Board issued an Exposure Draft, *Objectives of Financial Reporting by Nonbusiness Organizations,* on March 14, 1980. In preparing the Exposure Draft, the Board deliberated the issues at meetings which were open to public observation. FASB Board and staff members have met with and maintained close liaison with various groups and individuals in the community of nonbusiness organizations since the outset of this project. In addition, persons from academe, public accounting, and various nonbusiness organizations provided counsel to the Board and its staff in preparing the Exposure Draft. The Board received 77 letters of comment on the Exposure Draft and considered the issues raised by respondents in those comment letters at meetings which were open to public observation.

64. The major differences between this Statement and the Exposure Draft are revisions to the scope of the document. The types of organizations to which the objectives in this document apply have been clarified (paragraph 1 of the Exposure Draft), and a discussion has been added concerning the relationship of this Statement to Concepts Statement 1. Other significant changes are (a) the addition of examples of various types of nonbusiness organizations in the environment section (paragraphs 13-22); (b) greater emphasis on distinguishing flows that affect operations from those that do not (paragraph 49); (c) greater emphasis on the need for research to determine if measures of service accomplishments with the requisite characteristics of relevance, reliability, comparability, verifiability, and neutrality can be developed; and (d) acknowledgement that, in the absence of that financial reporting capability, information about service accomplishments may be furnished by managers' explanations and sources other than financial reporting.

State and Local Governmental Units

65. Others have been studying the objectives of financial reporting by governmental units during the period that the Board has been deliberating the issues and preparing this concepts Statement. The National Council on Governmental Accounting is sponsoring research in the broad area of a conceptual framework for governmental accounting, which includes the objectives of external financial reporting by state and local governmental units. A state accounting project that was commissioned by the Council of State Governments includes a study of objectives of accounting and financial reporting by state governments. The U.S. General Accounting Office is developing a statement of the objectives of financial reporting by the federal government and its agencies.

66. Since the publication of the Exposure Draft of this concepts Statement, the Board and its staff have monitored developments on the three projects discussed above. This monitoring has consisted of reviewing and analyzing working drafts of certain materials made available to the FASB by the NCGA and other researchers. On the basis of its study to date, the Board is aware of no persuasive evidence that the objectives in this Statement are inappropriate for general purpose external financial reports of governmental units.

Appendix B

COMPARISON OF OBJECTIVES IN THIS STATEMENT TO THOSE IN CONCEPTS STATEMENT 1

67. This Statement follows the *structure* of Concepts Statement 1. Both sets of objectives are based on the fundamental notion that financial accounting and reporting concepts and standards should be based on their decision usefulness. Thus, the objectives in this Statement and in Concepts Statement 1 focus on:

a. Types of users of the information provided by financial reporting and the types of decisions they make
b. The broad interests of the users identified and the information they need to assist them in making decisions
c. The type of information financial reporting can provide to help satisfy their informational needs.

The chart on pages 174-176 compares the similarities and differences of this Statement and Concepts Statement 1 in each of those areas.

Purpose of Objectives	Nonbusiness Organizations Concepts Statement 4	Business Enterprises Concepts Statement 1	Comparison of Objectives
a. Identifies (1) the types of users that financial reporting should focus on in providing information and (2) the types of decisions those users make.	a. Financial reporting by nonbusiness organizations should provide information that is useful to present and potential resource providers and other users in making rational decisions about the allocation of resources to those organizations (paragraph 35).	a. Financial reporting should provide information that is useful to present and potential investors and creditors and other users in making rational investment, credit, and similar decisions (paragraph 34).	a(1)Investors and creditors are major resource providers to business enterprises. Thus, resource providers, as a type of user, include investors and creditors as well as the other groups identified in Concepts Statement 4.
			a(2)Both Statements focus on providing information useful in deciding whether to provide resources to an entity. The reasons for providing the resources, in each case, are quite different. Investors and creditors of business enterprises seek monetary repayment of and a return on resources they provide. Nonbusiness organizations, in contrast, obtain significant resources from resource providers who either expect no economic benefits or expect benefits that are not proportionate to the resources provided.
b. Identifies the broad interests of the users identified and the information they need to assist them in making the type of decisions described above.	b(1) Financial reporting should provide information to help present and potential resource providers and other users in assessing the services that a nonbusiness organization provides and its ability to continue to provide those services (paragraph 38).	b(1) Financial reporting should provide information to help present and potential investors and creditors and other users in assessing the amounts, timing, and uncertainty of prospective cash receipts from dividends or interest and the proceeds from the sale, redemption, or maturity of securities or loans (paragraph 37).	b(1)These two objectives reflect the different interests of the respective resource providers. Those different interests lead to the other major area of difference in the objectives: the types of information financial reporting should provide about performance.
	b(2) Financial reporting should provide information that is useful to present and potential resource providers and other users in assessing how managers of a nonbusiness	b(2) Financial reporting should provide information about how	b(2) The substance of these two objectives is similar but their placement within the two Statements is different. In this concepts Statement, the objective is viewed as a

	organization have discharged their stewardship responsibilities and about other aspects of their performance (paragraph 40).	management of an enterprise has discharged its stewardship responsibility to owners (stockholders) for the use of enterprise resources entrusted to it (paragraph 50).	basic information need of users. In Concepts Statement 1, it was viewed as information financial reporting could provide to satisfy other basic information needs. That difference in placement arises from the importance of stewardship information in the environment of nonbusiness organizations. It is more important because the organization often is not self-sustaining (not profit oriented) and is dependent upon the continuing support of its resource providers. Consequently, there often is a more direct relationship between resource providers and the entity than for a business enterprise.
c. Identifies the type of information financial reporting can provide to help satisfy users' informational needs.	c. Financial reporting should provide information about the economic resources, obligations, and net resources of an organization and the effects of transactions, events and circumstances that change resources and interests in those resources (paragraph 43).	c. Financial reporting should provide information about the economic resources of an enterprise, the claims to those resources (obligations of the enterprise to transfer resources to other entities and owners' equity), and the effects of transactions, events, and circumstances that change resources and claims to those resources (paragraph 40).	c. The objectives are similar except for differences in terminology that reflect one of the distinguishing characteristics of nonbusiness organizations—the lack of ownership interests entitled to a residual distribution in the event of liquidation.
	(1) Financial reporting should provide information about an organization's economic resources, obligations, and net resources (paragraph 44).	(1) Financial reporting should provide information about an enterprise's economic resources, obligations, and owners' equity (paragraph 41).	(1) Except for differences in terminology, these objectives are the same.
	(2) Financial reporting should provide information about the performance of an organization during a		(2) The goals of the two objectives are the same but, because of the distinguishing characteristics of nonbusiness organizations, somewhat different information is

Purpose of Objectives	Nonbusiness Organizations Concepts Statement 4	Business Enterprises Concepts Statement 1	Comparison of Objectives
	period. Periodic measurement of the changes in the amount and nature of the net resources of a nonbusiness organization and information about the service efforts and accomplishments of an organization together represent the information most useful in assessing its performance (paragraph 47).	(2) Financial reporting should provide information about an enterprise's financial performance during a period. The primary focus of financial reporting is information about an enterprise's performance provided by measures of earnings and its components (paragraphs 42 and 43).	required to satisfy those goals. Both seek to measure the efforts and accomplishments of the entity but assessment of performance in nonbusiness lacks earnings as a focal measure. This creates the need for information on service efforts and accomplishments.
	(3) Financial reporting should provide information about how an organization obtains and spends cash or other liquid resources, about its borrowing and repayment of borrowing, and about other factors that may affect its liquidity (paragraph 54).	(3) Financial reporting should provide information about how an enterprise obtains and spends cash, about its borrowing and repayment of borrowing, about its capital transactions, including cash dividends and other distributions of enterprise resources to owners, and about other factors that may affect an enterprise's liquidity or solvency (paragraph 49).	(3) Except for differences in terminology and circumstances that reflect the lack of ownership interests entitled to receive cash dividends and other distributions of entity resources in nonbusiness organizations, these objectives are the same.
	(4) Financial reporting should include explanations and interpretations to help users understand financial information provided (paragraph 55).	(4) Financial reporting should include explanations and interpretations to help users understand financial information provided (paragraph 54).	(4) These objectives are the same.

Statement of Financial Accounting Concepts No. 5 Recognition and Measurement in Financial Statements of Business Enterprises

STATUS

Issued: December 1984

Affects: No other pronouncements

Affected by: No other pronouncements

HIGHLIGHTS

[Best understood in context of full Statement]

- This Statement sets forth recognition criteria and guidance on what information should be incorporated into financial statements and when. The Statement provides a basis for consideration of criteria and guidance by first addressing financial statements that should be presented and their contribution to financial reporting. It gives particular attention to statements of earnings and comprehensive income. The Statement also addresses certain measurement issues that are closely related to recognition.

- Financial statements are a central feature of financial reporting—a principal means of communicating financial information to those outside an entity. Some useful information is better provided by financial statements and some is better provided, or can only be provided, by notes to financial statements, supplementary information, or other means of financial reporting. For items that meet criteria for recognition, disclosure by other means is not a substitute for recognition in financial statements.

- Recognition is the process of formally incorporating an item into the financial statements of an entity as an asset, liability, revenue, expense, or the like. A recognized item is depicted in both words and numbers, with the amount included in the statement totals.

- A full set of financial statements for a period should show:
  - Financial position at the end of the period
  - Earnings for the period
  - Comprehensive income for the period
  - Cash flows during the period
  - Investments by and distributions to owners during the period.

- Financial statements individually and collectively contribute to meeting the objectives of financial reporting. No one financial statement is likely to provide all the financial statement information that is useful for a particular kind of decision.

- The parts of a financial statement also contribute to meeting the objectives of financial reporting and may be more useful to those who make investment, credit, and similar decisions than the whole.

- Financial statements result from simplifying, condensing, and aggregating masses of data. As a result, they convey information that would be obscured if great detail were provided. Although those simplifications, condensations, and aggregations are both necessary and useful, the Board believes that it is important to avoid focusing attention almost exclusively on "the bottom line," earnings per share, or other highly simplified condensations.

- A statement of financial position provides information about an entity's assets, liabilities, and equity and their relationships to each other at a moment in time. The statement delineates the entity's resource structure—major classes and amounts of assets—and its financing structure—major classes and amounts of liabilities and equity.

- A statement of financial position does not purport to show the value of a business enterprise but, together with other financial statements and other information, should provide information that is useful to those who desire to make their own estimates of the enterprise's value. Those estimates are part of financial analysis, not of financial reporting, but financial accounting aids financial analysis.

- Statements of earnings and of comprehensive income together reflect the extent to which and the ways in which the equity of an entity increased or decreased from all sources other than transactions with owners during a period.

- The concept of earnings set forth in this Statement is similar to net income for a period in present practice; however, it excludes certain accounting adjustments of earlier periods that are recognized in the current period—cumulative effect of a change in accounting principle is the principal example from present practice. The Board expects the concept of earnings to be subject to the process of gradual change or evolution that has characterized the development of net income.

- Earnings is a measure of entity performance during a period. It measures the extent to which asset inflows (revenues and gains) associated with cash-to-cash cycles substantially completed during the period exceed asset outflows (expenses and losses) associated, directly or indirectly, with the same cycles.

- Comprehensive income is a broad measure of the effects of transactions and other events on an entity, comprising all recognized changes in equity (net assets) of the entity during a period from transactions and other events and circumstances except those resulting from investments by owners and distributions to owners.

- A variety of terms are used for net income in present practice. The Board anticipates that a variety of terms will be used in future financial statements as names for earnings (for example, net income, profit, or net loss) and for comprehensive income (for example, total nonowner changes in equity or comprehensive loss).

- Earnings and comprehensive income are not the same because certain gains and losses are included in comprehensive income but are excluded from earnings. Those items fall into two classes that are illustrated by certain present practices:

  — Effects of certain accounting adjustments of earlier periods that are recognized in the current period (already described)

  — Certain other changes in net assets (principally certain holding gains and losses) that are recognized in the period but are excluded from earnings, such as some changes in market values of investments in marketable equity securities classified as noncurrent assets, some changes in market values of investments in industries having specialized accounting practices for marketable securities, and foreign currency translation adjustments.

- The full set of financial statements discussed in this Statement is based on the concept of financial capital maintenance.

- Future standards may change what is recognized as components of earnings. Future standards may also recognize certain changes in net assets as components of comprehensive income but not of earnings.

- A statement of cash flows directly or indirectly reflects an entity's cash receipts classified by major sources and its cash payments classified by major uses during a period, including cash flow information about its operating, financing, and investing activities.

- A statement of investments by and distributions to owners reflects an entity's capital transactions during a period—the extent to which and in what ways the equity of the entity increased or decreased from transactions with owners *as owners*.

- An item and information about it should meet four fundamental recognition criteria to be recognized and should be recognized when the criteria are met, subject to a cost-benefit constraint and a materiality threshold. Those criteria are:

  — *Definitions.* The item meets the definition of an element of financial statements.

  — *Measurability.* It has a relevant attribute measurable with sufficient reliability.

  — *Relevance.* The information about it is capable of making a difference in user decisions.

  — *Reliability.* The information is representationally faithful, verifiable, and neutral.

- Items currently reported in the financial statements are measured by different attributes (for example, historical cost, current [replacement] cost, current market value, net realizable value, and present value of future cash flows), depending on the nature of the item and the relevance and reliability of the attribute measured. The Board expects use of different attributes to continue.

- The monetary unit or measurement scale in current practice in financial statements is nominal units of money, that is, unadjusted for changes in purchasing power of money over time. The Board expects that nominal units of money will continue to be used to measure items recognized in financial statements.

- Further guidance in applying the criteria for recognizing components of earnings is necessary because of the widely acknowledged importance of earnings as a primary measure of entity performance. Guidance for recognizing components of earnings is concerned with identifying which cycles are substantially complete and with associating particular revenues, gains, expenses, and losses with those cycles.

- In assessing the prospect that as yet uncompleted transactions will be concluded successfully, a degree of skepticism is often warranted. As a reaction to uncertainty, more stringent requirements have historically been imposed for recognizing revenues and gains as components of earnings than for recognizing expenses and losses. Those conservative reactions influence the guidance for applying the recognition criteria to components of earnings.

- Guidance for recognizing revenues and gains is based on their being:

  — *Realized or realizable.* Revenues and gains are generally not recognized as components of earnings until realized or realizable and

  — *Earned.* Revenues are not recognized until earned. Revenues are considered to have been earned when the entity has substantially accomplished what it must do to be entitled to the benefits represented by the revenues. For gains, being earned is generally less significant than being realized or realizable.

- Guidance for expenses and losses is intended to recognize:

  — *Consumption of benefit.* Expenses are generally recognized when an entity's economic benefits are consumed in revenue-earning activities or otherwise or

  — *Loss or lack of benefit.* Expenses or losses are recognized if it becomes evident that previously recognized future economic benefits of assets have been reduced or eliminated, or that liabilities have been incurred or increased, without associated economic benefits.

- In a limited number of situations, the Board may determine that the most useful information results from recognizing the effects of certain events in comprehensive income but not in earnings, and set standards accordingly. Certain changes in net assets that meet the fundamental recognition criteria may qualify for recognition in comprehensive income even though they do not qualify for recognition as components of earnings.

- Information based on current prices should be recognized if it is sufficiently relevant and reliable to justify the costs involved and more relevant than alternative information.

- Most aspects of current practice are consistent with the recognition criteria and guidance in this Statement, but the criteria and guidance do not foreclose the possibility of future changes in practice. When evidence indicates that information that is more useful (relevant and reliable) than information currently reported is available at a justifiable cost, it should be included in financial statements.

Statement of Financial Accounting Concepts No. 5

Recognition and Measurement in Financial Statements of Business Enterprises

December 1984

CONTENTS

	Paragraph Numbers
Highlights	
Introduction, Scope, and Limitations	1– 4
Financial Statements	5– 57
Financial Statements, Financial Reporting, and Recognition	5– 9
Financial Statements and Objectives of Financial Reporting	10– 12
Full Set of Financial Statements	13– 14
Purposes and Limitations of Financial Statements	15– 24
General Purpose Financial Statements and Individual Users	15– 16
Usefulness of Financial Statements, Individually and Collectively	17– 24
Classification and Aggregation in Financial Statements	20– 22
Complementary Nature of Financial Statements	23– 24
Individual Financial Statements	25– 57
Statement of Financial Position	26– 29
Statements of Earnings and Comprehensive Income	30– 51
Earnings	33– 38
Comprehensive Income	39– 41
Relationships between Earnings and Comprehensive Income	42– 44
Financial Capital Maintenance	45– 48
Recognition Implications of Earnings	49– 51
Statement of Cash Flows	52– 54
Statement of Investments by and Distributions to Owners	55– 57
Recognition Criteria	58– 77
Purposes of Criteria	59– 60
Structure of Recognition Criteria	61– 62
Fundamental Recognition Criteria	63– 77
Definitions	64
Measurability	65– 72
Measurement Attributes	66– 70
Monetary Unit or Measurement Scale	71– 72
Relevance	73 74
Reliability	75– 77

Guidance in Applying Criteria to Components of Earnings............. 78– 87
Revenues and Gains 83– 84
Expenses and Losses 85– 87
Consumption of Benefits 86
Loss or Lack of Future Benefit 87
Recognition of Changes in Assets and Liabilities 88– 90
Summary 91
Appendix: Background Information 92–108
Summary Index of Concepts Defined or Discussed

Statements of Financial Accounting Concepts

This Statement of Financial Accounting Concepts is one of a series of publications in the Board's conceptual framework for financial accounting and reporting. Statements in the series are intended to set forth objectives and fundamentals that will be the basis for development of financial accounting and reporting standards. The objectives identify the goals and purposes of financial reporting. The fundamentals are the underlying concepts of financial accounting—concepts that guide the selection of transactions, events, and circumstances to be accounted for; their recognition and measurement; and the means of summarizing and communicating them to interested parties. Concepts of that type are fundamental in the sense that other concepts flow from them and repeated reference to them will be necessary in establishing, interpreting, and applying accounting and reporting standards.

The conceptual framework is a coherent system of interrelated objectives and fundamentals that is expected to lead to consistent standards and that prescribes the nature, function, and limits of financial accounting and reporting. It is expected to serve the public interest by providing structure and direction to financial accounting and reporting to facilitate the provision of evenhanded financial and related information that helps promote the efficient allocation of scarce resources in the economy and society, including assisting capital and other markets to function efficiently.

Establishment of objectives and identification of fundamental concepts will not directly solve financial accounting and reporting problems. Rather, objectives give direction, and concepts are tools for solving problems.

The Board itself is likely to be the most direct beneficiary of the guidance provided by the Statements in this series. They will guide the Board in developing accounting and reporting standards by providing the Board with a common foundation and basic reasoning on which to consider merits of alternatives.

However, knowledge of the objectives and concepts the Board will use in developing standards also should enable those who are affected by or interested in financial accounting standards to understand better the purposes, content, and characteristics of information provided by financial accounting and reporting. That knowledge is expected to enhance the usefulness of, and confidence in, financial accounting and reporting. The concepts also may provide some guidance in analyzing new or emerging problems of financial accounting and reporting in the absence of applicable authoritative pronouncements.

Statements of Financial Accounting Concepts do not establish standards prescribing accounting procedures or disclosure practices for particular items or events, which are issued by the Board as Statements of Financial Accounting Standards. Rather, Statements in this series describe concepts and relations that will underlie

future financial accounting standards and practices and in due course serve as a basis for evaluating existing standards and practices.*

The Board recognizes that in certain respects current generally accepted accounting principles may be inconsistent with those that may derive from the objectives and concepts set forth in Statements in this series. However, a Statement of Financial Accounting Concepts does not (a) require a change in existing generally accepted accounting principles; (b) amend, modify, or interpret Statements of Financial Accounting Standards, Interpretations of the FASB, Opinions of the Accounting Principles Board, or Bulletins of the Committee on Accounting Procedure that are in effect; or (c) justify either changing existing generally accepted accounting and reporting practices or interpreting the pronouncements listed in item (b) based on personal interpretations of the objectives and concepts in the Statements of Financial Accounting Concepts.

Since a Statement of Financial Accounting Concepts does not establish generally accepted accounting principles or standards for the disclosure of financial information outside of financial statements in published financial reports, it is not intended to invoke application of Rule 203 or 204 of the Rules of Conduct of the Code of Professional Ethics of the American Institute of Certified Public Accountants (or successor rules or arrangements of similar scope and intent).†

Like other pronouncements of the Board, a Statement of Financial Accounting Concepts may be amended, superseded, or withdrawn by appropriate action under the Board's *Rules of Procedure.*

---

*Pronouncements such as APB Statement No. 4, *Basic Concepts and Accounting Principles Underlying Financial Statements of Business Enterprises,* and the Accounting Terminology Bulletins will continue to serve their intended purpose—they describe objectives and concepts underlying standards and practices existing at the time of their issuance.

†Rule 203 prohibits a member of the American Institute of Certified Public Accountants from expressing an opinion that financial statements conform with generally accepted accounting principles if those statements contain a material departure from an accounting principle promulgated by the Financial Accounting Standards Board, unless the member can demonstrate that because of unusual circumstances the financial statements otherwise would have been misleading. Rule 204 requires members of the Institute to justify departures from standards promulgated by the Financial Accounting Standards Board for the disclosure of information outside of financial statements in published financial reports.

Statement of Financial Accounting Concepts No. 5

Recognition and Measurement in Financial Statements of Business Enterprises

December 1984

INTRODUCTION, SCOPE, AND LIMITATIONS

1. This Statement sets forth fundamental recognition criteria and guidance on what information should be formally incorporated into financial statements and when. It builds on the foundation laid by earlier concepts Statements, bringing those concepts together to apply them to broad recognition issues. As a basis for considering recognition criteria, the Statement first addresses financial statements that should be presented and how those financial statements contribute to the objectives of financial reporting. Both that discussion and the later discussion of recognition give particular attention to statements of earnings and comprehensive income.

2. The recognition criteria and guidance in this Statement are generally consistent with current practice and do not imply radical change. Nor do they foreclose the possibility of future changes in practice. The Board intends future change to occur in the gradual, evolutionary way that has characterized past change.

3. This Statement also addresses certain measurement issues that are closely related to recognition. Measurement involves choice of an attribute by which to quantify a recognized item and choice of a scale of measurement (often called "unit of measure"). The Statement notes that different attributes are currently used to measure different items in financial statements and that the Board expects the use of different attributes to continue. The Statement further notes that the measurement scale in current practice is nominal units of money (that is, unadjusted for changes in purchasing power over time) and that the Board expects use of nominal units to continue.

4. This Statement is not intended to apply to organizations other than business enterprises. Recognition criteria and guidance on what information should be formally incorporated into financial statements of nonbusiness organizations can be considered only after completion of another Board project that concerns significant underlying concepts upon which recognition criteria and guidance are built. The Board issued its Exposure Draft, *Proposed Amendments to FASB Concepts Statements 2 and 3 to Apply Them to Nonbusiness Organizations,* on July 7, 1983 and

held public hearings on that matter on November 14 and 15, 1983. Since that project is still in progress, all references in this Statement are to the original Statements, FASB Concepts Statements No. 2, *Qualitative Characteristics of Accounting Information,* and No. 3, *Elements of Financial Statements of Business Enterprises.*

FINANCIAL STATEMENTS

Financial Statements, Financial Reporting, and Recognition

5. Financial statements are a central feature of financial reporting—a principal means of communicating financial information to those outside an entity. In external general purpose financial reporting, a financial statement is a formal tabulation of names and amounts of money derived from accounting records that displays either financial position of an entity at a moment in time or one or more kinds of changes in financial position of the entity during a period of time. Items that are recognized in financial statements are financial representations of certain resources (assets) of an entity, claims to those resources (liabilities and owners' equity), and the effects of transactions and other events and circumstances that result in changes in those resources and claims. The financial statements of an entity are a fundamentally related set that articulate with each other and derive from the same underlying data.[1]

6. Recognition is the process of formally recording or incorporating an item into the financial statements of an entity as an asset, liability, revenue, expense, or the like. Recognition includes depiction of an item in both words and numbers, with the amount included in the totals of the financial statements. For an asset or liability, recognition involves recording not only acquisition or incurrence of the item but also later changes in it, including changes that result in removal from the financial statements.[2]

---

[1]FASB Concepts Statement No. 1, *Objectives of Financial Reporting by Business Enterprises,* pars. 6 and 18; Concepts Statement 3, pars. 6 and 14 and 15. *Financial position* and *changes in financial position* are used here in a broad sense and do not refer to specific financial statements. "Used broadly, financial position refers to state or status of assets or claims to assets at moments in time, and changes in financial position refers to flows or changes in assets or claims to assets over time" (Concepts Statement 3, par. 14, footnote 6). "Through the financial accounting process, the myriad and complex effects of the economic activities of an enterprise are accumulated, analyzed, quantified, classified, recorded, summarized, and reported as information of two basic types: (1) financial position, which relates to a point in time, and (2) changes in financial position, which relate to a period of time" (APB Statement No. 4, *Basic Concepts and Accounting Principles Underlying Financial Statements of Business Enterprises,* par. 10).

[2]Concepts Statement 3, pars. 83, 6, 25, 26, and 34 and 35.

7. Although financial statements have essentially the same objectives as financial reporting, some useful information is better provided by financial statements and some is better provided, or can only be provided, by notes to financial statements or by supplementary information or other means of financial reporting:[3]

a. Information disclosed in notes or parenthetically on the face of financial statements, such as significant accounting policies or alternative measures for assets or liabilities, amplifies or explains information recognized in the financial statements.[4] That sort of information is essential to understanding the information recognized in financial statements and has long been viewed as an integral part of financial statements prepared in accordance with generally accepted accounting principles.
b. Supplementary information, such as disclosures of the effects of changing prices, and other means of financial reporting, such as management discussion and analysis, add information to that in the financial statements or notes, including information that may be relevant but that does not meet all recognition criteria.[5]

8. The scope of this concepts Statement is limited to recognition (and measurement) in financial statements. That limitation on scope does not alter the status of notes, supplementary information, or other means of financial reporting; those types of information remain important and useful for the reasons discussed in the preceding paragraph. To clarify the scope of this concepts Statement, the diagram on page 191 illustrates the types of information used in investment, credit, and similar decisions.

9. Since recognition means depiction of an item in both words and numbers, with the amount included in the totals of the financial statements, disclosure by other

---

[3]Concepts Statement 1, par. 5.

[4]For example, notes provide essential descriptive information for long-term obligations, including when amounts are due, what interest they bear, and whether important restrictions are imposed by related covenants. For inventory, the notes provide information on the measurement method used—FIFO cost, LIFO cost, current market value, etc. For an estimated litigation liability, an extended discussion of the circumstances, counsel's opinions, and the basis for management's judgment may all be provided in the notes. For sales, useful information about revenue recognition policies may appear only in the notes (FASB Statement No. 47, *Disclosure of Long-Term Obligations;* ARB No. 43, Chapter 4, "Inventory Pricing," statement 8; FASB Statement No. 5, *Accounting for Contingencies,* par. 10; and APB Statement 4, par. 199).

[5]Concepts Statement 1, pars. 6, 7, and 22. Supplementary financial statements, complete or partial, may be useful, especially to introduce and to gain experience with new kinds of information. Criteria for including information in supplementary statements may have much in common with recognition criteria for primary statements discussed here, but the criteria discussed in this Statement apply specifically to primary financial statements.

means is *not* recognition. Disclosure of information about the items in financial statements and their measures that may be provided by notes or parenthetically on the face of financial statements, by supplementary information, or by other means of financial reporting is not a substitute for recognition in financial statements for items that meet recognition criteria. Generally, the most useful information about assets, liabilities, revenues, expenses, and other items of financial statements and their measures (that with the best combination of relevance and reliability) should be recognized in the financial statements.

Financial Statements and Objectives of Financial Reporting

10. FASB Concepts Statement No. 1, *Objectives of Financial Reporting by Business Enterprises,* describes the broad purposes of financial reporting, including financial statements.[6] Financial reporting should provide:

> Information that is useful to present and potential investors and creditors and other users in making rational investment, credit, and similar decisions (paragraphs 34-36)
>
> Information to help investors, creditors, and others assess the amounts, timing, and uncertainty of prospective net cash inflows to the related enterprise because their prospects for receiving cash from investments in, loans to, or other participation in the enterprise depend significantly on its cash flow prospects (paragraphs 37-39)
>
> Information about the economic resources of an enterprise, the claims to those resources (obligations of the enterprise to transfer resources to other entities and owners' equity), and the effects of transactions, events, and circumstances that change resources and claims to those resources (paragraph 40).

11. Concepts Statement 1 also gives guidance about the kinds of information that financial reporting, including financial statements, should provide:

> Information about an enterprise's economic resources, obligations, and owners' equity (paragraph 41)

[6]Paragraphs 8-33 of Concepts Statement 1 give needed background. They describe factors affecting the objectives of general purpose external financial reporting, such as characteristics of the environment in the United States, characteristics and limitations of information provided, potential users and their interests, and the nature of the objectives. For example, "financial reporting is but one source of information needed by those who make economic decisions about business enterprises" (par. 22).

All Information Useful for Investment, Credit, and Similar Decisions
(Concepts Statement 1, paragraph 22; partly quoted in footnote 6)

Financial Reporting
(Concepts Statement 1, paragraphs 5–8)

Area Directly Affected by Existing FASB Standards

Basic Financial Statements
(in AICPA Auditing Standards Literature)

Scope of Recognition and Measurement Concepts Statement

Financial Statements

- Statement of Financial Position
- Statements of Earnings and Comprehensive Income
- Statement of Cash Flows
- Statement of Investments by and Distributions to Owners

Notes to Financial Statements (& parenthetical disclosures)

Examples:

- Accounting Policies
- Contingencies
- Inventory Methods
- Number of Shares of Stock Outstanding
- Alternative Measures (market values of items carried at historical cost)

Supplementary Information

Examples:

- Changing Prices Disclosures (FASB Statement 33 as amended)
- Oil and Gas Reserves Information (FASB Statement 69)

Other Means of Financial Reporting

Examples:

- Management Discussion and Analysis
- Letters to Stockholders

Other Information

Examples:

- Discussion of Competition and Order Backlog in SEC Form 10-K (under SEC Reg. S-K)
- Analysts' Reports
- Economic Statistics
- News Articles about Company

Information about an enterprise's performance provided by measures of earnings and comprehensive income[7] and their components measured by accrual accounting (paragraphs 42-48)

Information about how an enterprise obtains and spends cash, about its borrowing and repayment of borrowing, about its capital (equity) transactions, including cash dividends and other distributions of enterprise resources to owners, and about other factors that may affect an enterprise's liquidity or solvency (paragraph 49)

Information about how management of an enterprise has discharged its stewardship responsibility to owners (stockholders) for the use of enterprise resources entrusted to it (paragraphs 50-53).

12. A full, articulated set of several financial statements that provide those various kinds of information about an entity's financial position and changes in its financial position is necessary to satisfy the broad purposes of financial reporting.

Full Set of Financial Statements

13. The amount and variety of information that financial reporting should provide about an entity require several financial statements. A full set of financial statements for a period should show:

Financial position at the end of the period

Earnings (net income)[8] for the period

Comprehensive income (total nonowner changes in equity)[8] for the period

Cash flows during the period

Investments by and distributions to owners during the period.

Information about earnings, comprehensive income, cash flows, and transactions with owners have in common that they are different kinds of information about the effects of transactions and other events and circumstances that change assets and liabilities during a period.

---

[7]Concepts Statement 3 used the term *comprehensive income* for the concept that was called *earnings* in Concepts Statement 1 and reserved the term *earnings* for possible use to designate a component part of comprehensive income (par. 1, footnote 1). Earnings, including its relationship to comprehensive income, is a major topic of this Statement.

[8]Pars. 33 and 40.

14. This Statement does not consider details of displaying those different kinds of information and does not preclude the possibility that some entities might choose to combine some of that information in a single statement. In present practice, for example, a reconciliation of beginning and ending balances of retained earnings is sometimes appended to an income statement.

Purposes and Limitations of Financial Statements

General Purpose Financial Statements and Individual Users

15. General purpose financial statements, to which the objectives of financial reporting apply, are directed toward the common interest of various potential users in the ability of a business enterprise to generate favorable cash flows.[9] General purpose financial statements are feasible only because groups of users of financial information have generally similar needs. But "general purpose" does not mean "all purpose," and financial statements do not necessarily satisfy all users equally well.

16. Each decision maker judges what accounting information is useful, and that judgment is influenced by factors such as the decisions to be made, the methods of decision making to be used, the information already possessed or obtainable from other sources, and the decision maker's capacity (alone or with professional help) to process the information. Even users of financial statement information who make generally similar kinds of decisions differ from each other in those matters.[10]

Usefulness of Financial Statements, Individually and Collectively

17. Financial statements of an entity individually and collectively contribute to meeting the objectives of financial reporting. Component parts of financial statements also contribute to meeting the objectives.

18. Each financial statement provides a different kind of information, and, with limited exceptions (paragraph 14), the various kinds of information cannot be combined into a smaller number of statements without unduly complicating the information. Moreover, the information each provides is used for various purposes, and particular users may be especially interested in the information in one of the state-

---

[9]Concepts Statement 1, par. 30.

[10]Concepts Statement 2, pars. 23-26 and 32-41. For example, information cannot be useful to decision makers who cannot understand it, even though it may otherwise be relevant to a decision and be reliable. Understandability of information is related to the characteristics of the decision maker as well as to the characteristics of the information itself.

ments. Paragraphs 26-57 of this Statement summarize how individual financial statements provide the information listed in paragraph 13.

19. The following two sections first describe how classification and aggregation, if done and used with care, enhance the decision usefulness of financial statements and how financial statements complement each other.

Classification and Aggregation in Financial Statements

20. Classification in financial statements facilitates analysis by grouping items with essentially similar characteristics and separating items with essentially different characteristics. Analysis aimed at objectives such as predicting amounts, timing, and uncertainty of future cash flows requires financial information segregated into reasonably homogeneous groups. For example, components of financial statements that consist of items that have similar characteristics in one or more respects, such as continuity or recurrence, stability, risk, and reliability, are likely to have more predictive value than if their characteristics are dissimilar.

21. Financial statements result from processing vast masses of data and involve needs to simplify, to condense, and to aggregate.[11] Real things and events that affect a dynamic and complex business enterprise are represented in financial statements by words and numbers, which are necessarily highly simplified symbols of the real thing. Real transactions and other events are voluminous and are interpreted, combined, and condensed to be reflected in financial statements. Numerous items and components are aggregated into sums or totals. The resulting financial statements convey information that would be obscured from most users if great detail, such as descriptions of each transaction or event, were provided.

22. Although those simplifications, condensations, and aggregations are both necessary and useful, the Board believes it is important to avoid focusing attention almost exclusively on "the bottom line," earnings per share, or other highly simplified condensations. Summary data, such as the amounts of net assets, comprehensive income, earnings, or earnings per share, may be useful as general indicators of the amount of investment or overall past performance and are often used in efforts to compare an entity with many other entities. But, in a complex business enterprise,

---

[11]". . . It is a very fundamental principle indeed that knowledge is always gained by the *orderly* loss of information, that is, by condensing and abstracting and indexing the great buzzing confusion of information that comes from the world around us into a form which we can appreciate and comprehend" (Kenneth E. Boulding, *Economics as a Science* [New York: McGraw-Hill Book Company, 1970], p. 2, emphasis added).

summary amounts include many heterogeneous things and events. Components of a financial statement often reflect more homogeneous classes of items than the whole statement. The individual items, subtotals, or other parts of a financial statement may often be more useful than the aggregate to those who make investment, credit, and similar decisions.

Complementary Nature of Financial Statements

23. Financial statements interrelate (articulate) because they reflect different aspects of the same transactions or other events affecting an entity.[12] Although each presents information different from the others, none is likely to serve only a single purpose or provide all the financial statement information that is useful for a particular kind of assessment or decision. Significant tools of financial analysis, such as rates of return and turnover ratios, depend on interrelationships between financial statements and their components.

24. Financial statements complement each other. For example:

a. Statements of financial position include information that is often used in assessing an entity's liquidity and financial flexibility,[13] but a statement of financial position provides only an incomplete picture of either liquidity or financial flexibility unless it is used in conjunction with at least a cash flow statement.
b. Statements of earnings and comprehensive income generally reflect a great deal about the profitability of an entity during a period, but that information can be interpreted most meaningfully or compared with that of the entity for other periods or that of other entities only if it is used in conjunction with a statement of financial position, for example, by computing rates of return on assets or equity.
c. Statements of cash flows commonly show a great deal about an entity's current cash receipts and payments, but a cash flow statement provides an incomplete basis for assessing prospects for future cash flows because it cannot show interperiod relationships. Many current cash receipts, especially from operations, stem from activities of earlier periods, and many current cash payments are intended or expected to result in future, not current, cash receipts. Statements of earnings and comprehensive income, especially if used in conjunction with statements of financial position, usually provide a better basis for assessing future

---

[12]Concepts Statement 3, pars. 14 and 15.

[13]Liquidity reflects an asset's or liability's nearness to cash. Financial flexibility is the ability of an entity to take effective actions to alter amounts and timing of cash flows so it can respond to unexpected needs and opportunities.

cash flow prospects of an entity than do cash flow statements alone.[14]

d. Statements of investments by and distributions to owners provide information about significant sources of increases and decreases in assets, liabilities, and equity, but that information is of little practical value unless used in conjunction with other financial statements, for example, by comparing distributions to owners with earnings and comprehensive income or by comparing investments by and distributions to owners with borrowings and repayments of debt.

Individual Financial Statements

25. This discussion summarizes how individual financial statements provide the information listed in paragraph 13. It also introduces recognition considerations, which are the subject of the sections following.

Statement of Financial Position

26. A statement of financial position provides information about an entity's assets, liabilities, and equity and their relationships to each other at a moment in time. The statement delineates the entity's resource structure—major classes and amounts of assets—and its financing structure—major classes and amounts of liabilities and equity.

27. A statement of financial position does not purport to show the value of a business enterprise[15] but, together with other financial statements and other information, should provide information that is useful to those who desire to make their own estimates of the enterprise's value. As a result of limitations stemming from uncertainty and cost-benefit considerations, not all assets and not all liabilities are included in a statement of financial position, and some assets and liabilities that are included are affected by events, such as price changes or accretion, that are not recognized. Statements of financial position also commonly use different attributes to measure different assets and liabilities.[16]

28. Uncertainty and related limitations of financial accounting put the burden of estimating values of business enterprises and of investments in them on investors, creditors, and others. Information about components of earnings and comprehensive income often plays a significant part in that analysis. For example, investors

[14]Concepts Statement 1, pars. 42-46.

[15]Ibid., par. 41.

[16]The different attributes are defined and their current use illustrated in paragraphs 66-70 of this Statement.

may use that information to help estimate "earning power," or other amounts that they perceive as representative of long-term earning ability of an enterprise, as a significant step in comparing the market price of an equity security with its "intrinsic value." Those estimates and analyses are part of financial analysis, not financial reporting,[17] but financial accounting facilitates financial analysis by, among other things, classifying financial statement information in homogeneous groups.[18]

29. Important uses of information about an entity's financial position include helping users to assess factors such as the entity's liquidity, financial flexibility, profitability, and risk. Comparisons among entities and computations of rates of return are enhanced to the extent that significant asset and liability groupings are homogeneous in general characteristics and measurement.

Statements of Earnings and Comprehensive Income

30. Statements of earnings and comprehensive income together reflect the extent to which and the ways in which the equity of an entity increased or decreased from all sources other than transactions with owners during a period. Investors, creditors, managers, and others need information about the causes of changes in an entity's assets and liabilities—including results of its ongoing major or central operations, results of its incidental or peripheral transactions, and effects of other events and circumstances stemming from the environment that are often partly or wholly beyond the control of the entity and its management.

31. Effects of an entity's various activities, transactions, and events differ in stability, risk, and predictability, indicating a need for information about various components of earnings and comprehensive income. That need underlies the distinctions between revenues and gains, between expenses and losses, between various kinds of gains and losses, and between measures found in present practice such as income from continuing operations and net income.[19]

---

[17]". . . [A]ccrual accounting provides measures of earnings rather than evaluations of management's performance, estimates of 'earning power,' predictions of earnings, assessments of risk, or confirmations or rejections of predictions or assessments. Investors, creditors, and other users of the information do their own evaluating, estimating, predicting, assessing, confirming, or rejecting. For example, procedures such as averaging or normalizing reported earnings for several periods and ignoring or averaging out the financial effects of 'nonrepresentative' transactions and events are commonly used in estimating 'earning power.' However, both the concept of 'earning power' and the techniques for estimating it are part of financial analysis and are beyond the scope of financial reporting" (Concepts Statement 1, par. 48).

[18]Pars. 20-22 of this Statement.

[19]Concepts Statement 3, pars. 61 and 151.

32. Since the parts of a financial statement may be more useful to decision makers than the whole (paragraphs 20-22), this Statement emphasizes usefulness of components, interrelationships, and different perspectives as well as usefulness, collectively and individually, of financial statements.

Earnings

33. The concept of earnings described in this Statement is similar to net income in present practice. It includes almost all of what is in present net income for a period, and a statement of earnings based on it will be much like a present income statement. Present practice accepts a variety of terms for net income, and the Board anticipates that net income, profit, net loss, and other equivalent terms will continue to be used in financial statements as names for earnings. However, earnings is not exactly the same as present net income, and this Statement uses the term *earnings* in part to distinguish the concept described here from present net income.

34. Earnings does not include the cumulative effect of certain accounting adjustments of earlier periods that are recognized in the current period.[20] The principal example that is included in present net income but excluded from earnings is the cumulative effect of a change in accounting principle, but others may be identified in the future. Earnings is a measure of performance for a period and to the extent feasible excludes items that are extraneous to that period—items that belong primarily to other periods.[21] The following condensed statements show the similarities and major existing difference between earnings and present net income.

---

[20]That is, the cumulative effect on equity at the beginning of the period for which an earnings statement is provided, sometimes called a "catch-up adjustment."

[21]Prior period adjustments as defined in FASB Statement No. 16, *Prior Period Adjustments,* are not included in net income in present practice and are not, therefore, differences between earnings in this Statement and present net income. Statement 16 narrowed considerably the definition of prior period adjustments in APB Opinions No. 9, *Reporting the Results of Operations,* and No. 30, *Reporting the Results of Operations—Reporting the Effects of Disposal of a Segment of a Business, and Extraordinary, Unusual and Infrequently Occurring Events and Transactions.* Some items that were prior period adjustments under those Opinions are included in net income in present practice, and some argue that the existing definition is too narrow because as a result net income includes items that belong to other periods.

	Present Net Income		Earnings	
Revenues		100		100
Expenses		80		80
Gain from unusual source		(3)		(3)
Income from continuing operations		23		23
Loss on discontinued operations				
Income from operating discontinued segment	10		10	
Loss on disposal of discontinued segment	12	2	12	2
Income before extraordinary items				21
and effect of a change in accounting principle		21		
Extraordinary loss	6			6
Cumulative effect on prior years of a change in accounting principle	2	8		—
Earnings				15
Net Income		13		

35. The Board expects the concept of earnings to be subject to the process of gradual change or evolution that has characterized the development of net income. Present practice has developed over a long time, and that evolution has resulted in significant changes in what net income reflects, such as a shift toward what is commonly called an "all-inclusive" income statement. Those changes have resulted primarily from standard-setting bodies' responses to several factors, such as changes in the business and economic environment and perceptions about the nature and limitations of financial statements, about the needs of users of financial statements, and about the need to prevent or cure perceived abuse(s) in financial reporting. Those factors sometimes may conflict or appear to conflict. For example, an all-inclusive income statement is intended, among other things, to avoid discretionary omissions of losses (or gains) from an income statement, thereby avoiding presentation of a more (or less) favorable report of performance or stewardship than is justified. However, because income statements also are used as a basis for estimating future performance and assessing future cash flow prospects, arguments have been advanced urging exclusion of unusual or nonrecurring gains and losses that might reduce the usefulness of an income statement for any one year for predictive purposes.

36. Earnings is a measure of performance during a period that is concerned primarily with the extent to which asset inflows associated with cash-to-cash cycles[22] substantially completed (or completed) during the period exceed (or are less than) asset outflows associated, directly or indirectly, with the same cycles. Both an entity's ongoing major or central activities and its incidental or peripheral transactions involve a number of overlapping cash-to-cash cycles of different lengths. At any time, a significant proportion of those cycles is normally incomplete, and prospects for their successful completion and amounts of related revenues, expenses, gains, and losses vary in degree of uncertainty. Estimating those uncertain results of incomplete cycles is costly and involves risks, but the benefits of timely financial reporting based on sales or other more relevant events, rather than on cash receipts or other less relevant events, outweigh those costs and risks.

37. Final results of incomplete cycles usually can be reliably measured at some point of substantial completion (for example, at the time of sale, usually meaning delivery) or sometimes earlier in the cycle (for example, as work proceeds on certain long-term, construction-type contracts), so it is usually not necessary to delay recognition until the point of full completion (for example, until after receivables have been collected and warranty obligations have been satisfied). Guidance for applying recognition criteria to components of earnings (paragraphs 78-87) helps define earnings by aiding in making those determinations.

38. Earnings focuses on what the entity has received or reasonably expects to receive for its output (revenues) and what it sacrifices to produce and distribute that output (expenses). Earnings also includes results of the entity's incidental or peripheral transactions and some effects of other events and circumstances stemming from the environment (gains and losses).[23]

Comprehensive Income

39. Comprehensive income is a broad measure of the effects of transactions and other events on an entity, comprising all recognized changes in equity (net assets) of

[22]The patterns of cash-to-cash cycles vary by industry. "Descriptions of operations of business enterprises commonly describe a cycle that begins with cash outlays and ends with cash receipts. That description . . . generally fits manufacturing, merchandising, financial, and service enterprises whose operations comprise primarily activities such as acquiring goods and services, increasing their value by adding time, place, or form utility, selling them, and collecting the selling price. Cash receipts may precede cash payments, however, and commonly do in the operations of some service and financial enterprises" (Concepts Statement 1, par. 39, footnote 8).

[23]Concepts Statement 3, paragraphs 50 and 63-73, defines revenues, expenses, gains, and losses.

the entity during a period from transactions and other events and circumstances except those resulting from investments by owners and distributions to owners.[24]

40. Just as a variety of terms are used for net income in present practice, the Board anticipates that total nonowner changes in equity, comprehensive loss, and other equivalent terms will be used in future financial statements as names for comprehensive income.

41. Components of comprehensive income other than those that are included in earnings present no recognition problems in addition to those involved in recognizing assets and liabilities, for which fundamental criteria are described later (paragraphs 58-77).

Relationships between Earnings and Comprehensive Income

42. Earnings and comprehensive income have the same broad components—revenues, expenses, gains, and losses—but are not the same because certain classes of gains and losses are included in comprehensive income but are excluded from earnings.[25] Those items fall into two classes that are illustrated by certain present practices:

a. Effects of certain accounting adjustments of earlier periods that are recognized in the period, such as the principal example in present practice—cumulative effects of changes in accounting principles—which are included in present net income but are excluded from earnings as set forth in this Statement (paragraphs 33 and 34)

b. Certain other changes in net assets (principally certain holding gains and losses) that are recognized in the period, such as some changes in market values of investments in marketable equity securities classified as noncurrent assets, some changes in market values of investments in industries having specialized account-

[24]Ibid., pars. 50, 56-62, and 147-152.

[25]That possibility was noted in Concepts Statement 3: ". . . the reason for using *comprehensive income* rather than *earnings* in this Statement is that the Board has decided to reserve *earnings* for possible use to designate a different concept that is a component part of—that is, is narrower than or less than—comprehensive income. . . ." (par. 58, footnote reference omitted).

ing practices for marketable securities, and foreign currency translation adjustments.[26]

Both classes and the items they comprise are subject to evolutionary change (paragraph 35).

43. Differences between earnings and comprehensive income require some distinguishing terms. The items in both classes described in paragraph 42 are gains and losses under the definitions in Concepts Statement 3 (paragraphs 67-73), but to refer to *some* gains and losses that are included in earnings and *other* gains and losses that are included in comprehensive income but are excluded from earnings is not only clumsy but also likely to be confusing. This Statement therefore uses *gains* and *losses* for those included in earnings and uses *cumulative accounting adjustments* and *other nonowner changes in equity* for those excluded from earnings but included in comprehensive income.

44. The relationships between earnings and comprehensive income described in the foregoing paragraphs mean that statements of earnings and comprehensive income complement each other something like this:[27]

+ Revenues	100	+ Earnings	15
− Expenses	80	− Cumulative accounting adjustments	2
+ Gains	3		
− Losses	8	+ Other nonowner changes in equity	1
= Earnings	15	= Comprehensive income	14

[26]FASB Statements No. 12, *Accounting for Certain Marketable Securities;* No. 60, *Accounting and Reporting by Insurance Enterprises;* and No. 52, *Foreign Currency Translation.* Changes in market values of marketable securities are included in earnings by some other entities having specialized accounting practices for marketable securities (for example, securities brokers and dealers and investment companies) and for some classes of marketable securities (for example, securities held in trading accounts of banks and futures contracts that are considered speculative [FASB Statement No. 80, *Accounting for Futures Contracts*]).

[27]Earnings and its components are the same as in the example in paragraph 34. Both *cumulative accounting adjustments* and *other nonowner changes in equity* may be either additions to or deductions from earnings. The signs used in the example are for illustration only.

Financial Capital Maintenance

45. The full set of articulated financial statements discussed in this Statement is based on the concept of financial capital maintenance.

46. An enterprise receives a return only after its capital has been maintained or recovered. The concept of capital maintenance, therefore, is critical in distinguishing an enterprise's return *on* investment from return *of* its investment. Both investors and the enterprises in which they acquire an interest invest financial resources with the expectation that the investment will generate more financial resources than they invested.

47. A return on financial capital results only if the financial (money) amount of an enterprise's net assets at the end of a period exceeds the financial amount of net assets at the beginning of the period after excluding the effects of transactions with owners. The financial capital concept is the traditional view and is the capital maintenance concept in present financial statements.[28] In contrast, a return on physical capital results only if the physical productive capacity of the enterprise at the end of the period (or the resources needed to achieve that capacity) exceeds the physical productive capacity at the beginning of the period, also after excluding the effects of transactions with owners. The physical capital maintenance concept can be implemented only if inventories and property, plant, and equipment (and perhaps other assets) are measured by their current costs, while the financial capital maintenance concept does not require measurement by a particular attribute.

48. The principal difference between the two capital maintenance concepts involves the effects of price changes during a period on assets while held and liabilities while owed. Under the financial capital concept, if the effects of those price changes are recognized, they are conceptually holding gains and losses (though they are commonly reported under other names)[29] and are included in the return on capital. Under the physical capital concept, those changes would be recognized but conceptually would be capital maintenance adjustments that would be included directly in equity and not included in return on capital. Both earnings and comprehensive income as set forth in this Statement, like present net income, include holding gains and losses that would be excluded from income under a physical capital maintenance concept.

[28]Concepts Statement 3, par. 58. "Comprehensive income as defined in paragraph 56 is a return *on* financial capital" (Ibid.).

[29]For example, under the FIFO method in present practice, gains from price increases on inventory while held reduce cost of goods sold.

Recognition Implications of Earnings

49. Although recognition involves considerations of relevance and comparability, recognition criteria, conventions, and rules are primarily intended to increase reliability—they are means of coping with the uncertainty that surrounds business and economic activities. Uncertainty in business and economic affairs is a continuum, ranging from mere lack of absolute sureness to a degree of vagueness that precludes anything other than guesswork. Since uncertainty surrounds an entity's incomplete cash-to-cash cycles in varying degrees, measuring progress reliably involves determining whether uncertainty about future cash flows has been reduced to an acceptable level.

50. In response to uncertainty, there has been a general tendency to emphasize purchase and sale transactions and to apply conservative procedures in accounting recognition. Perceptions about characteristics such as realizability and volatility may also help to explain why some events are recognized in present practice while others are not. For example, revenues are sometimes recognized before sale if readily realizable (if sale is a more-or-less effortless or perfunctory activity, and uncertainty about amounts involved is reduced to an acceptable level by quoted prices for interchangeable units in active markets or other reliable measures).[30] Those characteristics may also help to explain certain special recognition rules. For example, so-called translation adjustments from translating foreign currency financial statements are excluded from net income but are reported separately in comprehensive income (paragraphs 39 and 42) because they are considered not only unrealized but also unrealizable short of sale or liquidation of the investment in the entity. Effects of exchange rate changes on the net investment are considered too uncertain and remote to be included in operating results.[31] Similarly, a reason commonly given for the same treatment for certain changes in market values of investments in marketable equity securities is that they may be temporary, and temporary fluctuations in market values of long-term investments should not be included in net income.[32]

51. Since earnings in this Statement is similar to net income for a period in present practice, criteria and guidance given in the Statement for recognizing components of earnings (paragraphs 58-87) are generally similar to revenue and expense recognition criteria or rules in present practice. Future standards may change what is recognized as components of earnings (paragraph 35). Moreover, because of the differences between earnings and comprehensive income, future standards also may recognize

[30]ARB No. 43, Chapter 4, par. 16; FASB Statement 12, pars. 14-16, 27, and 28.

[31]Statement 52, pars. 111-113.

[32]Statement 12, pars. 21, 29, and 30.

certain changes in net assets as components of comprehensive income but not as components of earnings.[33]

Statement of Cash Flows

52. A statement of cash flows directly or indirectly reflects an entity's cash receipts classified by major sources and its cash payments classified by major uses during a period. It provides useful information about an entity's activities in generating cash through operations to repay debt, distribute dividends, or reinvest to maintain or expand operating capacity; about its financing activities, both debt and equity; and about its investing or spending of cash. Important uses of information about an entity's current cash receipts and payments include helping to assess factors such as the entity's liquidity, financial flexibility, profitability, and risk.

53. Since neither earnings nor comprehensive income measured by accrual accounting is the same as cash flow from operations, cash flow statements provide significant information about amounts, causes, and intervals of time between earnings and comprehensive income and cash receipts and outlays. Users commonly consider that information in assessing the relationship between earnings or comprehensive income and associated cash flows.

54. Statements of cash flows present few recognition problems because all cash receipts and payments are recognized when they occur. Reporting cash flows involves no estimates or allocations and few judgments except regarding classification in cash flow statements.[34]

Statement of Investments by and Distributions to Owners

55. A statement of investments by and distributions to owners reflects the extent to which and in what ways the equity of an entity increased or decreased from transactions with owners as owners[35] during a period. That is, it reflects the capital transac-

[33]A possibility that has been suggested is the "inventory profits" that would result if cost of goods sold were reported on LIFO while inventories were reported on FIFO.

[34]Determinations about the particular items to be reported within cash flow statements and the form of those statements are matters that may be developed further in Statements of Financial Accounting Standards or in practice.

[35]Rather than as its employees, suppliers, customers, lenders, or the like (Concepts Statement 3, par. 44); that Statement defines investments by and distributions to owners in paragraphs 52-55.

tions[36] of the entity, in contrast to its income transactions—those with nonowners—which are reflected in statements of earnings and comprehensive income. Statements of comprehensive income and statements of transactions with owners together include all changes in equity (net assets) recognized during a period.

56. Investments by owners establish or increase ownership interests in the entity and may be received in the form of cash, goods or services, or satisfaction or conversion of the entity's liabilities. Distributions decrease ownership interests and include not only cash dividends when declared (or other cash withdrawals by owners of noncorporate entities) but also transactions such as reacquisitions of the entity's equity securities and distributions "in kind" of noncash assets. Information about those events is useful, in conjunction with other financial statement information, to investors, creditors, and other users as an aid in assessing factors such as the entity's financial flexibility, profitability, and risk.

57. Transactions with owners are now normally recognized when they occur. Recognition problems concerning them can be difficult; for example, problems sometimes arise in distinguishing transactions with owners from transactions with certain creditors, and investments and dividends in kind may present measurement problems.[37] However, the recognition implications of earnings that lead to special guidance do not apply to transactions with owners, and that sort of special guidance is not needed for them.

RECOGNITION CRITERIA

58. As noted in paragraphs 6-9, recognition is the process of formally recording or incorporating an item into the financial statements of an entity as an asset, liability, revenue, expense, or the like. A recognized item is depicted in both words and numbers, with the amount included in the statement totals. Recognition comprehends

[36]Capital transactions are transactions with owners that affect ownership interests (equity) in an entity:

> Although *capital* is not a precise term in referring to ownership interests because it is also applied to assets and liabilities in various ways, it is used in this discussion because *capital* is part of so many terms commonly used to describe aspects of ownership interests; for example, investments by owners are commonly called capital contributions, distributions to owners are commonly called capital distributions, and discussions of comprehensive income and its components often refer to capital maintenance. [Concepts Statement 3, par. 144]

[37]Concepts Statement 3, par. 49, and APB Opinion No. 29, *Accounting for Nonmonetary Transactions.*

both initial recognition of an item and recognition of subsequent changes in or removal of a previously recognized item.

Purposes of Criteria

59. Criteria are set forth in this Statement to provide direction for resolving issues that involve accounting recognition. An entity's assets and liabilities and the effects of events on them and on its equity are candidates for recognition in its financial statements.

60. Some events that affect assets, liabilities, or equity are not recognized in financial statements at the time they occur. Some events that result in future benefits, for example, creation of product awareness by advertising and promotion, may perhaps never be recognized as separate assets. Other events, for example, a disaster loss of unknown dimension, are recognized only when sufficient information about the effects of the event has become available at a justifiable cost to reduce uncertainty to an acceptable level. Recognition criteria aid in making those determinations.

Structure of Recognition Criteria

61. The recognition criteria in this Statement are derived from the qualitative characteristics of financial information in Concepts Statement 2 and are helpful in making the definitions of elements of financial statements in Concepts Statement 3 operational in resolving financial reporting issues.

62. The fundamental criteria apply to all recognition decisions. Further guidance is provided in paragraphs 78-87 for applying the fundamental criteria to components of earnings.

Fundamental Recognition Criteria

63. An item and information about it should meet four fundamental recognition criteria to be recognized and should be recognized when the criteria are met, subject to a cost-benefit constraint and a materiality threshold. Those criteria are:

> *Definitions*—The item meets the definition of an element of financial statements.
>
> *Measurability*—It has a relevant attribute measurable with sufficient reliability.

Relevance—The information about it is capable of making a difference in user decisions.

Reliability—The information is representationally faithful, verifiable, and neutral.

All four criteria are subject to a pervasive cost-benefit constraint: the expected benefits from recognizing a particular item should justify perceived costs of providing and using the information.[38] Recognition is also subject to a materiality threshold: an item and information about it need not be recognized in a set of financial statements if the item is not large enough to be material and the aggregate of individually immaterial items is not large enough to be material to those financial statements.[39]

Definitions

64. The definitions are those in FASB Concepts Statement No. 3, *Elements of Financial Statements of Business Enterprises.*[40] To be recognized in financial statements, a resource must meet the definition of an asset, and an obligation must meet the definition of a liability. A change in equity must meet the definition of a revenue, expense, gain, or loss to be recognized as a component of comprehensive income.[41]

Measurability

65. The asset, liability, or change in equity must have a relevant attribute[42] that can be quantified in monetary units with sufficient reliability. Measurability must be considered together with both relevance and reliability.

[38]Concepts Statement 2, pars. 32 and 33 and 133-144.

[39]"Individual judgments are required to assess materiality. . . . The essence of the materiality concept is clear. The omission or misstatement of an item in a financial report is material if, in the light of surrounding circumstances, the magnitude of the item is such that it is probable that the judgment of a reasonable person relying upon the report would have been changed or influenced by the inclusion or correction of the item" (Concepts Statement 2, par. 132).

[40]Concepts Statement 3 does not define elements of cash flow statements but notes classes of items that may be called elements of financial statements, for example, cash provided by operations, cash provided by borrowing, cash provided by issuing equity securities, and so forth (par. 4). However, all items in cash flow statements involve cash receipts or payments, which for recognition purposes are covered by the definitions in that Statement.

[41]As already noted (pars. 42 and 43), the items called *cumulative accounting adjustments* and *other nonowner changes in equity* are gains and losses under the definitions in Concepts Statement 3.

[42]*Attribute* "refers to the traits or aspects of an element to be quantified or measured, such as historical cost/historical proceeds, current cost/current proceeds, etc. Attribute is a narrower concept than measurement, which includes not only identifying the attribute to be measured but also selecting a scale of measurement (for example, units of money or units of constant purchasing power)" (Concepts Statement 1, par. 2, footnote 2).

Measurement Attributes

66. Items currently reported in financial statements are measured by different attributes, depending on the nature of the item and the relevance and reliability of the attribute measured. The Board expects the use of different attributes to continue.

67. Five different attributes of assets (and liabilities) are used in present practice:

a. *Historical cost (historical proceeds).* Property, plant, and equipment and most inventories are reported at their historical cost, which is the amount of cash, or its equivalent, paid to acquire an asset, commonly adjusted after acquisition for amortization or other allocations. Liabilities that involve obligations to provide goods or services to customers are generally reported at historical proceeds, which is the amount of cash, or its equivalent, received when the obligation was incurred and may be adjusted after acquisition for amortization or other allocations.
b. *Current cost.* Some inventories are reported at their current (replacement) cost, which is the amount of cash, or its equivalent, that would have to be paid if the same or an equivalent asset were acquired currently.
c. *Current market value.* Some investments in marketable securities are reported at their current market value, which is the amount of cash, or its equivalent, that could be obtained by selling an asset in orderly liquidation. Current market value is also generally used for assets expected to be sold at prices lower than previous carrying amounts. Some liabilities that involve marketable commodities and securities, for example, the obligations of writers of options or sellers of common shares who do not own the underlying commodities or securities, are reported at current market value.
d. *Net realizable (settlement) value.* Short-term receivables and some inventories are reported at their net realizable value, which is the nondiscounted amount of cash, or its equivalent, into which an asset is expected to be converted in due course of business less direct costs, if any, necessary to make that conversion. Liabilities that involve known or estimated amounts of money payable at unknown future dates, for example, trade payables or warranty obligations, generally are reported at their net settlement value, which is the nondiscounted amounts of cash, or its equivalent, expected to be paid to liquidate an obligation in the due course of business, including direct costs, if any, necessary to make that payment.
e. *Present (or discounted) value of future cash flows.* Long-term receivables are reported at their present value (discounted at the implicit or historical rate), which

is the present or discounted value of future cash inflows into which an asset is expected to be converted in due course of business less present values of cash outflows necessary to obtain those inflows. Long-term payables are similarly reported at their present value (discounted at the implicit or historical rate), which is the present or discounted value of future cash outflows expected to be required to satisfy the liability in due course of business.

68. The different attributes often have the same amounts, particularly at initial recognition. As a result, there may be agreement about the appropriate amount for an item but disagreement about the attribute being used. Present financial statements frequently are characterized as being based on the historical cost (historical proceeds) attribute. That no doubt reflects the fact that, for most enterprises, a great many of the individual events recognized in financial statements are acquisitions of goods or services for cash or equivalent that are recorded at historical cost. Although the "historical cost system" description may be convenient and describes well present practice for some major classes of assets (most inventories, property, plant, and equipment, and intangibles), it describes less well present practice for a number of other classes of assets and liabilities—for example, trade receivables, notes payable, and warranty obligations.

69. "Historical exchange price" is more descriptive of the quantity most generally reflected in financial statements in present practice (and "transaction-based system" would be a better description of the present accounting model than "historical cost system"). Amounts initially recorded for trade receivables and long-term notes payable, for example, generally fit the historical exchange price description. But some assets are acquired, and some liabilities are incurred, without exchanges—for example, assets found or received as contributions and income tax or litigation liabilities. There is no historical exchange price in those situations, and some other attribute must be used. Moreover, carrying amounts of assets (liabilities) are frequently reduced (increased) from historical exchange price to a lower (higher) current cost, current market value, or net realizable value, even though no subsequent exchange of the assets held or liabilities owed has occurred. And some assets are carried at current market value, independent of historical exchange price.

70. Rather than attempt to characterize present practice as being based on a single attribute with numerous major exceptions for diverse reasons, this concepts Statement characterizes present practice as based on different attributes. Rather than attempt to select a single attribute and force changes in practice so that all classes of assets and liabilities use that attribute, this concepts Statement suggests that use of

different attributes will continue, and discusses how the Board may select the appropriate attribute in particular cases.[43]

Monetary Unit or Measurement Scale

71. The monetary unit or measurement scale in financial statements in current practice is nominal units of money, that is, unadjusted for changes in purchasing power of money over time. An ideal measurement scale would be one that is stable over time. At low rates of change in general purchasing power (inflation or deflation), nominal units of money are relatively stable. Also, preparation and use of financial statements is simpler with nominal units than with other units of measure, such as units of constant general purchasing power (used, for example, in supplementary disclosures of the effects of changing prices),[44] artificial monetary units (for example, the European Currency Unit or ECU), or units of a commodity (for example, ounces of gold). However, as rates of change in general purchasing power increase, financial statements expressed in nominal units of money become progressively less useful and less comparable.

72. The Board expects that nominal units of money will continue to be used to measure items recognized in financial statements. However, a change from present circumstances (for example, an increase in inflation to a level at which distortions became intolerable) might lead the Board to select another, more stable measurement scale.

Relevance

73. Relevance is a primary qualitative characteristic. To be relevant, information about an item must have feedback value or predictive value (or both) for users and must be timely.[45] Information is relevant if it has the capacity to make a difference in investors', creditors', or other users' decisions. To be recognized, the information conveyed by including an asset, liability, or change therein in the financial statements must be relevant.

74. The relevance of particular information about an item being considered for recognition cannot be determined in isolation. Relevance should be evaluated in the

---

[43]This discussion of measurement attributes is based in part on the FASB Discussion Memorandum, *Conceptual Framework for Financial Accounting and Reporting: Elements of Financial Statements and Their Measurement* (December 2, 1976), paragraphs 388-574, which further describes and illustrates each of the attributes and remains a useful reference.

[44] FASB Statement No. 33, *Financial Reporting and Changing Prices,* as amended.

[45]Concepts Statement 2, pars. 46-57.

context of the principal objective of financial reporting: providing information that is useful in making rational investment, credit, and similar decisions.[46] Relevance should also be evaluated in the context of the full set of financial statements—with consideration of how recognition of a particular item contributes to the aggregate decision usefulness.

Reliability

75. Reliability is the other primary qualitative characteristic. To be reliable, information about an item must be representationally faithful, verifiable, and neutral.[47] To be reliable, information must be sufficiently faithful in its representation of the underlying resource, obligation, or effect of events and sufficiently free of error and bias to be useful to investors, creditors, and others in making decisions. To be recognized, information about the existence and amount of an asset, liability, or change therein must be reliable.

76. Reliability may affect the timing of recognition. The first available information about an event that may have resulted in an asset, liability, or change therein is sometimes too uncertain to be recognized: it may not yet be clear whether the effects of the event meet one or more of the definitions or whether they are measurable, and the cost of resolving those uncertainties may be excessive. Information about some items that meet a definition may never become sufficiently reliable at a justifiable cost to recognize the item. For other items, those uncertainties are reduced as time passes, and reliability is increased as additional information becomes available.

77. Unavailability or unreliability of information may delay recognition of an item, but waiting for virtually complete reliability or minimum cost may make the information so untimely that it loses its relevance. At some intermediate point, uncertainty may be reduced at a justifiable cost to a level tolerable in view of the perceived relevance of the information. If other criteria are also met, that is the appropriate point for recognition. Thus, recognition may sometimes involve a trade-off between relevance and reliability.

GUIDANCE IN APPLYING CRITERIA TO COMPONENTS OF EARNINGS

78. This section discusses the need for and provides further guidance in applying the fundamental criteria in recognizing components of earnings. Changes in net assets

[46]Concepts Statement 1, pars. 34-40.

[47]Concepts Statement 2, pars. 58-110.

are recognized as components of earnings if they qualify under the guidance in paragraphs 83-87. Certain changes in net assets (discussed in paragraphs 42-44 and 49-51) that meet the four fundamental recognition criteria just described may qualify for recognition in comprehensive income even though they do not qualify for recognition as components of earnings based on that guidance.

79. Further guidance in applying the recognition criteria to components of earnings is necessary because of the widely acknowledged importance of information about earnings and its components as a primary measure of performance for a period. The performance measured is that of the entity, not necessarily that of its management, and includes the recognized effects upon the entity of events and circumstances both within and beyond the control of the entity and its management.[48] The widely acknowledged importance of earnings information leads to guidance intended in part to provide more stringent requirements for recognizing components of earnings than for recognizing other changes in assets or liabilities.

80. As noted in paragraph 36, earnings measures the extent to which asset inflows (revenues and gains) associated with substantially completed cash-to-cash cycles exceed asset outflows (expenses and losses) associated, directly or indirectly, with the same cycles. Guidance for recognizing components of earnings is concerned with identifying which cycles are substantially complete and with associating particular revenues, gains, expenses, and losses with those cycles.

81. In assessing the prospect that as yet uncompleted transactions will be concluded successfully, a degree of skepticism is often warranted.[49] Moreover, as a reaction to uncertainty, more stringent requirements historically have been imposed for recognizing revenues and gains than for recognizing expenses and losses, and those conservative reactions influence the guidance for applying the recognition criteria to components of earnings.

82. The guidance stated here is intended to summarize key considerations in a form useful for guidance for future standard setting—guidance which also is consistent with the vast bulk of current practice. The following paragraphs provide guidance separately for recognition of revenues and gains and for expenses and losses as components of earnings.

---

[48]"What happens to a business enterprise is usually so much a joint result of a complex interaction of many factors that neither accounting nor other statistical analysis can discern with reasonable accuracy the degree to which management, or any other factor, affected the joint result" (Concepts Statement 1, par. 53).

[49]Concepts Statement 2, par. 97.

Revenues and Gains

83. Further guidance for recognition of revenues and gains is intended to provide an acceptable level of assurance of the existence and amounts of revenues and gains before they are recognized. Revenues and gains of an enterprise during a period are generally measured by the exchange values of the assets (goods or services) or liabilities involved, and recognition involves consideration of two factors, (a) being realized or realizable and (b) being earned, with sometimes one and sometimes the other being the more important consideration.

a. *Realized or realizable.* Revenues and gains generally are not recognized until realized or realizable.[50] Revenues and gains are realized when products (goods or services), merchandise, or other assets are exchanged for cash or claims to cash. Revenues and gains are realizable when related assets received or held are readily convertible to known amounts of cash or claims to cash. Readily convertible assets have (i) interchangeable (fungible) units and (ii) quoted prices available in an active market that can rapidly absorb the quantity held by the entity without significantly affecting the price.
b. *Earned.* Revenues are not recognized until earned. An entity's revenue-earning activities involve delivering or producing goods, rendering services, or other activities that constitute its ongoing major or central operations,[51] and revenues are considered to have been earned when the entity has substantially accomplished what it must do to be entitled to the benefits represented by the revenues. Gains commonly result from transactions and other events that involve no "earning process," and for recognizing gains, being earned is generally less significant than being realized or realizable.

---

[50]The terms *realized* and *realizable* are used in the Board's conceptual framework in precise senses, focusing on conversion or convertibility of noncash assets into cash or claims to cash (Concepts Statement 3, par. 83). *Realized* has sometimes been used in a different, broader sense: for example, some have used that term to include *realizable* or to include certain conversions of noncash assets into other assets that are also not cash or claims to cash. APB Statement 4, paragraphs 148-153, used the term *realization* even more broadly as a synonym for *recognition*.

[51]"Most types of revenue are the joint result of many profit-directed activities of an enterprise and revenue is often described as being 'earned' gradually and continuously by the whole of enterprise activities. *Earning* in this sense is a technical term that refers to the activities that give rise to the revenue—purchasing, manufacturing, selling, rendering service, delivering goods, allowing other entities to use enterprise assets, the occurrence of an event specified in a contract, and so forth. All of the profit-directed activities of an enterprise that comprise the process by which revenue is earned may be called the *earning process*" (APB Statement 4, par. 149). Concepts Statement 3, paragraph 64, footnote 31, contains the same concept.

84. In recognizing revenues and gains:

a. The two conditions (being realized or realizable and being earned) are usually met by the time product or merchandise is delivered or services are rendered to customers, and revenues from manufacturing and selling activities and gains and losses from sales of other assets are commonly recognized at time of sale (usually meaning delivery).[52]
b. If sale or cash receipt (or both) precedes production and delivery (for example, magazine subscriptions), revenues may be recognized as earned by production and delivery.
c. If product is contracted for before production, revenues may be recognized by a percentage-of-completion method as earned—as production takes place—provided reasonable estimates of results at completion and reliable measures of progress are available.[53]
d. If services are rendered or rights to use assets extend continuously over time (for example, interest or rent), reliable measures based on contractual prices established in advance are commonly available, and revenues may be recognized as earned as time passes.
e. If products or other assets are readily realizable because they are salable at reliably determinable prices without significant effort (for example, certain agricultural products, precious metals, and marketable securities), revenues and some gains or losses may be recognized at completion of production or when prices of the assets change. Paragraph 83(a) describes readily realizable (convertible) assets.
f. If product, services, or other assets are exchanged for nonmonetary assets that are not readily convertible into cash, revenues or gains or losses may be recognized on the basis that they have been earned and the transaction is completed. Gains or losses may also be recognized if nonmonetary assets are received or distributed in nonreciprocal transactions. Recognition in both kinds of transactions depends on the provision that the fair values involved can be determined within reasonable limits.[54]

---

[52]The requirement that revenue be earned before it is recorded "usually causes no problems because the earning process is usually complete or nearly complete by the time of [sale]" (APB Statement 4, par. 153).

[53]If production is long in relation to reporting periods, such as for long-term, construction-type contracts, recognizing revenues as earned has often been deemed to result in information that is significantly more relevant and representationally faithful than information based on waiting for delivery, although at the sacrifice of some verifiability. (Concepts Statement 2, paragraphs 42-45, describes trade-offs of that kind.)

[54]APB Opinion 29.

g. If collectibility of assets received for product, services, or other assets is doubtful, revenues and gains may be recognized on the basis of cash received.

Expenses and Losses

85. Further guidance for recognition of expenses and losses is intended to recognize consumption (using up) of economic benefits or occurrence or discovery of loss of future economic benefits during a period. Expenses and losses are generally recognized when an entity's economic benefits are used up in delivering or producing goods, rendering services, or other activities that constitute its ongoing major or central operations or when previously recognized assets are expected to provide reduced or no further benefits.

Consumption of Benefits

86. Consumption of economic benefits during a period may be recognized either directly or by relating it to revenues recognized during the period:[55]

a. Some expenses, such as cost of goods sold, are matched with revenues—they are recognized upon recognition of revenues that result directly and jointly from the same transactions or other events as the expenses.
b. Many expenses, such as selling and administrative salaries, are recognized during the period in which cash is spent or liabilities are incurred for goods and services that are used up either simultaneously with acquisition or soon after.
c. Some expenses, such as depreciation and insurance, are allocated by systematic and rational procedures to the periods during which the related assets are expected to provide benefits.

Loss or Lack of Future Benefit

87. An expense or loss is recognized if it becomes evident that previously recognized future economic benefits of an asset have been reduced or eliminated, or that a liability has been incurred or increased, without associated economic benefits.

[55]Concepts Statement 3, pars. 84-89.

RECOGNITION OF CHANGES IN ASSETS AND LIABILITIES

88. Initial recognition of assets acquired and liabilities incurred generally involves measurement based on current exchange prices at the date of recognition. Once an asset or a liability is recognized, it continues to be measured at the amount initially recognized until an event that changes the asset or liability or its amount occurs and meets the recognition criteria.

89. Events that change assets and liabilities are of two types: (a) inflows (acquisitions of assets or incurrences of liabilities) and outflows (sale or other disposal or loss of assets and settlement or cancellation of liabilities) and (b) changes of amounts of assets while held or of liabilities while owed by the entity. The latter also are of two types: (i) changes in utility or substance and (ii) changes in price. Examples of changes in utility or substance that are recognized in current practice include use of assets in production, depreciation of assets used in administrative activities, and fire damage to assets.

90. Information based on current prices should be recognized if it is sufficiently relevant and reliable to justify the costs involved and more relevant than alternative information. The merits of recognizing changes in prices may be clear in certain cases, and, as already noted, some price changes are recognized in present practice. In other cases, the relative merits of information based on current prices and alternative information may be unclear or may be a matter of dispute. In considering the application of the fundamental recognition criteria, those relative merits must be evaluated in the light of the circumstances of each case.

SUMMARY

91. Most aspects of current practice are consistent with the recognition criteria and guidance in this Statement, but the criteria and guidance do not foreclose the possibility of future changes in practice. This Statement is intended to provide guidance for orderly change in accounting standards when needed. When evidence indicates that information about an item that is more useful (relevant and reliable) than information currently reported is available at a justifiable cost, it should be included in financial statements.

This Statement was adopted by the affirmative vote of six members of the Financial Accounting Standards Board. Mr. March dissented.

Mr. March dissents from this Statement because (a) it does not adopt measurement concepts oriented toward what he believes is the most useful single attribute for recognition purposes, the cash equivalent of recognized transactions reduced by subsequent impairments or loss of service value—instead it suggests selecting from several different attributes without providing sufficient guidance for the selection process; (b) it identifies all nonowner changes in assets and liabilities as comprehensive income and return on equity, thereby including in income, incorrectly in his view, capital inputs from nonowners, unrealized gains from price changes, amounts that should be deducted to maintain capital in real terms, and foreign currency translation adjustments; (c) it uses a concept of income that is fundamentally based on measurements of assets, liabilities, and changes in them, rather than adopting the Statement's concept of earnings as the definition of income; and (d) it fails to provide sufficient guidance for initial recognition and derecognition of assets and liabilities.

Mr. March would not, in general, recognize increases in prices of assets and decreases in prices of liabilities before they are realized. He believes present measurement practice can be characterized as largely using a single attribute, the cash equivalent of recognized transactions reduced by subsequent impairments or loss of service value, and that present practices that recognize revenues or gains from changes in prices before realization, such as the uses of current market values and net realizable values cited in paragraphs 67(c) and (d) and 69, are exceptions to the general use of that single attribute. Mr. March is concerned that the guidance in paragraph 90 would permit, and perhaps point toward, more recognition of changes in current prices before realization. He believes that income, recognition, and measurement concepts based largely on the single attribute that he proposes are most relevant to reporting capital committed, performance, and the investment and realization of resources.

Mr. March objects to comprehensive income, defined in Concepts Statement 3 and confirmed in this Statement, as a concept of income because it includes all recognized changes (including price changes) in assets and liabilities other than investments by owners and distributions to owners. He would exclude from income, and include in the amount of capital to be maintained (in addition to transactions with owners), what he would consider to be direct capital inputs to the enterprise from nonowner sources. Those include governmental and other capital contributions or grants and capital arising in reorganizations, recapitalizations, and extinguishments or restatements of debt capital.

Mr. March would also require that income must first deduct a provision for maintenance of capital in real terms (adjusted for changes in purchasing power of money over time, paragraphs 71-72). He believes that is necessary to avoid reporting a return of capital as income. Complex implementation should not be necessary to provide for the erosion of capital caused by the effects of inflation on the unit of measure. A "rubber yardstick" is a poor measuring tool. Mr. March would also exclude from income foreign currency translation adjustments (excluded from earnings but included in comprehensive income by paragraph 42(b)), which he believes are analogous to provisions for maintenance of capital in real terms.

The description of earnings (paragraphs 33-38) and the guidance for applying recognition criteria to components of earnings (paragraphs 78-87) is consistent with Mr. March's view that income should measure performance and that performance flows primarily from an entity's fulfillment of the terms of its transactions with outside entities that result in revenues, other proceeds on resource dispositions (gains), costs (expenses) associated with those revenues and proceeds, and losses sustained. However, Mr. March believes that those concepts are fundamental and should be embodied in definitions of the elements of financial statements and in basic income recognition criteria rather than basing income on measurements of assets, liabilities, and changes in them.

Disregarding the foregoing objections, Mr. March believes this Statement offers insufficient guidance for the near-term future work of the Board. To be useful, it needs to be supplemented with more specific guidance for selecting measurement attributes for specific assets, liabilities, and transactions and for deciding when the criteria require recognition or derecognition of an asset or a liability.

Members of the Financial Accounting Standards Board:

Donald J. Kirk, *Chairman*
Frank E. Block
Victor H. Brown
Raymond C. Lauver
John W. March
David Mosso
Robert T. Sprouse

Appendix

BACKGROUND INFORMATION

92. The Board's study of recognition and measurement concepts has spanned several years. The need to develop those concepts was identified early in the conceptual framework project, and the first FASB concepts Statement, *Objectives of Financial Reporting by Business Enterprises,* listed them among several separate matters to be covered:

> . . . Later Statements are expected to cover the elements of financial statements and their recognition, measurement, and display . . . , criteria for distinguishing information to be included in financial statements from that which should be provided by other means of financial reporting, and criteria for evaluating and selecting accounting information (qualitative characteristics). [paragraph 2]

93. During that period, three FASB Research Reports,[56] a Discussion Memorandum,[57] a concepts Statement,[58] and an Exposure Draft[59] have dealt in whole or in part with recognition and measurement matters, and the Board has discussed those matters extensively.

94. The once-separate projects on recognition and on measurement were combined, principally because in the Board's view certain recognition questions, which are among the most important to be dealt with, are so closely related to measurement issues that it is not productive to discuss them separately. For example, the question of whether the appropriate attribute to measure a particular item is a past exchange price or a current exchange price is not easily separable from the question of whether events such as price changes should be recognized.

---

[56] *Recognition of Contractual Rights and Obligations: An Exploratory Study of Conceptual Issues,* by Yuji Ijiri, December 1980; *Survey of Present Practices in Recognizing Revenues, Expenses, Gains, and Losses,* by Henry R. Jaenicke, January 1981; and *Recognition in Financial Statements: Underlying Concepts and Practical Conventions,* by L. Todd Johnson and Reed K. Storey, July 1982.

[57] FASB Discussion Memorandum, *Conceptual Framework for Financial Accounting and Reporting: Elements of Financial Statements and Their Measurement,* December 2, 1976, Part III.

[58] FASB Concepts Statement No. 3, *Elements of Financial Statements of Business Enterprises,* pars. 16 and 17, 37-43, and 74-89.

[59] FASB Exposure Draft, *Reporting Income, Cash Flows, and Financial Position of Business Enterprises,* November 1981, pars. 13-16 and elsewhere. This Statement supersedes that Exposure Draft.

95. The Board issued an Exposure Draft, *Recognition and Measurement in Financial Statements of Business Enterprises,* on December 30, 1983 and received 104 letters of comment on it.

96. The changes made to the Exposure Draft were largely in response to suggestions in those comment letters and are intended to improve the clarity and organization of the ideas presented in the Exposure Draft. The Board believes that the substance of this Statement is not significantly changed from the Exposure Draft. Noteworthy changes made and changes suggested but not made are discussed below.

97. The discussion of financial statements, financial reporting, and recognition in paragraphs 5-12 has been expanded and reorganized in response to comments that the status of notes, supplementary information, and other means of financial reporting outside of financial statements (all of which are outside the scope of this concepts Statement) was unclear.

98. The term *full set* of financial statements has been used in paragraph 13 and elsewhere in response to comments that *complete set,* the term used in the Exposure Draft, implied that no further information beyond the listed financial statements was needed and to comments that *complete set* had been used in some standards in a different way.

99. A number of respondents inferred from the discussion of cash flow statements in the Exposure Eraft that the Board had decided one or more specific issues about cash flow reporting. Those issues include the direct and indirect methods of presentation; whether or not "cash" should include equivalents to cash and, if so, what instruments qualify; whether or not the nonmonetary transactions currently reported in statements of changes in financial position should appear in cash flow statements; and the definitions of cash provided by (or used for) operations, financing activities, and investing activities. Those and other specific cash flow statement issues mentioned by respondents are beyond the scope of this concepts Statement. The discussion of the statement of cash flows was revised to emphasize that.

100. Many respondents criticized the term *comprehensive income* and some criticized the term *earnings* as unwarranted innovations likely to cause confusion and legal difficulties. Those terms are not new. They were first used in their present senses in Concepts Statement 3, in which the Board defined comprehensive income as an element of financial statements and reserved the term *earnings* for possible later use to designate a component part of comprehensive income. This Statement carries forward the concept of comprehensive income and describes a concept for earnings. The Board retained the idea of two separate measures both to reflect

present practice for the items discussed in paragraph 42(b) and to allow for the possibility that future standards may recognize some items, for example, the cumulative accounting adjustments discussed in paragraph 42(a), in comprehensive income but not in earnings.

101. The Board explored the alternative terms for *comprehensive income* and *earnings* suggested by respondents, as well as other possibilities suggested by its staff, but concluded that the other terms had disadvantages greater than those attaching to the terms originally selected. The Statement was revised to indicate that the Board anticipates that, as with net income in present practice, a variety of terms will be used in future financial statements as names for earnings (for example, net income, profit, or net loss) and for comprehensive income (for example, total nonowner changes in equity or comprehensive loss).

102. Some respondents urged the Board to clarify the concept of earnings. The discussion in paragraphs 36-38, the table in paragraph 44, and footnote 26 have been rewritten to explain more fully what the Board intended.

103. The materiality threshold for recognition, implicit in the conceptual framework, has been made explicit in paragraph 63 at the suggestion of several respondents. Some respondents suggested that materiality and cost-benefit considerations should be fundamental recognition criteria. No change was made because the Board believes that, while those considerations affect the application of the criteria, they are different in character from the four fundamental recognition criteria.

104. Several respondents urged the Board to include the question of the monetary unit or measurement scale within the scope of the Statement. The Exposure Draft described present practice as using nominal units of money but left the unit of measure outside its scope. The Board clarified the matter by indicating in paragraph 72 that it expects that nominal units of money will continue to be used to measure items recognized in financial statements.

105. The discussion of measurement has been expanded, in response to the suggestions of several respondents, to explain and illustrate the different attributes more fully and to discuss why different attributes are needed to describe present practice and are expected to continue to be used to measure items in financial statements.

106. Some respondents expressed concern that the guidance in paragraph 84(e) (concerning circumstances under which revenue or gain may be recognized at completion of production or when prices of assets change) and the guidance in paragraph 87 (concerning recognition of losses when it becomes evident that assets have been

reduced or eliminated or liabilities incurred or increased without associated benefits) meant significant change from present practice. Those paragraphs describe concepts that the Board believes underlie many current practices and standards, just as do the other parts of the guidance for recognition of components of earnings. They have been retained and clarified.

107. Several respondents urged the Board to address in this Statement certain specific recognition and measurement issues including definitive guidance for recognition of contracts that are fully executory (that is, contracts as to which neither party has as yet carried out any part of its obligations, which are generally not recognized in present practice) and selection of measurement attributes for particular assets and liabilities. Those issues have long been, and remain, unresolved on a general basis. As noted in the introductory statement to this and earlier concepts Statements (page 185), establishment of objectives and identification of fundamental concepts will not directly solve specific financial accounting and reporting problems. Rather, objectives give direction, and concepts are tools for solving problems.

108. The Board and others who use this Statement will be guided and aided by the concepts it sets forth, but judgments, based on the particular circumstances of each case, will continue to play a major role in solving problems of recognition and measurement in financial statements. The Board believes that further development of recognition, measurement, and display matters will occur as the concepts are applied at the standards level.

Summary Index of Concepts Defined or Discussed

	Paragraph Number
Articulation	5, 12, 23, 45
Attributes measured	66–70, footnote 42, 105, 107
Capital maintenance	45–48
Cash flow, statement of	13, 24, 52–54, 99
Comprehensive income	13, 24, 30–32, 39–44, 100–101
Consumption of benefit	86
Cumulative accounting adjustments	42–44, 100
Current market value	67, 69
Current prices	90
Current (replacement) cost	67, 69
Definitions	63–64
Distributions to owners, statement of	13, 24, 55–57
Earned	83–84
Earnings	13, 24, 30–38, 42–44, 49–51, 100–102
Expenses	85–87
Financial flexibility	24, footnote 13
Financial position, statement of	13, 24, 26–30
Financial statements	5–57, 97
Full set of financial statements	13, 98
Gains	83–84
Guidance for components of earnings	78–87, 106
Historical cost	67–69
Investments by owners, statement of	13, 24, 55–57
Liquidity	24, footnote 13
Losses	85–87, 106
Loss of benefit	87
Measurability	63, 65–72
Net realizable (settlement) value	67
Notes to financial statements	7–9, footnote 4, 97
Other means of financial reporting	7–9, 92, 97
Other nonowner changes in equity	42–44, footnote 27
Present value	67
Realized and realizable	83–84, footnote 50
Recognition	6–7, 58, 94, 97, 108
Recognition criteria	63, 103
Relevance	63, 73–74

Reliability 63, 75–77
Revenues 83–84
Supplementary information 7–9, 97
Unit of measure 71–72, 104

Statement of Financial Accounting Concepts No. 6
Elements of Financial Statements
a replacement of FASB Concepts Statement No. 3
(incorporating an amendment of FASB Concepts Statement No. 2)

STATUS

Issued: December 1985

Affects: Supersedes CON 2, paragraph 4 and footnote 2
Supersedes CON 3

Affected by: No other pronouncements

HIGHLIGHTS

[*Best understood in context of full Statement*]

- Elements of financial statements are the building blocks with which financial statements are constructed—the classes of items that financial statements comprise. The items in financial statements represent in words and numbers certain entity resources, claims to those resources, and the effects of transactions and other events and circumstances that result in changes in those resources and claims.

- This Statement replaces FASB Concepts Statement No.3, *Elements of Financial Statements of Business Enterprises,* expanding its scope to encompass not-for-profit organizations as well.

- This Statement defines 10 interrelated elements that are directly related to measuring performance and status of an entity. (Other possible elements of financial statements are not addressed.)

  — Assets are probable future economic benefits obtained or controlled by a particular entity as a result of past transactions or events.

- Liabilities are probable future sacrifices of economic benefits arising from present obligations of a particular entity to transfer assets or provide services to other entities in the future as a result of past transactions or events.
- Equity or net assets is the residual interest in the assets of an entity that remains after deducting its liabilities. In a business enterprise, the equity is the ownership interest. In a not-for-profit organization, which has no ownership interest in the same sense as a business enterprise, net assets is divided into three classes based on the presence or absence of donor-imposed restrictions—permanently restricted, temporarily restricted, and unrestricted net assets.
- Investments by owners are increases in equity of a particular business enterprise resulting from transfers to it from other entities of something valuable to obtain or increase ownership interests (or equity) in it. Assets are most commonly received as investments by owners, but that which is received may also include services or satisfaction or conversion of liabilities of the enterprise.
- Distributions to owners are decreases in equity of a particular business enterprise resulting from transferring assets, rendering services, or incurring liabilities by the enterprise to owners. Distributions to owners decrease ownership interest (or equity) in an enterprise.
- Comprehensive income is the change in equity of a business enterprise during a period from transactions and other events and circumstances from nonowner sources. It includes all changes in equity during a period except those resulting from investments by owners and distributions to owners.
- Revenues are inflows or other enhancements of assets of an entity or settlements of its liabilities (or a combination of both) from delivering or producing goods, rendering services, or other activities that constitute the entity's ongoing major or central operations.
- Expenses are outflows or other using up of assets or incurrences of liabilities (or a combination of both) from delivering or producing goods, rendering services, or carrying out other activities that constitute the entity's ongoing major or central operations.
- Gains are increases in equity (net assets) from peripheral or incidental transactions of an entity and from all other transactions and other events and circumstances affecting the entity except those that result from revenues or investments by owners.
- Losses are decreases in equity (net assets) from peripheral or incidental transactions of an entity and from all other transactions and other events and circumstances affecting the entity except those that result from expenses or distributions to owners.

- The Statement defines three classes of net assets of not-for-profit organizations and the changes in those classes during a period. Each class is composed of the revenues, expenses, gains, and losses that affect that class and of reclassifications from or to other classes.

  — Change in permanently restricted net assets during a period is the total of (a) contributions and other inflows during the period of assets whose use by the organization is limited by donor-imposed stipulations that neither expire by passage of time nor can be fulfilled or otherwise removed by actions of the organization, (b) other asset enhancements and diminishments during the period that are subject to the same kinds of stipulations, and (c) reclassifications from (or to) other classes of net assets during the period as a consequence of donor-imposed stipulations.

  — Change in temporarily restricted net assets during a period is the total of (a) contributions and other inflows during the period of assets whose use by the organization is limited by donor-imposed stipulations that either expire by passage of time or can be fulfilled and removed by actions of the organization pursuant to those stipulations, (b) other asset enhancements and diminishments during the period subject to the same kinds of stipulations, and (c) reclassifications to (or from) other classes of net assets during the period as a consequence of donor-imposed stipulations, their expiration by passage of time, or their fulfillment and removal by actions of the organization pursuant to those stipulations.

  — Change in unrestricted net assets during a period is the total change in net assets during the period less change in permanently restricted net assets and change in temporarily restricted net assets for the period. It is the change during the period in the part of net assets of a not-for-profit organization that is not limited by donor-imposed stipulations. Changes in unrestricted net assets include (a) revenues and gains that change unrestricted net assets, (b) expenses and losses that change unrestricted net assets, and (c) reclassifications from (or to) other classes of net assets as a consequence of donor-imposed stipulations, their expiration by passage of time, or their fulfillment and removal by actions of the organization pursuant to those stipulations.

- The Statement also defines or describes certain other concepts that underlie or are otherwise closely related to the 10 elements and 3 classes defined in the Statement.

- Earnings is not defined in this Statement. FASB Concepts Statement 5 has now described earnings for a period as excluding certain cumulative accounting adjustments and other nonowner changes in equity that are included in comprehensive income for a period.

- The Board expects most assets and liabilities in present practice to continue to qualify as assets or liabilities under the definitions in this Statement. The Board emphasizes that the definitions neither require nor presage upheavals in present practice, although they may in due time lead to some evolutionary changes in practice or at least in the ways certain items are viewed. They should be especially helpful in understanding the content of financial statements and in analyzing and resolving new financial accounting issues as they arise.

- The appendixes are not part of the definitions but are intended for readers who may find them useful. They describe the background of the Statement and elaborate on the descriptions of the essential characteristics of the elements and classes, including some discussions and illustrations of how to apply the definitions.

- This Statement amends FASB Concepts Statement No. 2, *Qualitative Characteristics of Accounting Information,* to apply it to financial reporting by not-for-profit organizations.

Statement of Financial Accounting Concepts No. 6

Elements of Financial Statements

December 1985

CONTENTS

	Paragraph Numbers
Highlights	
Introduction	1– 23
Scope and Content of Statement	1– 8
Other Possible Elements of Financial Statements	3– 4
Elements and Financial Representations	5– 7
Other Scope and Content Matters	8
Objectives, Qualitative Characteristics, and Elements	9– 19
Interrelation of Elements—Articulation	20– 21
Definition, Recognition, Measurement, and Display	22– 23
Definitions of Elements	24–133
Assets	25– 34
Characteristics of Assets	26– 31
Transactions and Events That Change Assets	32– 33
Valuation Accounts	34
Liabilities	35– 43
Characteristics of Liabilities	36– 40
Transactions and Events That Change Liabilities	41– 42
Valuation Accounts	43
Effects of Uncertainty	44– 48
Equity or Net Assets	49– 59
Equity of Business Enterprises and Net Assets of Not-for-Profit Organizations	50– 53
Equity and Liabilities	54– 59
Equity of Business Enterprises	60– 65
Characteristics of Equity of Business Enterprises	60– 63
Transactions and Events That Change Equity of Business Enterprises	64– 65
Investments by and Distributions to Owners	66– 69
Characteristics of Investments by and Distributions to Owners	68– 69

	Paragraph Numbers
Comprehensive Income of Business Enterprises	70– 77
Concepts of Capital Maintenance	71– 72
Characteristics, Sources, and Components of Comprehensive Income	73– 77
Revenues	78– 79
Characteristics of Revenues	79
Expenses	80– 81
Characteristics of Expenses	81
Gains and Losses	82– 89
Characteristics of Gains and Losses	84– 86
Revenues, Expenses, Gains, and Losses	87– 89
Net Assets of Not-for-Profit Organizations	90–106
Characteristics of Net Assets of Not-for-Profit Organizations	90– 91
Classes of Net Assets	92–102
Donor-Imposed Restrictions	95– 97
Temporary and Permanent Restrictions	98–100
Restrictions Affect Net Assets Rather Than Particular Assets	101–102
Maintenance of Net Assets	103–106
Transactions and Events That Change Net Assets of Not-for-Profit Organizations	107–116
Revenues, Expenses, Gains, and Losses	111–113
Reclassifications	114–116
Changes in Classes of Net Assets of Not-for-Profit Organizations	117–133
Change in Permanently Restricted Net Assets	119–122
Characteristics of Change in Permanently Restricted Net Assets	120–122
Change in Temporarily Restricted Net Assets	123–126
Characteristics of Change in Temporarily Restricted Net Assets	124–126
Change in Unrestricted Net Assets	127–133
Characteristics of Change in Unrestricted Net Assets	128–133
Accrual Accounting and Related Concepts	134–152
Transactions, Events, and Circumstances	135–138
Accrual Accounting	139–140
Accrual and Deferral (Including Allocation and Amortization)	141–142
Realization and Recognition	143
Recognition, Matching, and Allocation	144–152
Appendix A: Background Information	153–163

	Paragraph Numbers
Appendix B: Characteristics of Assets, Liabilities, and Equity or Net Assets and of Changes in Them	164–255
Purpose and Summary of Appendix	164–170
Characteristics of Assets	171–191
Future Economic Benefits	172–182
Assets and Costs	178–182
Control by a Particular Entity	183–189
Control and Legal Rights	186–187
Noncontrolled Benefits	188–189
Occurrence of a Past Transaction or Event	190–191
Characteristics of Liabilities	192–211
Required Future Sacrifice of Assets	193–198
Liabilities and Proceeds	198
Obligation of a Particular Entity	199–205
Occurrence of a Past Transaction or Event	206–211
Characteristics of Equity of Business Enterprises	212–214
Residual Interest	213
Invested and Earned Equity	214
Characteristics of Comprehensive Income of Business Enterprises and Its Components	215–220
Interest in Information about Sources of Comprehensive Income	219–220
Characteristics of Net Assets and Changes in the Classes of Net Assets of Not-for-Profit Organizations	221–228
Residual Interest	222
Interest in Information about Changes in Classes of Net Assets	223–228
Examples to Illustrate Concepts	229–255
Deferred Gross Profit on Installment Sales	232–234
Debt Discount, Premium, and Issue Cost	235–239
Deferred Income Tax Credits	240–242
Deferred Investment Tax Credits	243–245
Deferred Costs of Assets	246–250
Estimated Loss on Purchase Commitments	251–253
Minority Interests and Stock Purchase Warrants	254
Examples Do Not Govern Practice	255
Summary Index of Concepts Defined or Discussed	page 325
Amendment of FASB Concepts Statement No. 2, *Qualitative Characteristics of Accounting Information*	page 329

STATEMENTS OF FINANCIAL ACCOUNTING CONCEPTS

This Statement of Financial Accounting Concepts is one of a series of publications in the Board's conceptual framework for financial accounting and reporting. Statements in the series are intended to set forth objectives and fundamentals that will be the basis for development of financial accounting and reporting standards. The objectives identify the goals and purposes of financial reporting. The fundamentals are the underlying concepts of financial accounting—concepts that guide the selection of transactions, events, and circumstances to be accounted for; their recognition and measurement; and the means of summarizing and communicating them to interested parties. Concepts of that type are fundamental in the sense that other concepts flow from them and repeated reference to them will be necessary in establishing, interpreting, and applying accounting and reporting standards.

The conceptual framework is a coherent system of interrelated objectives and fundamentals that is expected to lead to consistent standards and that prescribes the nature, function, and limits of financial accounting and reporting. It is expected to serve the public interest by providing structure and direction to financial accounting and reporting to facilitate the provision of evenhanded financial and related information that helps promote the efficient allocation of scarce resources in the economy and society, including assisting capital and other markets to function efficiently.

Establishment of objectives and identification of fundamental concepts will not directly solve financial accounting and reporting problems. Rather, objectives give direction, and concepts are tools for solving problems.

The Board itself is likely to be the most direct beneficiary of the guidance provided by the Statements in this series. They will guide the Board in developing accounting and reporting standards by providing the Board with a common foundation and basic reasoning on which to consider merits of alternatives.

However, knowledge of the objectives and concepts the Board will use in developing standards also should enable those who are affected by or interested in financial accounting standards to understand better the purposes, content, and characteristics of information provided by financial accounting and reporting. That knowledge is expected to enhance the usefulness of, and confidence in, financial accounting and reporting. The concepts also may provide some guidance in analyzing new or emerging problems of financial accounting and reporting in the absence of applicable authoritative pronouncements.

Statements of Financial Accounting Concepts do not establish standards prescribing accounting procedures or disclosure practices for particular items or events, which are issued by the Board as Statements of Financial Accounting Standards. Rather, Statements in this series describe concepts and relations that will underlie

future financial accounting standards and practices and in due course serve as a basis for evaluating existing standards and practices.*

The Board recognizes that in certain respects current generally accepted accounting principles may be inconsistent with those that may derive from the objectives and concepts set forth in Statements in this series. However, a Statement of Financial Accounting Concepts does not (a) require a change in existing generally accepted accounting principles; (b) amend, modify, or interpret Statements of Financial Accounting Standards, Interpretations of the FASB, Opinions of the Accounting Principles Board, or Bulletins of the Committee on Accounting Procedure that are in effect; or (c) justify either changing existing generally accepted accounting and reporting practices or interpreting the pronouncements listed in item (b) based on personal interpretations of the objectives and concepts in the Statements of Financial Accounting Concepts.

Since a Statement of Financial Accounting Concepts does not establish generally accepted accounting principles or standards for the disclosure of financial information outside of financial statements in published financial reports, it is not intended to invoke application of Rule 203 or 204 of the Rules of Conduct of the Code of Professional Ethics of the American Institute of Certified Public Accountants (or successor rules or arrangements of similar scope and intent).†

Like other pronouncements of the Board, a Statement of Financial Accounting Concepts may be amended, superseded, or withdrawn by appropriate action under the Board's *Rules of Procedure.*

---

*Pronouncements such as APB Statement No. 4, *Basic Concepts and Accounting Principles Underlying Financial Statements of Business Enterprises,* and the Accounting Terminology Bulletins will continue to serve their intended purpose—they describe objectives and concepts underlying standards and practices existing at the time of their issuance.

†Rule 203 prohibits a member of the American Institute of Certified Public Accountants from expressing an opinion that financial statements conform with generally accepted accounting principles if those statements contain a material departure from an accounting principle promulgated by the Financial Accounting Standards Board, unless the member can demonstrate that because of unusual circumstances the financial statements otherwise would have been misleading. Rule 204 requires members of the Institute to justify departures from standards promulgated by the Financial Accounting Standards Board for the disclosure of information outside of financial statements in published financial reports.

Statement of Financial Accounting Concepts No. 6

Elements of Financial Statements

December 1985

INTRODUCTION

Scope and Content of Statement

1. This Statement defines 10 elements of financial statements: 7 elements of financial statements of both business enterprises and not-for-profit organizations—assets, liabilities, equity (business enterprises) or net assets (not-for-profit organizations), revenues, expenses, gains, and losses—and 3 elements of financial statements of business enterprises only—investments by owners, distributions to owners, and comprehensive income.[1] It also defines three classes of net assets of not-for-profit organizations and the changes in those classes during a period—change in permanently restricted net assets, change in temporarily restricted net assets, and change in unrestricted net assets. The Statement also defines or describes certain other concepts that underlie or are otherwise related to those elements and classes (Summary Index, pages 325-327).

2. This Statement replaces FASB Concepts Statement No. 3, *Elements of Financial Statements of Business Enterprises,* extending that Statement's definitions to not-for-profit organizations.[2] It confirms conclusions in paragraph 2 of Concepts State-

[1]*Comprehensive income* is the name used in this Statement and in FASB Concepts Statement No. 3, *Elements of Financial Statements of Business Enterprises,* for the concept that was called *earnings* in FASB Concepts Statement No. 1, *Objectives of Financial Reporting by Business Enterprises,* and other conceptual framework documents previously issued (*Tentative Conclusions on Objectives of Financial Statements of Business Enterprises* [December 1976]; FASB Discussion Memorandum, *Elements of Financial Statements and Their Measurement* [December 1976]; FASB Exposure Draft, *Objectives of Financial Reporting and Elements of Financial Statements of Business Enterprises* [December 1977], and FASB Discussion Memorandum, *Reporting Earnings* [July 1979]). Concepts Statement 3 did not define *earnings* because the Board decided to reserve the term for possible use to designate a component part, then undetermined, of comprehensive income.

FASB Concepts Statement No. 5, *Recognition and Measurement in Financial Statements of Business Enterprises* (December 1984), has now described earnings for a period as excluding certain cumulative accounting adjustments and other nonowner changes in equity that are included in comprehensive income for a period.

[2]The term *not-for-profit organizations* in this Statement encompasses private sector organizations described in FASB Concepts Statement No. 4, *Objectives of Financial Reporting by Nonbusiness Organizations* (December 1980). Financial reporting by state and local governmental units is within the purview of the Governmental Accounting Standards Board (GASB), and the FASB has not considered the applicability of this Statement to those units.

ment 3 that (a) assets and liabilities are common to all organizations and can be defined the same for business and not-for-profit organizations, (b) the definitions of equity (net assets), revenues, expenses, gains, and losses fit both business and not-for-profit organizations, and (c) not-for-profit organizations have no need for elements such as investments by owners, distributions to owners, and comprehensive income. Thus, this Statement continues unchanged the elements defined in Concepts Statement 3, although it contains added explanations stemming from characteristics of not-for-profit organizations and their operations. It also defines three classes of net assets of not-for-profit organizations, distinguished by the presence or absence of donor-imposed restrictions, and the changes in those classes during a period—change in permanently restricted, temporarily restricted, and unrestricted net assets.

Other Possible Elements of Financial Statements

3. Although the elements defined in this Statement include basic elements and are probably those most commonly identified as elements of financial statements, they are not the only elements of financial statements. The elements defined in this Statement are a related group with a particular focus—on assets, liabilities, equity, and other elements directly related to measuring performance and status of an entity. Information about an entity's performance and status provided by accrual accounting is the primary focus of financial reporting (FASB Concepts Statement No. 1, *Objectives of Financial Reporting by Business Enterprises,* paragraphs 40-48, and FASB Concepts Statement No. 4, *Objectives of Financial Reporting by Nonbusiness Organizations,* paragraphs 38-53). Other statements or focuses may require other elements.[3]

4. Variations of possible statements showing the effects on assets and liabilities of transactions or other events and circumstances during a period are almost limitless, and all of them have classes of items that may be called elements of financial statements. For example, a statement showing funds flows or cash flows during a period may include categories for funds or cash provided by (a) operations, (b) borrowing, (c) issuing equity securities, (d) sale of assets, and so forth. Other projects may define additional elements of financial statements as needed.

[3]Some respondents to the 1977 Exposure Draft on elements of financial statements of business enterprises (par. 157) interpreted the discussion of other possible elements to mean that financial statements now called balance sheets and income statements might have elements other than those defined. However, the other elements referred to pertain to other possible financial statements. Although this Statement contains no conclusions about the identity, number, or form of financial statements, it defines all elements for balance sheets and income statements of business enterprises in their present forms, except perhaps *earnings* (par. 1, footnote 1), and for balance sheets and statements of changes in net assets of not-for-profit organizations in their present forms.

Elements and Financial Representations

5. Elements of financial statements are the building blocks with which financial statements are constructed—the classes of items that financial statements comprise. *Elements* refers to broad classes, such as assets, liabilities, revenues, and expenses. Particular economic things and events, such as cash on hand or selling merchandise, that may meet the definitions of elements are not elements as the term is used in this Statement. Rather, they are called *items* or other descriptive names. This Statement focuses on the broad classes and their characteristics instead of defining particular assets, liabilities, or other items. Although notes to financial statements are described in some authoritative pronouncements as an integral part of financial statements, they are not elements. They serve different functions, including amplifying or complementing information about items in financial statements.[4]

6. The items that are formally incorporated in financial statements are financial representations (depictions in words and numbers) of certain resources of an entity, claims to those resources, and the effects of transactions and other events and circumstances that result in changes in those resources and claims. That is, symbols (words and numbers) in financial statements stand for cash in a bank, buildings, wages due, sales, use of labor, earthquake damage to property, and a host of other economic things and events pertaining to an entity existing and operating in what is sometimes called the "real world."

7. This Statement follows the common practice of calling by the same names both the financial representations in financial statements and the resources, claims, transactions, events, or circumstances that they represent. For example, *inventory* or *asset* may refer either to merchandise on the floor of a retail enterprise or to the words and numbers that represent that merchandise in the entity's financial statements; and *sale* or *revenue* may refer either to the transaction by which some of that merchandise is transferred to a customer or to the words and numbers that represent the transaction in the entity's financial statements.[5]

---

[4]Paragraphs 5-9 of Concepts Statement 5 discuss the role of notes and their relation to financial statements.

[5]The 1977 Exposure Draft on elements of financial statements of business enterprises attempted to distinguish the representations from what they represent by giving them different names. For example, *assets* referred only to the financial representations in financial statements, and *economic resources* referred to the real-world things that assets represented in financial statements. That aspect of the Exposure Draft caused considerable confusion and was criticized by respondents. The revised Exposure Draft, *Elements of Financial Statements of Business Enterprises* (December 28, 1979), reverted to the more common practice of using the same names for both, and this Statement adopts the same usage.

Other Scope and Content Matters

8. Appendix A of this Statement contains background information. Appendix B contains explanations and examples pertaining to the characteristics of elements of financial statements of business enterprises and not-for-profit organizations.

Objectives, Qualitative Characteristics, and Elements

9. The focus of the FASB concepts Statements that underlie this one is usefulness of financial reporting information in making economic decisions—reasoned choices among alternative uses of scarce resources. Concepts Statement No. 1, *Objectives of Financial Reporting by Business Enterprises,* emphasizes usefulness to present and potential investors, creditors, and others in making rational investment, credit, and similar decisions. Concepts Statement No. 4, *Objectives of Financial Reporting by Nonbusiness Organizations,* emphasizes usefulness to present and potential resource providers and others in making rational decisions about allocating resources to not-for-profit organizations.[6] Concepts Statement No. 2, *Qualitative Characteristics of Accounting Information,* emphasizes that usefulness of financial reporting information for those decisions rests on the cornerstones of relevance and reliability.

10. The definitions in this Statement are of economic things and events that are relevant to investment, credit, and other resource-allocation decisions and thus are relevant to financial reporting.[7] Those decisions involve committing (or continuing to commit) resources to an entity. The elements defined are an entity's resources, the claims to or interests in those resources, and the changes therein from transactions and other events and circumstances involved in its use of resources to produce and distribute goods or services and, if it is a business enterprise, to earn a profit. Rele-

---

[6]Those who make decisions about allocating resources to not-for-profit organizations include both (a) lenders, suppliers, employees, and the like who expect repayment or other direct pecuniary compensation from an entity and have essentially the same interest in and make essentially the same kinds of decisions about the entity whether it is a not-for-profit organization or a business enterprise and (b) members, contributors, donors, and the like who provide resources to not-for-profit organizations for reasons other than expectations of direct and proportionate pecuniary compensation (Concepts Statement 4, pars. 15-19, 29).

[7]Decision usefulness of information provided about those relevant economic things and events depends not only on their relevance but also on the reliability (especially representational faithfulness) of the financial representations called assets, liabilities, revenues, expenses, and so forth in financial statements. Representational faithfulness depends not only on the way the definitions are applied but also on recognition and measurement decisions that are beyond the scope of this Statement (pars. 22 and 23).

vance of information about items that meet those definitions stems from the significance of an entity's resources and changes in resources (including those affecting profitability).

11. Economic resources or assets and changes in them are central to the existence and operations of an individual entity. Both business enterprises and not-for-profit organizations and are in essence resource or asset processors, and a resource's capacity to be exchanged for cash or other resources or to be combined with other resources to produce needed or desired scarce goods or services gives it utility and value (future economic benefit) to an entity.

12. Business enterprises and not-for-profit organizations obtain the resources they need from various sources. Business enterprises and some not-for-profit organizations sell the goods and services they produce for cash or claims to cash. Both buy goods and services for cash or by incurring liabilities to pay cash. Business enterprises receive resources from investments in the enterprise by owners, while not-for-profit organizations commonly receive significant amounts of resources from contributors who do not expect to receive either repayment or economic benefits proportionate to resources provided. Those contributions are the major source of resources for many not-for-profit organizations but are not significant for other not-for-profit organizations or for most business enterprises.[8]

13. A not-for-profit organization obtains and uses resources to provide certain types of goods or services to members of society, and the nature of those goods or services or the identity of the groups or individuals who receive them is often critical in donors' or other resource providers' decisions to contribute or otherwise provide cash or other assets to a particular organization. Many donors provide resources to support certain types of services or for the benefit of certain groups and may stipulate how or when (or both) an organization may use the cash or other resources they contribute to it. Those donor-imposed restrictions on a not-for-profit organization's use of assets may be either permanent or temporary.

[8]Concepts Statement 4 (par. 6) lists as the distinguishing characteristics of not-for-profit organizations (a) contributions from resource providers who do not expect pecuniary return, (b) operating purposes other than to provide goods or services at a profit, and (c) absence of ownership interests like those of business enterprises. Not-for-profit organizations have those characteristics in varying degrees. "The line between nonbusiness [not-for-profit] organizations and business enterprises is not always sharp since the incidence and relative importance of those characteristics in any organization are different. . . . As happens with any distinction, there will be borderline cases. . . . especially for organizations that possess some of the distinguishing characteristics of nonbusiness [not-for-profit] organizations but not others. Some organizations have no ownership interests but are essentially self-sustaining from fees they charge for goods and services. . . . the objectives of Concepts Statement 1 may be more appropriate for those organizations" (Concepts Statement 4, pars. 7 and 8).

14. Resources or assets are the lifeblood of a not-for-profit organization, and an organization cannot long continue to achieve its operating objectives unless it can obtain at least enough resources to provide goods or services at levels and of a quality that are satisfactory to resource providers. Organizations that do not provide adequate goods or services often find it increasingly difficult to obtain the resources they need to continue operations.

15. Economic resources or assets are also the lifeblood of a business enterprise. Since resources or assets confer their benefits on an enterprise by being exchanged, used, or otherwise invested, changes in resources or assets are the purpose, the means, and the result of an enterprise's operations, and a business enterprise exists primarily to acquire, use, produce, and distribute resources. Through those activities it both provides goods or services to members of society and obtains cash and other assets with which it compensates those who provide it with resources, including its owners.

16. Although the relation between profit of an enterprise[9] and compensation received by owners is complex and often indirect, profit is the basic source of compensation to owners for providing equity or risk capital to an enterprise. Profitable operations generate resources that can be distributed to owners or reinvested in the enterprise, and investors' expectations about both distributions to owners and reinvested profit may affect market prices of the enterprise's equity securities. Expectations that owners will be adequately compensated—that they will receive returns *on* their investments commensurate with their risks—are as necessary to attract equity capital to an enterprise as are expectations of wages and salaries to attract employees' services, expectations of repayments of borrowing with interest to attract borrowed funds, or expectations of payments on account to attract raw materials or merchandise.

17. Repayment or compensation of lenders, employees, suppliers, and other nonowners for resources provided is also related to profit or loss in the sense that profitable enterprises (and those that break even) generally are able to repay borrowing with interest, pay adequate wages and salaries, and pay for other goods and services received, while unprofitable enterprises often become less and less able to pay and

---

[9]*Profit* is used in this and the following paragraphs in a broad descriptive sense to refer to an enterprise's successful performance during a period. It is not intended to have a technical accounting meaning or to imply resolution of classification and display matters that are beyond the scope of this Statement, and no specific relation between *profit* and either *comprehensive income* or *earnings* (par. 1, footnote 1) is implied. *Loss* as in *profit or loss* (in contrast to *gain or loss*) is also used in a broad descriptive sense to refer to negative profit or unsuccessful performance and is not intended to have a technical accounting meaning.

thus find it increasingly difficult to obtain the resources they need to continue operations. Thus, information about profit and its components is of interest to suppliers, employees, lenders, and other providers of resources as well as to owners.

18. In contrast to business enterprises, not-for-profit organizations do not have defined ownership interests that can be sold, transferred, or redeemed, or that convey entitlement to a share of a residual distribution of resources in the event of liquidation of the organization. A not-for-profit organization is required to use its resources to provide goods and services to its constituents and beneficiaries as specified in its articles of incorporation (or comparable document for an unincorporated association) or by-laws and generally is prohibited from distributing assets as dividends to its members, directors, officers, or others.[10] Thus, not-for-profit organizations have operating purposes that are other than to provide goods or services at a profit or profit equivalent, and resource providers do not focus primarily on profit as an indicator of a not-for-profit organization's performance.[11]

19. Instead, providers of resources to a not-for-profit organization are interested in the services the organization provides and its ability to continue to provide them. Since profit indicators are not the focus of their resource-allocation decisions, resource providers need other information that is useful in assessing an organization's performance during a period and in assessing how its managers have discharged their stewardship responsibilities, not only for the custody and safekeeping of the organization's resources, but also for their efficient and effective use—that is, information about the amounts and kinds of inflows and outflows of resources during a period and the relations between them and information about service efforts and, to the extent possible, service accomplishments.[12]

Interrelation of Elements—Articulation

20. Elements of financial statements are of two different types, which are sometimes explained as being analogous to photographs and motion pictures. The ele-

---

[10]Some not-for-profit organizations, for example, many membership organizations, may be permitted under law to distribute assets to members upon dissolution or final liquidation. However, assets of many other not-for-profit organizations are held subject to limitations (a) permitting their use only for religious, charitable, eleemosynary, benevolent, educational, or similar purposes or (b) requiring their return to donors or their designees if the organization is dissolved. Thus, upon dissolution of a not-for-profit organization, its assets, or a significant part of them, must often be transferred to another not-for-profit organization engaged in activities substantially similar to those of the dissolving organization, to donors, or, in some cases, to other unrelated entities.

[11]Concepts Statement 4, pars. 6-9.

[12]Concepts Statement 4, pars. 9, 38, 41, and 47-53.

ments defined in this Statement include three of one type and seven of the other. (Three of the latter apply only to business enterprises.) Assets, liabilities, and equity (net assets) describe levels or amounts of resources or claims to or interests in resources at a moment in time. All other elements describe effects of transactions and other events and circumstances that affect an entity during intervals of time (periods). In a business enterprise, the second type includes comprehensive income and its components—revenues, expenses, gains, and losses—and investments by owners and distributions to owners. In a not-for-profit organization, it includes revenues, expenses, gains, and losses.[13]

21. The two types of elements are related in such a way that (a) assets, liabilities, and equity (net assets) are changed by elements of the other type and at any time are their cumulative result and (b) an increase (decrease) in an asset cannot occur without a corresponding decrease (increase) in another asset or a corresponding increase (decrease) in a liability or equity (net assets). Those relations are sometimes collectively referred to as "articulation." They result in financial statements that are fundamentally interrelated so that statements that show elements of the second type depend on statements that show elements of the first type and vice versa.[14]

Definition, Recognition, Measurement, and Display

22. All matters of recognition, measurement, and display have purposely been separated from the definitions of the elements of financial statements in the Board's con-

---

[13]The two types can also be distinguished as financial position and changes in financial position, without meaning to imply or describe particular financial statements. Used broadly, *financial position* refers to state or status of assets or claims to assets at moments in time, and *changes in financial position* refers to flows or changes in assets or claims to assets over time. In that sense, for example, both income statements and funds statements (now commonly called statements of changes in financial position for business enterprises) show changes in financial position in present practice. Other statements, such as statements of retained earnings or analyses of property, plant, and equipment, may show aspects of both financial position at the beginning and end of a period and changes in financial position during a period. The other possible elements of financial statements referred to in paragraphs 3 and 4 also fall into this second type. That is, they are changes in financial position, describing effects of transactions and other events and circumstances that affect assets, liabilities, or equity during a period, for example, acquisitions and dispositions of assets, borrowing, and repayments of borrowing. Financial statements of not-for-profit organizations may have different names from those of business enterprises but have the same distinctions between financial position and changes in financial position.

[14]The two relations described in this paragraph are commonly expressed as (a) balance at beginning of period + changes during period = balance at end of period and (b) assets = liabilities + equity. "Double entry," the mechanism by which accrual accounting formally includes particular items that qualify under the elements definitions in articulated financial statements, incorporates those relations.

ceptual framework project. The definitions in this Statement are concerned with the essential characteristics of elements of financial statements. Other phases of the conceptual framework project are concerned with questions such as which financial statements should be provided; which items that qualify under the definitions should be included in those statements; when particular items that qualify as assets, liabilities, revenues, expenses, and so forth should be formally recognized in the financial statements; which attributes of those items should be measured; which unit of measure should be used; and how the information included should be classified and otherwise displayed.[15]

23. Definitions of elements of financial statements are a significant first screen in determining the content of financial statements. An item's having the essential characteristics of one of the elements is a necessary but not a sufficient condition for formally recognizing the item in the entity's financial statements. To be included in a particular set of financial statements, an item must not only qualify under the definition of an element but also must meet criteria for recognition and have a relevant attribute (or surrogate for it) that is capable of reasonably reliable measurement or estimate.[16] Thus, some items that meet the definitions may have to be excluded from formal incorporation in financial statements because of recognition or measurement considerations (paragraphs 44-48).

DEFINITIONS OF ELEMENTS

24. All elements are defined in relation to a particular entity, which may be a business enterprise, an educational or charitable organization, a natural person, or the like. An item that qualifies under the definitions is a particular entity's asset, liability, revenue, expense, or so forth. An entity may comprise two or more affiliated entities and does not necessarily correspond to what is often described as a "legal entity." The definitions may also refer to "other entity," "other entities," or "entities other

---

[15]FASB Concepts Statement No. 5, *Recognition and Measurement in Financial Statements of Business Enterprises,* addresses those questions for business enterprises. Those conceptual questions as they relate to not-for-profit organizations and more detailed development of those concepts for all entities may be the subject of further concepts Statements or standards.

[16]Decisions about recognizing, measuring, and displaying elements of financial statements depend significantly on evaluations such as what information is most relevant for investment, credit, and other resource-allocation decisions and whether the information is reliable enough to be trusted. Other significant evaluations of the information involve its comparability with information about other periods or other entities, its materiality, and whether the benefits from providing it exceed the costs of providing it. Those matters are discussed in Concepts Statement 2, and criteria and guidance for business enterprises based on them are set forth in Concepts Statement 5.

than the enterprise," which may include individuals, business enterprises, not-for-profit organizations, and the like. For example, employees, suppliers, customers or beneficiaries, lenders, stockholders, donors, and governments are all "other entities" to a particular entity. A subsidiary company that is part of the same entity as its parent company in consolidated financial statements is an "other entity" in the separate financial statements of its parent.[17]

Assets

25. Assets are probable[18] future economic benefits obtained or controlled by a particular entity as a result of past transactions or events.

Characteristics of Assets

26. An asset has three essential characteristics: (a) it embodies a probable future benefit that involves a capacity, singly or in combination with other assets, to contribute directly or indirectly to future net cash inflows, (b) a particular entity can obtain the benefit and control others' access to it, and (c) the transaction or other event giving rise to the entity's right to or control of the benefit has already occurred. Assets commonly have other features that help identify them—for example, assets may be acquired at a cost[19] and they may be tangible, exchangeable, or legally enforceable. However, those features are not essential characteristics of assets. Their absence, by itself, is not sufficient to preclude an item's qualifying as an asset. That is, assets may be acquired without cost, they may be intangible, and although not exchangeable they may be usable by the entity in producing or distributing other goods or services. Similarly, although the ability of an entity to obtain benefit from

---

[17]The concept of a "reporting entity" for general-purpose external financial reporting is the subject of a separate Board project that includes consolidated financial statements, the equity method, and related matters.

[18]*Probable* is used with its usual general meaning, rather than in a specific accounting or technical sense (such as that in FASB Statement No. 5, *Accounting for Contingencies,* par. 3), and refers to that which can reasonably be expected or believed on the basis of available evidence or logic but is neither certain nor proved (*Webster's New World Dictionary of the American Language,* 2d college ed. [New York: Simon and Schuster, 1982], p. 1132). Its inclusion in the definition is intended to acknowledge that business and other economic activities occur in an environment characterized by uncertainty in which few outcomes are certain (pars. 44-48).

[19]*Cost* is the sacrifice incurred in economic activities—that which is given up or forgone to consume, to save, to exchange, to produce, and so forth. For example, the value of cash or other resources given up (or the present value of an obligation incurred) in exchange for a resource measures the cost of the resource acquired. Similarly, the expiration of future benefits caused by using a resource in production is the cost of using it.

an asset and to control others' access to it generally rests on a foundation of legal rights, legal enforceability of a claim to the benefit is not a prerequisite for a benefit to qualify as an asset if the entity has the ability to obtain and control the benefit in other ways.

27. The kinds of items that qualify as assets under the definition in paragraph 25 are also commonly called economic resources. They are the scarce means that are useful for carrying out economic activities, such as consumption, production, and exchange.

28. The common characteristic possessed by all assets (economic resources) is "service potential" or "future economic benefit," the scarce capacity to provide services or benefits to the entities that use them. In a business enterprise, that service potential or future economic benefit eventually results in net cash inflows to the enterprise. In a not-for-profit organization, that service potential or future economic benefit is used to provide desired or needed goods or services to beneficiaries or other constituents, which may or may not directly result in net cash inflows to the organization. Some not-for-profit organizations rely significantly on contributions or donations of cash to supplement selling prices or to replace cash or other assets used in providing goods or services. The relationship between service potential or future economic benefit of its assets and net cash inflows to an entity is often indirect in both business enterprises and not-for-profit organizations.

29. Money (cash, including deposits in banks) is valuable because of what it can buy. It can be exchanged for virtually any good or service that is available or it can be saved and exchanged for them in the future. Money's "command over resources"—its purchasing power—is the basis of its value and future economic benefits.[20]

30. Assets other than cash benefit an entity by being exchanged for cash or other goods or services, by being used to produce goods or services or otherwise increase the value of other assets, or by being used to settle liabilities. To carry out their operating purposes, both business enterprises and not-for-profit organizations commonly produce scarce goods or services that have the capacity to satisfy human wants or needs. Both create utility and value in essentially the same way—by using goods or services to produce other goods or services that their customers or constituents desire or need. Business enterprises expect customers to pay for the utility and

---

[20]Money's command over resources, or purchasing power, declines during periods of inflation and increases during periods of deflation (increases and decreases, respectively, in the level of prices in general). Since matters of measurement, including unit of measure, are beyond the scope of this Statement, it recognizes but does not emphasize that characteristic of money.

value added, and they price their outputs accordingly. Many not-for-profit organizations also distribute some or all of their outputs of goods or services at prices that include the utility and value they have added. Other not-for-profit organizations commonly distribute the goods or services they produce to beneficiaries gratis or at nominal prices. Although that may make measuring the value of their outputs difficult, it does not deprive them of value.

31. Services provided by other entities, including personal services, cannot be stored and are received and used simultaneously. They can be assets of an entity only momentarily—as the entity receives and uses them—although their use may create or add value to other assets of the entity. Rights to receive services of other entities for specified or determinable future periods can be assets of particular entities.

Transactions and Events That Change Assets

32. Assets of an entity are changed both by its transactions and activities and by events that happen to it. An entity obtains cash and other assets from other entities and transfers cash and other assets to other entities. It adds value to noncash assets through operations by using, combining, and transforming goods and services to make other desired goods or services. Some transactions or other events decrease one asset and increase another. An entity's assets or their values are also commonly increased or decreased by other events and circumstances that may be partly or entirely beyond the control of the entity and its management, for example, price changes, interest rate changes, technological changes, impositions of taxes and regulations, discovery, growth or accretion, shrinkage, vandalism, thefts, expropriations, wars, fires, and natural disasters.

33. Once acquired, an asset continues as an asset of the entity until the entity collects it, transfers it to another entity, or uses it up, or some other event or circumstance destroys the future benefit or removes the entity's ability to obtain it.

Valuation Accounts

34. A separate item that reduces or increases the carrying amount of an asset is sometimes found in financial statements. For example, an estimate of uncollectible amounts reduces receivables to the amount expected to be collected, or a premium on a bond receivable increases the receivable to its cost or present value. Those "valuation accounts" are part of the related assets and are neither assets in their own right nor liabilities.

Liabilities

35. Liabilities are probable[21] future sacrifices of economic benefits arising from present obligations[22] of a particular entity to transfer assets or provide services to other entities in the future as a result of past transactions or events.

Characteristics of Liabilities

36. A liability has three essential characteristics: (a) it embodies a present duty or responsibility to one or more other entities that entails settlement by probable future transfer or use of assets at a specified or determinable date, on occurrence of a specified event, or on demand, (b) the duty or responsibility obligates a particular entity, leaving it little or no discretion to avoid the future sacrifice, and (c) the transaction or other event obligating the entity has already happened. Liabilities commonly have other features that help identify them—for example, most liabilities require the obligated entity to pay cash to one or more identified other entities and are legally enforceable. However, those features are not essential characteristics of liabilities. Their absence, by itself, is not sufficient to preclude an item's qualifying as a liability. That is, liabilities may not require an entity to pay cash but to convey other assets, to provide or stand ready to provide services, or to use assets. And the identity of the recipient need not be known to the obligated entity before the time of settlement. Similarly, although most liabilities rest generally on a foundation of legal rights and duties, existence of a legally enforceable claim is not a prerequisite for an obligation to qualify as a liability if for other reasons the entity has the duty or responsibility to pay cash, to transfer other assets, or to provide services to another entity.

37. Most liabilities stem from human inventions—such as financial instruments, contracts, and laws—that facilitate the functioning of a highly developed economy and are commonly embodied in legal obligations and rights (or the equivalent) with no existence apart from them. Liabilities facilitate the functioning of a highly developed economy primarily by permitting delay—delay in payment, delay in delivery, and so on.[23]

---

[21]*Probable* is used with its usual general meaning, rather than in a specific accounting or technical sense (such as that in Statement 5, par. 3), and refers to that which can reasonably be expected or believed on the basis of available evidence or logic but is neither certain nor proved (*Webster's New World Dictionary*, p. 1132). Its inclusion in the definition is intended to acknowledge that business and other economic activities occur in an environment characterized by uncertainty in which few outcomes are certain (pars. 44-48).

[22]*Obligations* in the definition is broader than *legal obligations*. It is used with its usual general meaning to refer to duties imposed legally or socially; to that which one is bound to do by contract, promise, moral responsibility, and so forth (*Webster's New World Dictionary*, p. 981). It includes equitable and constructive obligations as well as legal obligations (pars. 37-40).

[23]A common feature of liabilities is interest—the time value of money or the price of delay.

38. Entities routinely incur most liabilities to acquire the funds, goods, and services they need to operate and just as routinely settle the liabilities they incur. For example, borrowing cash obligates an entity to repay the amount borrowed, usually with interest; acquiring assets on credit obligates an entity to pay for them, perhaps with interest to compensate for the delay in payment; using employees' knowledge, skills, time, and efforts obligates an enterprise to pay for their use, often including fringe benefits; selling products with a warranty or guarantee obligates an entity to pay cash or to repair or replace those that prove defective; and accepting a cash deposit or prepayment obligates an entity to provide goods or services or to refund the cash. In short, most liabilities are incurred in exchange transactions to obtain needed resources or their use, and most liabilities incurred in exchange transactions are contractual in nature—based on written or oral agreements to pay cash or to provide goods or services to specified or determinable entities on demand, at specified or determinable dates, or on occurrence of specified events.

39. Although most liabilities result from agreements between entities, some obligations are imposed on entities by government or courts or are accepted to avoid imposition by government or courts (or costly efforts related thereto), and some relate to other nonreciprocal transfers from an entity to one or more other entities. Thus, taxes, laws, regulations, and other governmental actions commonly require business enterprises (and sometimes not-for-profit organizations) to pay cash, convey other assets, or provide services either directly to specified governmental units or to others for purposes or in ways specified by government. An entity may also incur liabilities for donations pledged to educational or charitable organizations or for cash dividends declared but not paid.

40. Similarly, although most liabilities stem from legally enforceable obligations, some liabilities rest on equitable or constructive obligations, including some that arise in exchange transactions. Liabilities stemming from equitable or constructive obligations are commonly paid in the same way as legally binding contracts, but they lack the legal sanction that characterizes most liabilities and may be binding primarily because of social or moral sanctions or custom. An equitable obligation stems from ethical or moral constraints rather than from rules of common or statute law, that is, from a duty to another entity to do that which an ordinary conscience and sense of justice would deem fair, just, and right—to do what one ought to do rather than what one is legally required to do. For example, a business enterprise may have an equitable obligation to complete and deliver a product to a customer that has no other source of supply even though its failure to deliver would legally require only return of the customer's deposit. A constructive obligation is created, inferred, or construed from the facts in a particular situation rather than contracted by agreement with another entity or imposed by government. For example, an entity may

create a constructive obligation to employees for vacation pay or year-end bonuses by paying them every year even though it is not contractually bound to do so and has not announced a policy to do so. The line between equitable or constructive obligations and obligations that are enforceable in courts of law is not always clear, and the line between equitable or constructive obligations and no obligations may often be even more troublesome because to determine whether an entity is actually bound by an obligation to a third party in the absence of legal enforceability is often extremely difficult. Thus, the concepts of equitable and constructive obligations must be applied with great care. To interpret equitable and constructive obligations too narrowly will tend to exclude significant actual obligations of an entity, while to interpret them too broadly will effectively nullify the definition by including items that lack an essential characteristic of liabilities.

Transactions and Events That Change Liabilities

41. Liabilities of an entity are changed both by its transactions and activities and by events that happen to it. The preceding paragraphs note most major sources of changes in liabilities. An entity's liabilities are also sometimes affected by price changes, interest rate changes, or other events and circumstances that may be partly or wholly beyond the control of an entity and its management.

42. Once incurred, a liability continues as a liability of the entity until the entity settles it, or another event or circumstance discharges it or removes the entity's responsibility to settle it.

Valuation Accounts

43. A separate item that reduces or increases the carrying amount of a liability is sometimes found in financial statements. For example, a bond premium or discount increases or decreases the face value of a bond payable to its proceeds or present value. Those "valuation accounts" are part of the related liability and are neither liabilities in their own right nor assets.

Effects of Uncertainty

44. Uncertainty about economic and business activities and results is pervasive, and it often clouds whether a particular item qualifies as an asset or a liability of a particular entity at the time the definitions are applied. The presence or absence of future economic benefit that can be obtained and controlled by the entity or of the entity's legal, equitable, or constructive obligation to sacrifice assets in the future can often be discerned reliably only with hindsight. As a result, some items that with hindsight

actually qualified as assets or liabilities of the entity under the definitions may, as a practical matter, have been recognized as expenses, losses, revenues, or gains or remained unrecognized in its financial statements because of uncertainty about whether they qualified as assets or liabilities of the entity or because of recognition and measurement considerations stemming from uncertainty at the time of assessment. Conversely, some items that with hindsight did not qualify under the definitions may have been included as assets or liabilities because of judgments made in the face of uncertainty at the time of assessment.

45. An effect of uncertainty is to increase the costs of financial reporting in general and the costs of recognition and measurement in particular. Some items that qualify as assets or liabilities under the definitions may therefore be recognized as expenses, losses, revenues, or gains or remain unrecognized as a result of cost and benefit analyses indicating that their formal incorporation in financial statements is not useful enough to justify the time and effort needed to do it. It may be possible, for example, to make the information more reliable in the face of uncertainty by exerting greater effort or by spending more money, but it also may not be worth the added cost.

46. A highly significant practical consequence of the features described in the preceding two paragraphs is that the existence or amount (or both) of most assets and many liabilities can be probable but not certain.[24] The definitions in this Statement are not intended to require that the existence and amounts of items be certain for them to qualify as assets, liabilities, revenues, expenses, and so forth, and estimates and approximations will often be required unless financial statements are to be restricted to reporting only cash transactions.

47. To apply the definitions of assets and liabilities (and other elements of financial statements) thus commonly requires assessments of probabilities, but degrees of probability are not part of the definitions. That is, the degree of probability of a future economic benefit (or of a future cash outlay or other sacrifice of future economic benefits) and the degree to which its amount can be estimated with reasonable reliability that are required to recognize an item as an asset (or a liability) are matters of recognition and measurement that are beyond the scope of this Statement. The distinction needs to be maintained between the definitions themselves and steps that may be needed to apply them. Matters involving measurement problems, effects of uncertainty, reliability, and numerous other factors may be significant in applying a definition, but they are not part of the definition. Particular items that

[24]The meaning of *probable* in these paragraphs is described in paragraph 25, footnote 18, and paragraph 35, footnote 21.

qualify as assets or liabilities under the definitions may need to be excluded from formal incorporation in financial statements for reasons relating to measurement, uncertainty, or unreliability, but they are not excluded by the definitions. Similarly, the attitude commonly known as conservatism may be appropriate in applying the definitions under uncertain conditions, but conservatism is not part of the definitions. Definition, recognition, measurement, and display are separate in the Board's conceptual framework (paragraphs 22 and 23).[25]

48. All practical financial accounting and reporting models have limitations. The preceding paragraphs describe one limit that may affect various models—how recognition or measurement considerations stemming from uncertainty may result in not recognizing as assets or liabilities some items that qualify as such under the definitions or may result in postponing recognition of some assets or liabilities until their existence becomes more probable or their measures become more reliable.

Equity or Net Assets

49. Equity or net assets is the residual interest in the assets of an entity that remains after deducting its liabilities.

Equity of Business Enterprises and Net Assets of Not-for-Profit Organizations

50. The equity or net assets[26] of both a business enterprise and a not-for-profit organization is the difference between the entity's assets and its liabilities. It is a residual, affected by all events that increase or decrease total assets by different amounts than they increase or decrease total liabilities. Thus, equity or net assets of both a business enterprise and a not-for-profit organization is increased or decreased by the entity's operations and other events and circumstances affecting the entity.

51. A major distinguishing characteristic of the equity of a business enterprise is that it may be increased through investments of assets by owners who also may, from time to time, receive distributions of assets from the entity. Owners invest in a business enterprise with the expectation of obtaining a return on their investment as a result of the enterprise's providing goods or services to customers at a profit. Owners

---

[25]The Board's Concepts Statements 2 and 5 bear directly on the matter discussed in paragraphs 44-48.

[26]This Statement generally applies the term *equity* to business enterprises, which is common usage, and the term *net assets* to not-for-profit organizations, for which the term *equity* is less commonly used. The two terms are interchangeable.

benefit if the enterprise is profitable but bear the risk that it may be unprofitable (paragraphs 11 and 12 and 15-17).

52. In contrast, a not-for-profit organization has no ownership interest or profit purpose in the same sense as a business enterprise and thus receives no investments of assets by owners and distributes no assets to owners. Rather, its net assets often is increased by receipts of assets from resource providers (contributors, donors, grantors, and the like) who do not expect to receive either repayment or economic benefits proportionate to the assets provided[27] but who are nonetheless interested in how the organization makes use of those assets and often impose temporary or permanent restrictions on their use (paragraphs 11-13, 18, and 19).

53. Since the interests of investor-owners of business enterprises and the interests of donors to not-for-profit organizations differ, this Statement discusses separately (a) equity of business enterprises (paragraphs 60-63) and the transactions and events that change equity (paragraphs 64-89) and (b) net assets of not-for-profit organizations (paragraphs 90-106) and the transactions and events that change net assets (paragraphs 107-133).

Equity and Liabilities

54. An entity's assets, liabilities, and equity (net assets) all pertain to the same set of probable future economic benefits. Assets are probable future economic benefits owned or controlled by the entity. Its liabilities are claims to the entity's assets by other entities and, once incurred, involve nondiscretionary future sacrifices of assets that must be satisfied on demand, at a specified or determinable date, or on occurrence of a specified event. In contrast, equity is a residual interest—what remains after liabilities are deducted from assets—and depends significantly on the profitability of a business enterprise or on fund raising or other major or central operations of a not-for-profit organization. A not-for-profit organization may provide goods or services to resource providers who are also employees, members, or beneficiaries, but except upon dissolution or final liquidation of the organization, it cannot distribute assets to members or other resource providers as owners. A business enterprise may distribute assets resulting from income to its owners, but distributions to owners are discretionary, depending on the volition of owners or their representatives after considering the needs of the enterprise and restrictions imposed by law, regulation, or agreement. An enterprise is generally not obligated to transfer assets to owners except in the event of the enterprise's liquidation. An enterprise's liabilities and equity are mutually exclusive claims to or interests in the enterprise's assets by

---

[27]Since, in common use, *grants* mean not only gifts but also exchange transactions in which the *grantor* expects to receive commensurate value, this Statement generally avoids those terms.

entities other than the enterprise, and liabilities take precedence over ownership interests.

55. Although the line between equity and liabilities is clear in concept, it may be obscured in practice. Applying the definitions to particular situations may involve practical problems because several kinds of securities issued by business enterprises seem to have characteristics of both liabilities and equity in varying degrees or because the names given some securities may not accurately describe their essential characteristics. For example, convertible debt instruments have both liability and residual-interest characteristics, which may create problems in accounting for them. (APB Opinion No. 14, *Accounting for Convertible Debt and Debt Issued with Stock Purchase Warrants,* and APB Opinion No. 15, *Earnings per Share,* both discuss problems of that kind.) Preferred stock also often has both debt and equity characteristics, and some preferred stocks may effectively have maturity amounts and dates at which they must be redeemed for cash.

56. Similarly, the line between net assets and liabilities of not-for-profit organizations may be obscured in practice because donors' restrictions that specify the use of contributed assets may seem to result in liabilities, although most do not. The essence of a not-for-profit organization is that it obtains and uses resources to provide specific types of goods or services, and the nature of those goods or services is often critical in donors' decisions to contribute cash or other assets to a particular organization. Most donors contribute assets (restricted as well as unrestricted) to an organization to increase its capacity to provide those goods or services, and receipt of donated assets not only increases the assets of the organization but also imposes a fiduciary responsibility on its management to use those assets effectively and efficiently in pursuit of those service objectives.

57. That responsibility pertains to all of the organization's assets and does not constitute an equitable or constructive obligation as described in paragraphs 36-40. In other words, a not-for-profit organization's fiduciary responsibility to use assets to provide services to beneficiaries does not itself create a duty of the organization to pay cash, transfer other assets, or provide services to one or more creditors. Rather, an obligation to a creditor results when the organization buys supplies for a project, its employees work on it, and the like, and the organization therefore owes suppliers, employees, and others for goods and services they have provided to it.[28]

[28]Most liabilities are legally enforceable, and the concepts of equitable and constructive obligations have a relatively narrow area of application. To assess all or most donor-restricted contributions to not-for-profit organizations as having the essential characteristics of liabilities is too broad an interpretation of the definition of liabilities. A not-for-profit organization's need to acquire goods and services to provide services to beneficiaries in the future, or to expand to provide new services, is analogous to a business enterprise's need to replace merchandise sold or raw materials or equipment used up (paragraph 200), or to buy new assets, not to its liability to provide magazines to customers who have paid in advance.

58. A donor's restriction focuses that fiduciary responsibility on a stipulated use for specified contributed assets but does not change the basic nature of the organization's fiduciary responsibility to use its assets to provide services to beneficiaries. A donor's gift of cash to be spent for a stipulated purpose or of another asset to be used for a stipulated purpose—for example, a mansion to be used as a museum, a house to be used as a dormitory, or a sculpture to be displayed in a cemetery—imposes a responsibility to spend the cash or use the asset in accordance with the donor's instructions. In its effect on the liabilities of the organization, a donor's restriction is essentially the same as management's designating a specified use for certain assets. That is, the responsibility imposed by earmarking assets for specified uses is fundamentally different, both economically and legally, from the responsibility imposed by incurring a liability, which involves a creditor's claim. Consequently, most donor-imposed restrictions on an organization's use of contributed assets do not create obligations that qualify as liabilities of the organization.

59. To determine whether liabilities or equity (net assets) result from issuing specific securities with both debt and equity characteristics or from specific donors' stipulations presents practical problems of applying definitions rather than problems of determining the essential characteristics of those definitions. Adequate definitions are the starting point. They provide a basis for assessing, for example, the extent to which a particular application meets the qualitative characteristic of representational faithfulness, which includes the notion of reporting economic substance rather than legal form (Concepts Statement 2, paragraphs 63-80 and 160).

Equity of Business Enterprises

Characteristics of Equity of Business Enterprises

60. In a business enterprise, the equity is the ownership interest.[29] It stems from ownership rights (or the equivalent)[30] and involves a relation between an enterprise

[29]This Statement defines equity of business enterprises only as a whole, although the discussion notes that different owners of an enterprise may have different kinds of ownership rights and that equity has various sources. In financial statements of business enterprises, various distinctions *within* equity, such as those between common stockholders' equity and preferred stockholders' equity, between contributed capital and earned capital, or between stated or legal capital and other equity, are primarily matters of display that are beyond the scope of this Statement.

[30]Other entities with proprietary or ownership interests in a business enterprise are commonly known by specialized names, such as stockholders, partners, and proprietors, and by more general names, such as investors, but all are also covered by the descriptive term *owners*. Equity of business enterprises is thus commonly known by several names, such as owners' equity, stockholders' equity, ownership, equity capital, partners' capital, and proprietorship. Some enterprises (for example, mutual organizations) do not have stockholders, partners, or proprietors in the usual sense of those terms but do have participants whose interests are essentially ownership interests, residual interests, or both.

and its owners *as owners* rather than as employees, suppliers, customers, lenders, or in some other nonowner role.[31] Since equity ranks after liabilities as a claim to or interest in the assets of the enterprise, it is a residual interest: (a) equity is the same as net assets, the difference between the enterprise's assets and its liabilities, and (b) equity is enhanced or burdened by increases and decreases in net assets from nonowner sources as well as investments by owners and distributions to owners.

61. Equity sets limits, often legal limits, on distributions by an enterprise to its owners, whether in the form of cash dividends or other distributions of assets. Owners' and others' expectations about distributions to owners may affect the market prices of an enterprise's equity securities, thereby indirectly affecting owners' compensation for providing equity or risk capital to the enterprise (paragraph 16). Thus, the essential characteristics of equity center on the conditions for transferring enterprise assets to owners. Equity—an excess of assets over liabilities—is a necessary but not sufficient condition; distributions to owners are at the discretion and volition of the owners or their representatives after satisfying restrictions imposed by law, regulation, or agreements with other entities. Generally, an enterprise is not obligated to transfer assets to owners except in the event of the enterprise's liquidation unless the enterprise formally acts to distribute assets to owners, for example, by declaring a dividend.[32] Owners may sell their interests in an enterprise to others and thus may be able to obtain a return *of* part or all of their investments and perhaps a return *on* investments through a securities market, but those transactions do not normally affect the equity of an enterprise or its assets or liabilities.

62. An enterprise may have several classes of equity (for example, one or more classes each of common stock or preferred stock) with different degrees of risk stemming from different rights to participate in distributions of enterprise assets or different priorities of claims on enterprise assets in the event of liquidation. That is,

---

[31] Distinctions between liabilities and equity generally depend on the nature of the claim rather than on the identity of the claimant. The same entities may simultaneously be both owners and employees, owners and creditors, owners and customers, creditors and customers, or some other combination. For example, an investor may hold both debt and equity securities of the same enterprise, or an owner of an enterprise may also become its creditor by lending to it or by receiving rights to unpaid cash dividends that it declares. Wages due, products or services due, accounts payable due, and other amounts due to owners in their roles as employees, customers, suppliers, and the like are liabilities, not part of equity. Exceptions involve situations in which relationships between the parties cast doubts that they are liabilities in substance rather than investments by owners.

[32] A controlling interest or an interest that confers an ability to exercise significant influence over the operations of an enterprise may have more potential than other ownership interests to control or affect assets of the enterprise or distributions of assets to owners. Procedures such as consolidated financial statements and the equity method of accounting for intercorporate investments have been developed to account for the rights and relations involved.

some classes of owners may bear relatively more of the risks of an enterprise's unprofitability or may benefit relatively more from its profitability (or both) than other classes of owners. However, all classes depend at least to some extent on enterprise profitability for distributions of enterprise assets, and no class of equity carries an unconditional right to receive future transfers of assets from the enterprise except in liquidation, and then only after liabilities have been satisfied.

63. Equity is originally created by owners' investments in an enterprise and may from time to time be augmented by additional investments by owners. Equity is reduced by distributions by the enterprise to owners. However, the distinguishing characteristic of equity is that it inevitably is affected by the enterprise's operations and other events and circumstances affecting the enterprise (which together constitute comprehensive income—paragraph 70).

Transactions and Events That Change Equity of Business Enterprises

64. The diagram on the next page shows the sources of changes in equity (class B) and distinguishes them from each other and from other transactions, events, and circumstances affecting an entity during a period (classes A and C). Specifically, the diagram shows that (a) class B (changes in equity) comprises two mutually exclusive classes of transactions and other events and circumstances, B1 and B2, each of which has significant subclasses, and (b) classes B1, B2, and A are the sources of all increases and decreases in assets and liabilities of an enterprise; class C includes no changes in assets or liabilities. In the diagram, dashed lines rather than solid boundary lines separate revenues and gains and separate expenses and losses because of display considerations that are beyond the scope of this Statement. Paragraphs 78-89 of this Statement define and discuss revenues, expenses, gains, and losses as elements of financial statements but do not precisely distinguish between revenues and gains on the one hand or between expenses and losses on the other. Fine distinctions between revenues and gains and between expenses and losses, as well as other distinctions *within* comprehensive income, are more appropriately considered as part of display or reporting.

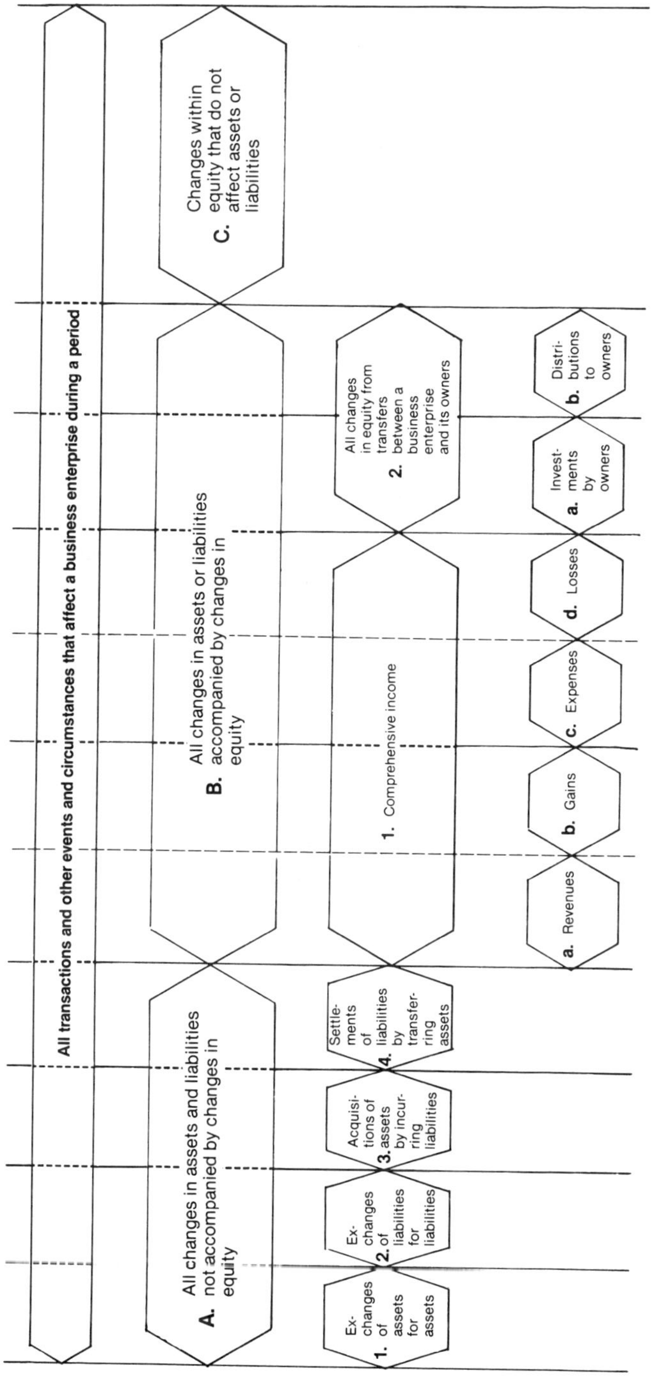
All transactions and other events and circumstances that affect a business enterprise during a period
A. All changes in assets and liabilities not accompanied by changes in equity
B. All changes in assets or liabilities accompanied by changes in equity
C. Changes within equity that do not affect assets or liabilities
1. Exchanges of assets for assets
2. Exchanges of liabilities for liabilities
3. Acquisitions of assets by incurring liabilities
4. Settlements of liabilities by transferring assets
1. Comprehensive income
2. All changes in equity from transfers between a business enterprise and its owners
a. Revenues
b. Gains
c. Expenses
d. Losses
a. Investments by owners
b. Distributions to owners

65. The full width of the diagram, represented by the two-pointed arrow labeled "All transactions and other events and circumstances that affect a business enterprise during a period," encompasses all potentially recordable events and circumstances affecting an entity. Moving from top to bottom of the diagram, each level divides the preceding level into classes that are significant for the definitions and related concepts in this Statement. (Size of classes does not indicate their relative volume or significance.)[33]

A. All changes in assets and liabilities not accompanied by changes in equity. This class comprises four kinds of exchange transactions that are common in most entities. (Exchanges that affect equity belong in class B rather than class A.)
   1. Exchanges of assets for assets, for example, purchases of assets for cash or barter exchanges
   2. Exchanges of liabilities for liabilities, for example, issues of notes payable to settle accounts payable or refundings of bonds payable by issuing new bonds to holders that surrender outstanding bonds
   3. Acquisitions of assets by incurring liabilities, for example, purchases of assets on account, borrowings, or receipts of cash advances for goods or services to be provided in the future
   4. Settlements of liabilities by transferring assets, for example, repayments of borrowing, payments to suppliers on account, payments of accrued wages or salaries, or repairs (or payments for repairs) required by warranties

B. All changes in assets or liabilities accompanied by changes in equity. This class is the subject of this section and comprises:
   1. Comprehensive income (defined in paragraph 70) whose components (broadly defined and discussed in paragraphs 78-89) are:
      a. Revenues
      b. Gains
      c. Expenses
      d. Losses
   2. All changes in equity from transfers between a business enterprise and its owners (defined in paragraphs 66 and 67):
      a. Investments by owners in the enterprise
      b. Distributions by the enterprise to owners

[33]The diagram reflects the concept that value added by productive activities increases assets as production takes place, which is the basis for the common observation that revenues are *earned* by the entire process of acquiring goods and services, using them to produce other goods or services, selling the output, and collecting the sales price or fee. However, that value added is commonly *recognized* after production is complete, usually when product is delivered or sold but sometimes when cash is received or product is completed. The diagram does not, of course, settle recognition issues.

C. Changes within equity that do not affect assets or liabilities (for example, stock dividends, conversions of preferred stock into common stock, and some stock recapitalizations). This class contains only changes *within* equity and does not affect the definition of equity or its amount.

The definitions in paragraphs 70-89 are those in class B1—comprehensive income—and its subclasses—revenues, expenses, gains, and losses.[34]

Investments by and Distributions to Owners

66. Investments by owners are increases in equity of a particular business enterprise resulting from transfers to it from other entities of something valuable to obtain or increase ownership interests (or equity) in it. Assets are most commonly received as investments by owners, but that which is received may also include services or satisfaction or conversion of liabilities of the enterprise.

67. Distributions to owners are decreases in equity of a particular business enterprise resulting from transferring assets, rendering services, or incurring liabilities by the enterprise to owners. Distributions to owners decrease ownership interest (or equity) in an enterprise.[35]

Characteristics of Investments by and Distributions to Owners

68. Investments by owners and distributions to owners are transactions between an enterprise and its owners *as owners.* Through investments by owners, an enterprise obtains resources it needs to begin or expand operations, to retire debt securities or other liabilities, or for other business purposes; as a result of investing resources in the enterprise, other entities obtain ownership interests in the enterprise or increase ownership interests they already have. Not all investments in the equity securities of an enterprise by other entities are investments by owners as that concept is defined in this Statement. In an investment by owners, the enterprise that issues the securities acquired by an owner always receives the proceeds or their benefits; its net assets increase. If the purchaser of equity securities becomes an owner or increases its ownership interest in an enterprise by purchasing those securities from another owner that is decreasing or terminating its ownership interest, the transfer does not affect the net assets of the enterprise.

[34]The definitions of revenues, expenses, gains, and losses in paragraphs 78-89 also apply to the changes in net assets of not-for-profit organizations as discussed in paragraphs 107-113.

[35]Investments by owners are sometimes called capital contributions. Distributions to owners are sometimes called capital distributions; distributions of earnings, profits, or income; or dividends.

69. Distributions by an enterprise to its owners decrease its net assets and decrease or terminate ownership interests of those that receive them. Reacquisition by an entity of its own equity securities by transferring assets or incurring liabilities to owners is a distribution to owners as that concept is defined in this Statement. Since owners become creditors for a dividend declared until it is paid, an enterprise's incurrence of a liability to transfer assets to owners in the future converts a part of the equity or ownership interest of the enterprise into creditors' claims; settlement of the liability by transfer of the assets is a transaction in class A4 in the diagram in paragraph 64 rather than in class B2(b). That is, equity is reduced by the incurrence of the liability to owners, not by its settlement.

Comprehensive Income of Business Enterprises

70. Comprehensive income is the change in equity of a business enterprise during a period from transactions and other events and circumstances from nonowner sources. It includes all changes in equity during a period except those resulting from investments by owners and distributions to owners.

Concepts of Capital Maintenance

71. A concept of maintenance of capital or recovery of cost is a prerequisite for separating return *on* capital from return *of* capital because only inflows in excess of the amount needed to maintain capital are a return *on* equity. Two major concepts of capital maintenance exist, both of which can be measured in units of either money or constant purchasing power: the financial capital concept and the physical capital concept (which is often expressed in terms of maintaining operating capability, that is, maintaining the capacity of an enterprise to provide a constant supply of goods or services). The major difference between them involves the effects of price changes on assets held and liabilities owed during a period. Under the financial capital concept, if the effects of those price changes are recognized, they are called "holding gains and losses" and are included in return on capital. Under the physical capital concept, those changes would be recognized but called "capital maintenance adjustments" and would be included directly in equity and would not be included in return on capital. Under that concept, capital maintenance adjustments would be a separate element rather than gains and losses.

72. The financial capital concept is the traditional view and is generally the capital maintenance concept in present primary financial statements. Comprehensive income as defined in paragraph 70 is a return *on* financial capital.[36]

[36]Concepts Statement 5, paragraphs 45-48 adopted financial capital maintenance as the concept on which the full set of articulated financial statements it discusses is based.

Characteristics, Sources, and Components of Comprehensive Income

73. Over the life of a business enterprise, its comprehensive income equals the net of its cash receipts and cash outlays, excluding cash (and cash equivalent of noncash assets) invested by owners and distributed to owners (Concepts Statement 1, paragraph 46). That characteristic holds whether the amounts of cash and comprehensive income are measured in nominal dollars or constant dollars. Although the amounts in constant dollars may differ from those in nominal dollars, the basic relationship is not changed because both nominal and constant dollars express the same thing using different measuring units. Matters such as recognition criteria and choice of attributes to be measured[37] also do not affect the amounts of comprehensive income and net cash receipts over the life of an enterprise but do affect the time and way parts of the total are identified with the periods that constitute the entire life. Timing of recognition of revenues, expenses, gains, and losses is also a major difference between accounting based on cash receipts and outlays and accrual accounting. Accrual accounting may encompass various timing possibilities—for example, when goods or services are provided, when cash is received, or when prices change.

74. Comprehensive income of a business enterprise results from (a) exchange transactions and other transfers between the enterprise and other entities that are not its owners, (b) the enterprise's productive efforts,[38] and (c) price changes, casualties, and other effects of interactions between the enterprise and the economic, legal, social, political, and physical environment of which it is part. An enterprise's productive efforts and most of its exchange transactions with other entities are ongoing major activities that constitute the enterprise's central operations by which it attempts to fulfill its basic function in the economy of producing and distributing

[37]"'Attributes to be measured' refers to the traits or aspects of an element to be quantified or measured, such as historical cost/historical proceeds, current cost/current proceeds, etc. Attribute is a narrower concept than measurement, which includes not only identifying the attribute to be measured but also selecting a scale of measurement (for example, units of money or units of constant purchasing power). 'Property' is commonly used in sciences to describe the trait or aspect of an object being measured, such as the length of a table or the weight of a stone. But 'property' may be confused with land and buildings in financial reporting contexts, and 'attribute' has become common in accounting literature and is used in this Statement" (Concepts Statement 1, par. 2, footnote 2). The choice of measurement attribute, measurement unit, and recognition criteria are discussed in Concepts Statement 5.

[38]An enterprise increases the values of goods or services it holds or acquires by adding time, place, or form utility. Thus, *productive efforts* and *producing and distributing activities* include not only manufacturing and other conversion processes but also other productive activities such as storing, transporting, lending, insuring, and providing professional services that might be overlooked if *producing* were narrowly equated with *manufacturing*.

goods or services at prices that are sufficient to enable it to pay for the goods and services it uses and to provide a satisfactory return to its owners.

75. Comprehensive income is a broad concept. Although an enterprise's ongoing major or central operations are generally intended to be the primary source of comprehensive income, they are not the only source. Most entities occasionally engage in activities that are peripheral or incidental to their central activities. Moreover, all entities are affected by the economic, legal, social, political, and physical environment of which they are part, and comprehensive income of each enterprise is affected by events and circumstances that may be partly or wholly beyond the control of individual enterprises and their managements.

76. Although cash resulting from various sources of comprehensive income is the same, receipts from various sources may vary in stability, risk, and predictability. That is, characteristics of various sources of comprehensive income may differ significantly from one another, indicating a need for information about various components of comprehensive income. That need underlies the distinctions between revenues and gains, between expenses and losses, between various kinds of gains and losses, and between measures found in present practice such as income from continuing operations and income after extraordinary item and cumulative effect of change in accounting principle.

77. Comprehensive income comprises two related but distinguishable types of components. It consists of not only its basic components—revenues, expenses, gains, and losses—but also various intermediate components that result from combining the basic components. Revenues, expenses, gains, and losses can be combined in various ways to obtain several measures of enterprise performance with varying degrees of inclusiveness. Examples of intermediate components in business enterprises are gross margin, income from continuing operations before taxes, income from continuing operations, and operating income. Those intermediate components are, in effect, subtotals of comprehensive income and often of one another in the sense that they can be combined with each other or with the basic components to obtain other intermediate measures of comprehensive income.[39]

---

[39]*Earnings* as adopted in Concepts Statement 5 and its relation to comprehensive income is discussed in paragraph 1, footnote 1.

Revenues

78. Revenues are inflows or other enhancements of assets of an entity or settlements of its liabilities (or a combination of both) from delivering or producing goods, rendering services, or other activities that constitute the entity's ongoing major or central operations.

Characteristics of Revenues

79. Revenues represent actual or expected cash inflows (or the equivalent) that have occurred or will eventuate as a result of the entity's ongoing major or central operations. The assets increased by revenues[40] may be of various kinds—for example, cash, claims against customers or clients, other goods or services received, or increased value of a product resulting from production. Similarly, the transactions and events from which revenues arise and the revenues themselves are in many forms and are called by various names—for example, output, deliveries, sales, fees, interest, dividends, royalties, and rent—depending on the kinds of operations involved and the way revenues are recognized.[41]

---

[40]In concept, revenues increase assets rather than decrease liabilities, but a convenient shortcut is often to directly record reduction of liabilities. Production is essentially an asset conversion process to create future economic benefit (par. 30; par. 65, footnote 33; and par. 74, footnote 38). It adds utility and value to assets and is the primary source of revenue, which may be recognized (as noted in footnote 41) when product is delivered, when cash is received, or when production is completed rather than as production takes place. Production does not directly incur or settle liabilities but is often closely related to exchange transactions in which liabilities are incurred or settled. Entities acquire assets (economic benefits), not expenses or losses, to carry out their production operations, and most expenses are at least momentarily assets. Since many goods and services acquired are used either simultaneously with acquisition or soon thereafter, it is common practice to record them as expenses at acquisition. However, to record an expense as resulting from incurring a liability is a useful shortcut that combines two conceptually separate events: (a) an exchange transaction in which an asset was acquired and (b) an internal event (production) in which an asset was used up. The assets produced by operations may be used to settle liabilities (for example, by delivering product that has been paid for in advance). However, again, to record a liability as being directly reduced by recording revenue is a useful shortcut that combines two conceptually separate events: (a) an internal event (production) that resulted in an asset and revenue and (b) an exchange transaction in which the asset was transferred to another entity to satisfy a liability. In the diagram in paragraph 64, the exchange transactions are in class A, while the internal events (production) that result in revenues or expenses are in class B1.

[41]Timing of recognition of revenues—including existing recognition procedures, which usually recognize revenues when goods are delivered or services are performed but may sometimes recognize them when cash is received, when production is completed, or as production progresses—is a subject of Concepts Statement 5. This Statement contains no conclusions about recognition of revenues or of any other elements.

Expenses

80. Expenses are outflows or other using up of assets or incurrences of liabilities (or a combination of both) from delivering or producing goods,[42] rendering services, or carrying out other activities that constitute the entity's ongoing major or central operations.

Characteristics of Expenses

81. Expenses represent actual or expected cash outflows (or the equivalent) that have occurred or will eventuate as a result of the entity's ongoing major or central operations. The assets that flow out or are used or the liabilities that are incurred[43] may be of various kinds—for example, units of product delivered or produced, employees' services used, kilowatt hours of electricity used to light an office building, or taxes on current income. Similarly, the transactions and events from which expenses arise and the expenses themselves are in many forms and are called by various names—for example, cost of goods sold, cost of services provided, depreciation, interest, rent, and salaries and wages—depending on the kinds of operations involved and the way expenses are recognized.

Gains and Losses

82. Gains are increases in equity (net assets) from peripheral or incidental transactions of an entity and from all other transactions and other events and circumstances affecting the entity except those that result from revenues or investments by owners.

83. Losses are decreases in equity (net assets) from peripheral or incidental transactions of an entity and from all other transactions and other events and circumstances affecting the entity except those that result from expenses or distributions to owners.

[42]If manufactured products are accounted for at accumulated costs until sold, as is common in present practice, production costs are recognized as expenses in the periods in which product is sold rather than in periods in which assets are used to produce output. For example, use of raw materials and depreciation of factory machinery are included in the cost of product and are recognized as expenses as part of the cost of goods sold. In contrast, if products are accounted for at net realizable value using a percentage-of-completion method, as output under construction contracts often is, production costs such as raw materials used and depreciation of construction equipment are recognized as expenses in the periods in which the assets are used to produce output.

[43]In concept, most expenses decrease assets rather than increase liabilities. They involve using (sacrificing) goods or services, not acquiring them. However, acquisition and use of many goods or services may occur simultaneously or during the same period, and a convenient shortcut is often to record directly increases of liabilities (par. 79, footnote 40). Taxes and other expenses resulting from nonreciprocal transfers to other entities commonly do result directly from incurring liabilities.

Characteristics of Gains and Losses

84. Gains and losses result from entities' peripheral or incidental transactions and from other events and circumstances stemming from the environment that may be largely beyond the control of individual entities and their managements. Thus, gains and losses are not all alike. There are several kinds, even in a single entity, and they may be described or classified in a variety of ways that are not necessarily mutually exclusive.

85. Gains and losses may be described or classified according to sources. Some gains or losses are net results of comparing the proceeds and sacrifices (costs) in peripheral or incidental transactions with other entities—for example, from sales of investments in marketable securities, from dispositions of used equipment, or from settlements of liabilities at other than their carrying amounts. Other gains or losses result from nonreciprocal transfers between an entity and other entities that are not its owners—for example, from gifts or donations,[44] from winning a lawsuit, from thefts, and from assessments of fines or damages by courts. Still other gains or losses result from holding assets or liabilities while their values change—for example, from price changes that cause inventory items to be written down from cost to market, from changes in market prices of investments in marketable equity securities accounted for at market values or at the lower of cost and market, and from changes in foreign exchange rates. And still other gains or losses result from other environmental factors, such as natural catastrophes—for example, damage to or destruction of property by earthquake or flood.

86. Gains and losses may also be described or classified as "operating" or "nonoperating," depending on their relation to an entity's major ongoing or central operations. For example, losses on writing down inventory from cost to market are usually considered to be operating losses, while major casualty losses are usually considered nonoperating losses.

Revenues, Expenses, Gains, and Losses

87. Revenues and gains are similar, and expenses and losses are similar, but some differences are significant in conveying information about an enterprise's performance. Revenues and expenses result from an entity's ongoing major or central operations and activities—that is, from activities such as producing or delivering goods, rendering services, lending, insuring, investing, and financing. In contrast, gains and losses

[44]Gifts or donations received by not-for-profit organizations may be revenues or gains (pars. 111-113).

result from incidental or peripheral transactions of an enterprise with other entities and from other events and circumstances affecting it. Some gains and losses may be considered "operating" gains and losses and may be closely related to revenues and expenses. Revenues and expenses are commonly displayed as gross inflows or outflows of net assets, while gains and losses are usually displayed as net inflows or outflows.

88. The definitions and discussion of revenues, expenses, gains, and losses in this Statement give broad guidance but do not distinguish precisely between revenues and gains or between expenses and losses. Distinctions between revenues and gains and between expenses and losses in a particular entity depend to a significant extent on the nature of the entity, its operations, and its other activities. Items that are revenues for one kind of entity may be gains for another, and items that are expenses for one kind of entity may be losses for another. For example, investments in securities that may be sources of revenues and expenses for insurance or investment companies may be sources of gains and losses in manufacturing or merchandising companies. Technological changes may be sources of gains or losses for most kinds of enterprises but may be characteristic of the operations of high-technology or research-oriented enterprises. Events such as commodity price changes and foreign exchange rate changes that occur while assets are being used or produced or liabilities are owed may directly or indirectly affect the *amounts* of revenues or expenses for most enterprises, but they are *sources* of revenues or expenses only for enterprises for which trading in foreign exchange or commodities is a major or central activity.

89. Since a primary purpose of distinguishing gains and losses from revenues and expenses is to make displays of information about an enterprise's sources of comprehensive income as useful as possible, fine distinctions between revenues and gains and between expenses and losses are principally matters of display or reporting (paragraphs 64, 219-220, and 228).

Net Assets of Not-for-Profit Organizations

Characteristics of Net Assets of Not-for-Profit Organizations

90. In a not-for-profit organization, as in a business enterprise, net assets (equity) is a residual, the difference between the entity's assets and its liabilities but, in contrast to equity of a business enterprise, it is not an ownership interest. Distinguishing characteristics of a not-for-profit organization include absence of ownership interest(s) in the same sense as a business enterprise, operating purposes not centered on profit, and significant receipts of contributions, many involving donor-imposed restrictions (paragraphs 11-15, 18 and 19, and 49-53).

91. Net assets of not-for-profit organizations is divided into three mutually exclusive classes, permanently restricted net assets, temporarily restricted net assets, and unrestricted net assets.[45]

Classes of Net Assets

92. Permanently restricted net assets is the part of the net assets of a not-for-profit organization resulting (a) from contributions and other inflows of assets whose use by the organization is limited by donor-imposed stipulations that neither expire by passage of time nor can be fulfilled or otherwise removed by actions of the organization, (b) from other asset enhancements and diminishments subject to the same kinds of stipulations, and (c) from reclassifications from (or to) other classes of net assets as a consequence of donor-imposed stipulations.

93. Temporarily restricted net assets is the part of the net assets of a not-for-profit organization resulting (a) from contributions and other inflows of assets whose use by the organization is limited by donor-imposed stipulations that either expire by passage of time or can be fulfilled and removed by actions of the organization pursuant to those stipulations, (b) from other asset enhancements and diminishments subject to the same kinds of stipulations, and (c) from reclassifications to (or from) other classes of net assets as a consequence of donor-imposed stipulations, their expiration by passage of time, or their fulfillment and removal by actions of the organization pursuant to those stipulations.

94. Unrestricted net assets is the part of net assets of a not-for-profit organization that is neither permanently restricted nor temporarily restricted by donor-imposed stipulations—that is, the part of net assets resulting (a) from all revenues, expenses, gains, and losses that are not changes in permanently or temporarily restricted net assets and (b) from reclassifications from (or to) other classes of net assets as a consequence of donor-imposed stipulations, their expiration by passage of time, or their fulfillment and removal by actions of the organization pursuant to those stipulations. The only limits on unrestricted net assets are broad limits resulting from the

[45]This Statement does not use the terms *funds* and *fund balances* because the most common meanings of those terms refer respectively to a common group of assets and related liabilities within a not-for-profit organization and to the net amount of those assets and liabilities. This Statement classifies net assets, not assets or liabilities. While some not-for-profit organizations may choose to classify assets and liabilities into fund groups, information about those groupings is not a necessary part of general purpose external financial reporting. Issues that affect how, if at all, classifications of assets and liabilities may be displayed in financial statements, for example, by using multicolumn presentations or disclosure in the notes, are outside the scope of this Statement and may be the subject of future Board projects.

nature of the organization and the purposes specified in its articles of incorporation (or comparable document for an unincorporated association) or bylaws and perhaps limits resulting from contractual agreements—for example, loan covenants—entered into by the organization in the course of its operations.

Donor-Imposed Restrictions

95. The three classes of net assets reflect differences in, or absence of, donor-imposed restrictions on a not-for-profit organization's use of its assets. Thus, *restriction* and *restricted* in this Statement refer to limits placed on a not-for-profit organization's use of assets by donors' stipulations that are more specific than broad limits resulting from the nature of the organization and the purposes specified in its articles of incorporation (or comparable document for an unincorporated association) or bylaws. Restrictions generally do not create liabilities (paragraphs 56-58), but they do restrain the organization from using part of its resources for purposes other than those specified, for example, to settle liabilities, purchase goods, or provide services not within the scope of the restrictions.

96. Donors need not explicitly limit uses of contributed assets for a not-for-profit organization to classify the increase in net assets as restricted if circumstances surrounding those receipts make clear the donor's implicit stipulation of restricted use. For example, use of contributed assets is restricted despite absence of a donor's explicit stipulation about use if the assets are received in a fund-raising drive declared to be for a specific purpose, such as to add to the organization's endowment, to acquire a particular property, or to obtain resources for next year's operations.

97. Only donors' explicit, or clearly evident implicit, stipulations that limit a not-for-profit organization's use of its assets can result in permanently or temporarily restricted net assets (as this Statement uses those terms). Decisions, resolutions, appropriations, or the like by the directors, trustees, or managers of a not-for-profit organization may impose seemingly similar limits on the use of net assets that were not stipulated by donors. However, unless limits are imposed by donors' stipulations that place them beyond the organization's discretion to change, they differ substantively from donor-imposed limits that result in restricted net assets. For example, a voluntary resolution by the trustees of an organization to earmark a portion of its unrestricted net assets to function as an endowment is a revocable internal designation that does not give rise to restricted net assets.[46] Only in the relatively few

[46]However, the nature and amounts of self-imposed limits on use of assets and of limits imposed by others as a condition of operating activities (for example, by debt covenants or other arrangements) may be significant information for financial statement users and may need to be disclosed.

instances in which self-imposed limits become legally irrevocable are they substantively equivalent to donor-imposed restrictions and the cause of restricted net assets.

Temporary and Permanent Restrictions

98. Contributions (or other enhancements) of assets with donor-imposed limits on their use increase assets and net assets of a not-for-profit organization in the period in which it receives them, but they do not increase unrestricted net assets, nor are they generally available for payment to creditors, as long as the restriction remains. Donor-imposed restrictions on use of assets may be either temporary or permanent.[47]

99. Some donors stipulate that their contributions be used in a later period or after a specified date rather than be expended immediately; those are often called time restrictions. Other donors stipulate that their contributions be used for a specified purpose, such as sponsoring a particular program or service, acquiring a particular building, or settling a particular liability; those are often called purpose restrictions. Time and purpose restrictions have in common that they can be satisfied, either by passage of time or by actions of the organization, and that the contributed assets can be expended. Those restrictions are temporary. Once the stipulation is satisfied, the restriction is gone.

100. Still other donors stipulate that resources be maintained permanently—not used up, expended, or otherwise exhausted—but permit the organization to use up or expend the income (or other economic benefits) derived from the donated assets. That type of restricted gift is often called an endowment. The restriction lasts in effect forever. It cannot be removed by actions of the organization or passage of time. The donations do not increase the organization's unrestricted net assets in any period, and the donated assets are not available for payment to creditors.

Restrictions Affect Net Assets Rather Than Particular Assets

101. Restrictions impose responsibilities on management to ensure that the organization uses donated resources in the manner stipulated by resource providers. Sometimes donor-imposed restrictions limit an organization's ability to sell or exchange

[47]This Statement makes distinctions among resource flows based on the presence or absence of donor-imposed restrictions on their use. In the past, other distinctions have been made, for example, between "nonoperating" and "operating," "nonexpendable" and "expendable," "noncapital" and "capital," and "restricted" and "unrestricted." Those terms have been used by not-for-profit organizations in practice to name groups of resource flows that, while similar in many respects, have differed in important details.

the particular asset received. For example, a donor may give a painting to a museum stipulating that it must be publicly displayed, properly maintained, and never sold.

102. More commonly, donors' stipulations permit the organization to pool the donated assets with other assets and to sell or exchange the donated assets for other suitable assets as long as the economic benefits of the donated assets are not consumed or used for a purpose that does not comply with the stipulation. For example, a donor may contribute 100 shares of Security A to an organization's endowment, thereby requiring that the amount of the gift be retained permanently but not requiring that the specific shares be held indefinitely. Thus, permanently restricted net assets and temporarily restricted net assets generally refer to amounts of net assets that are restricted by donor-imposed limits, not to specific assets.

Maintenance of Net Assets

103. Although not-for-profit organizations do not have ownership interests or profit in the same sense as business enterprises, they nonetheless need a concept of capital maintenance or its equivalent to reflect "the relation between inflows and outflows of resources during a period."[48] The activities of an organization during a period may draw upon resources received in past periods or may add resources that can be used in future periods.

104. Unless a not-for-profit organization maintains its net assets, its ability to continue to provide services dwindles; either future resource providers must make up the deficiency or services to future beneficiaries will decline. For example, use of an asset such as a building to provide goods or services to beneficiaries consumes part of the future economic benefits or service potential constituting the asset, and that decrease in future economic benefits is one of the costs (expenses) of using the asset for that purpose.[49] The organization's net assets decrease as it uses up an asset unless its revenues and gains at least equal its expenses and losses, including the cost of consuming part of the asset during the period (depreciation). Even if that organization plans to replace the asset through future contributions from donors, and probably will be able to do so, it has not maintained its net assets during the current period.

[48]FASB Concepts Statement 4, par. 49. The Statement also says, "A nonbusiness [not-for-profit] organization cannot, in the long run, continue to achieve its operating objectives unless the resources made available to it at least equal the resources needed to provide services at levels satisfactory to resource providers and other constituents" (par. 39).

[49]Some assets—for example, land and endowment investments in securities—are generally not used up or consumed by productive use. The extent, if any, to which the future economic benefits or service potential of particular kinds of assets are used up by productive use involves measurement issues beyond the scope of this Statement.

105. Maintenance of net assets in not-for-profit organizations, as in business enterprises (paragraph 72), is based on the maintenance of financial capital—that is, a not-for-profit organization's capital has been maintained if the financial (money) amount of its net assets at the end of a period equals or exceeds the financial amount of its net assets at the beginning of the period.

106. Since donor-imposed restrictions affect the types and levels of service a not-for-profit organization can provide, whether an organization has maintained certain classes of net assets may be more significant than whether it has maintained net assets in the aggregate. For example, if net assets were maintained in a period only because permanently restricted endowment contributions made up for a decline in unrestricted net assets, information focusing on the aggregate change might obscure the fact that the organization had not maintained the part of its net assets that is fully available to support services in the next period.

Transactions and Events That Change Net Assets of Not-for-Profit Organizations

107. The diagram on the next page shows the sources of changes in the amount of or the restrictions on a not-for-profit organization's net assets and distinguishes them from each other and from other transactions, events, and circumstances affecting the organization during a period. While similar in many respects to the diagram in paragraph 64 for business enterprises, it reflects the different characteristics and financial reporting objectives of not-for-profit organizations. The importance to those organizations of donor-imposed restrictions on use of some assets focuses financial reporting information on changes in restrictions on net assets as well as on changes in the amount of net assets.

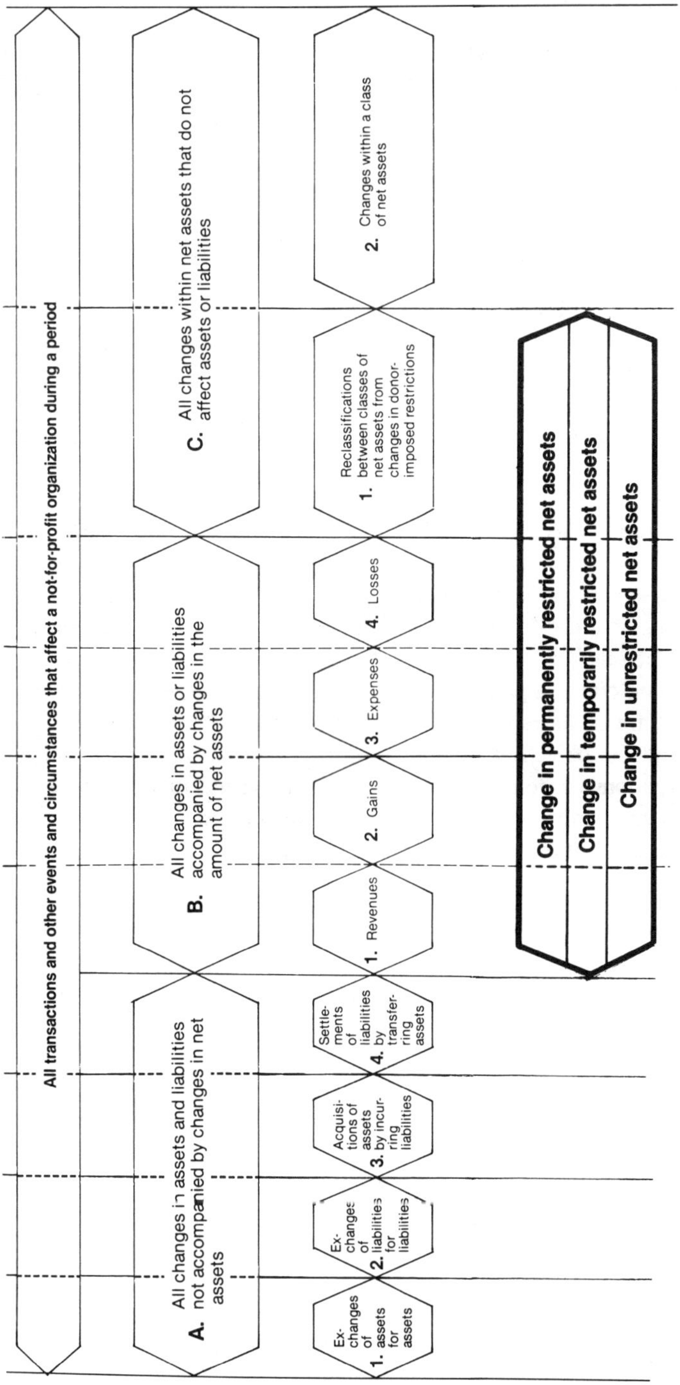
All transactions and other events and circumstances that affect a not-for-profit organization during a period
A. All changes in assets and liabilities not accompanied by changes in net assets
B. All changes in assets or liabilities accompanied by changes in the amount of net assets
C. All changes within net assets that do not affect assets or liabilities
1. Ex-changes of assets for assets
2. Ex-changes of liabilities for liabilities
3. Acquisi-tions of assets by incur-ring liabilities
4. Settle-ments of liabilities by transfer-ring assets
1. Revenues
2. Gains
3. Expenses
4. Losses
1. Reclassifications between classes of net assets from changes in donor-imposed restrictions
2. Changes within a class of net assets
Change in permanently restricted net assets
Change in temporarily restricted net assets
Change in unrestricted net assets

108. The full width of the diagram, represented by the two-pointed arrow labeled "All transactions and other events and circumstances that affect a not-for-profit organization during a period," encompasses all potentially recordable events and circumstances affecting a not-for-profit organization. Moving down the diagram, the next level is divided into three mutually exclusive classes that are the same as those of business enterprises (classes A, B, and C). Continuing down the diagram, however, classes B and C are divided differently from classes B and C in the business-enterprise diagram because not-for-profit organizations have no owners or transactions with owners in the same sense as business enterprises and because restrictions on net assets and changes in the restrictions are significant in not-for-profit organizations. (Size of classes does not indicate their relative volume or significance.)

A. All changes in assets and liabilities not accompanied by changes in net assets. This class comprises four kinds of exchange transactions that are common in most entities; paragraph 65 includes examples. (Exchanges that affect the amount of net assets belong in class B rather than A.)
   1. Exchanges of assets for assets
   2. Exchanges of liabilities for liabilities
   3. Acquisitions of assets by incurring liabilities
   4. Settlements of liabilities by transferring assets

B. All changes in assets or liabilities accompanied by changes in the amount of net assets. This class comprises four kinds of items that also exist for business enterprises:
   1. Revenues
   2. Gains
   3. Expenses
   4. Losses

C. All changes within net assets that do not affect assets or liabilities.
   1. Reclassifications between classes of net assets from changes in donor-imposed restrictions, for example, temporarily restricted net assets become unrestricted net assets when a donor-imposed time stipulation expires. This class comprises events that increase one class of net assets while decreasing another but do not change the amount of net assets.
   2. Changes within a class of net assets, for example, an internal designation by trustees to establish a working capital reserve from a portion of the entity's unrestricted net assets.

109. The shaded arrow* that is divided horizontally into three classes—change in permanently restricted net assets, change in temporarily restricted net assets, and change in unrestricted net assets—encompasses all transactions and other events and circumstances that change either the amount of net assets or the donor-imposed restrictions on net assets. It thus encompasses the transactions and other events and circumstances that comprise class B (revenues, expenses, gains, losses), and class C1 (reclassifications), combined.

110. In other words, the third and fourth levels of the diagram show in two different ways the same set of transactions and other events and circumstances affecting net assets of a not-for-profit organization and the composition of its three classes during a period. The third level emphasizes sources of changes in net assets—transactions or other events that result in revenues, expenses, gains, or losses or in reclassifications within net assets. The fourth level emphasizes the effects of those events on each of the three classes of net assets—permanently restricted net assets, temporarily restricted net assets, and unrestricted net assets. The components of class B—revenues, expenses, gains, and losses—are discussed collectively in paragraphs 111-113; reclassifications (class C1) are defined and discussed in paragraphs 114-116; and changes in classes of net assets (the fourth level) are defined and discussed in paragraphs 117-133.

Revenues, Expenses, Gains, and Losses

111. Revenues, expenses, gains, and losses are defined and discussed in paragraphs 78-89. Collectively, they include all transactions and other events and circumstances that change the amount of net assets of a not-for-profit organization. All resource inflows and other enhancements of assets of a not-for-profit organization or settlements of its liabilities that increase net assets are either revenues or gains and have characteristics similar to the revenues or gains of a business enterprise. Likewise, all resource outflows or other using up of assets or incurrences of liabilities that decrease net assets are either expenses or losses and have characteristics similar to expenses or losses of business enterprises.

112. Net assets of a not-for-profit organization change as a result of (a) exchange transactions, (b) contributions and other nonreciprocal transfers from or to other entities, (c) the organization's service-providing efforts,[50] and (d) price changes,

[50]A not-for-profit organization, like a business enterprise, increases the values of goods or services it acquires by adding time, place, or form utility. Thus, *service-providing efforts* and *producing and distributing activities* include conversion processes and other utility-adding activities such as storing, transporting, distributing, providing professional services, and many others. Since a not-for-profit organization may provide goods, services, or cash to its beneficiaries, the term *service-providing efforts* may refer to activities for producing and distributing goods or cash as well as services.

*Editor's Note: The arrow is highlighted in this edition by a bold-faced outline rather than by shading.

casualties, and other effects of interactions between the organization and the economic, legal, social, political, and physical environment of which it is a part.

113. A not-for-profit organization's service-providing efforts, most of its fund-raising activities, and most of its exchange transactions with other entities are generally ongoing major activities that constitute the organization's central operations by which it attempts to fulfill its basic function of providing goods or services to its constituency and thus are the sources of its revenues and expenses. Its gains and losses result from activities that are peripheral or incidental to its central operations and from interactions with its environment, which give rise to price changes, casualties, and other effects that may be partly or wholly beyond the control of individual organizations and their managements. Items that are revenues (or expenses) for one kind of organization may be gains (or losses) for another. For example, donors' contributions are revenues to many not-for-profit organizations but are gains to others that do not actively seek them and receive them only occasionally. Similarly, contributions such as those for endowments are usually gains because they occur only occasionally for most not-for-profit organizations.

Reclassifications

114. Reclassifications between classes of net assets result from donor-imposed stipulations, their expiration by passage of time, or their fulfillment and removal by actions of the organization pursuant to those stipulations. Reclassifications simultaneously increase one class and decrease another class of net assets; they do not involve inflows, outflows, or other changes in assets or liabilities.

115. Reclassifications include events that remove or impose restrictions on an organization's use of its existing resources. Restrictions are removed from temporarily restricted net assets when stipulated conditions expire or are fulfilled by the organization. Time-restricted net assets generally become unrestricted when the stipulated time arrives; for example, net assets that are restricted by contribution of assets during 1985 for use in 1986 become unrestricted on January 1, 1986. Purpose-restricted net assets generally become unrestricted when the organization undertakes activities pursuant to the specified purpose, perhaps over several periods, depending on the nature of donors' stipulations. The resulting reclassifications increase unrestricted net assets, often at the same time that the activities that remove the restrictions result in expenses that decrease unrestricted net assets (paragraphs 151 and 152). Temporarily restricted net assets may become unrestricted when an organization incurs liabilities to vendors or employees as it undertakes the activities required by donor stipulations, rather than at the time those liabilities are paid. Restrictions occasionally may be withdrawn by the donor or removed by judicial action.

116. A donor's gift may impose restrictions on otherwise unrestricted net assets. For example, some donors provide endowment gifts on the condition that the organization agree to "match" them by permanently restricting a stated amount of its unrestricted net assets. "Matching agreements" that are not reversible without donors' consent result in a reclassification of unrestricted net assets to permanently restricted net assets or to temporarily restricted net assets.

Changes in Classes of Net Assets of Not-for-Profit Organizations

117. Those who provide, or may provide, resources to a not-for-profit organization usually need information not only about sources of changes in its net assets—about transactions and other events that result in revenues, expenses, gains, and losses—but also about their effects, and the effects of events that change donor-imposed restrictions, on classes of net assets. Effects on classes of net assets often may be more significant to them than sources of changes because donor-imposed restrictions may significantly affect the types and levels of services that a not-for-profit organization can provide.

118. Events that result in reclassifications within net assets and revenues, expenses, gains, and losses together encompass the transactions and other events and circumstances that comprise change in permanently restricted net assets, change in temporarily restricted net assets, and change in unrestricted net assets (paragraphs 108-110).

Change in Permanently Restricted Net Assets

119. Change in permanently restricted net assets of a not-for-profit organization during a period is the total of (a) contributions and other inflows during the period of assets whose use by the organization is limited by donor-imposed stipulations that neither expire by passage of time nor can be fulfilled or otherwise removed by actions of the organization, (b) other asset enhancements and diminishments during the period that are subject to the same kinds of stipulations, and (c) reclassifications from (or to) other classes of net assets during the period as a consequence of donor-imposed stipulations.

Characteristics of Change in Permanently Restricted Net Assets

120. Most increases in permanently restricted net assets of a not-for-profit organization are from its accepting contributions of assets that donors stipulate must be maintained in perpetuity. Receipt of a contribution increases permanently restricted net assets if the donor stipulates that the resources received must be maintained per-

manently and those resources are capable of providing future economic benefit indefinitely. Only assets that are not by their nature used up in carrying out the organization's activities are capable of providing economic benefits indefinitely. Gifts of cash, securities, or nonexhaustible property, such as land and art objects, to be added to an organization's endowment or collections are common examples of those types of assets.

121. Donors' permanent restrictions on the use of contributed assets may also extend to enhancements of those assets or to inflows that result from them. For example, increases in the value of endowment investments that by donor stipulation or law become part of endowment principal also increase permanently restricted net assets. Events that diminish permanently restricted net assets may also occur. Examples include destruction of or damage to a permanently restricted work of art by fire, flood, or vandalism; decline in value of endowment investments that by donor stipulation or law reduces endowment principal; or external mandate (by judicial or similar authority) to transfer endowment securities to another organization.

122. Reclassifications also may increase the amount of permanently restricted net assets or occasionally decrease it (paragraphs 114-116).

Change in Temporarily Restricted Net Assets

123. Change in temporarily restricted net assets of a not-for-profit organization during a period is the total of (a) contributions and other inflows during the period of assets whose use by the organization is limited by donor-imposed stipulations that either expire by passage of time or can be fulfilled and removed by actions of the organization pursuant to those stipulations, (b) other asset enhancements and diminishments during the period subject to the same kinds of stipulations, and (c) reclassifications to (or from) other classes of net assets during the period as a consequence of donor-imposed stipulations, their expiration by passage of time, or their fulfillment and removal by actions of the organization pursuant to those stipulations.

Characteristics of Change in Temporarily Restricted Net Assets

124. Most increases in temporarily restricted net assets of a not-for-profit organization are from its accepting contributions of assets that donors limit to use after a specified future time—for example, to be used for next year's operations or to be invested for 10 years before becoming available for operations—or for a specified purpose—for example, sponsoring a particular program activity or acquiring a particular building or piece of equipment. Temporary restrictions pertain to contributions with donor stipulations that expire or can be fulfilled and removed by using

assets as specified. And, in contrast to permanent restrictions, which pertain to assets that can provide economic benefits indefinitely and must be maintained in perpetuity by the receiving organization, temporary restrictions pertain to assets that by their nature are spent or used up in carrying out the receiving organization's activities or, if capable of providing economic benefits indefinitely, need not be retained after a stipulated time.

125. Donors' restrictions on the use of contributed assets may also extend to enhancements of those assets or to inflows that result from them. For example, if a donor stipulates that interest income derived from investment of contributed assets is limited to use after a specified date or for a specified operating purpose, the interest income is a restricted inflow that increases temporarily restricted net assets. Events that diminish temporarily restricted net assets, other than expirations and removals of restrictions (next paragraph), may also occur and are much like those that affect permanently restricted net assets (paragraph 121).

126. Reclassifications are the most common source of decreases in temporarily restricted net assets. Events resulting in the expiration or removal of temporary restrictions result in reclassifications from temporarily restricted net assets to unrestricted net assets.

Change in Unrestricted Net Assets

127. Change in unrestricted net assets of a not-for-profit organization during a period is the total change in net assets during the period less change in permanently restricted net assets and change in temporarily restricted net assets for the period. It is the change during the period in the part of net assets of a not-for-profit organization that is not limited by donor-imposed stipulations.

Characteristics of Change in Unrestricted Net Assets

128. Changes in unrestricted net assets include (a) revenues and gains that change unrestricted net assets, (b) expenses and losses that change unrestricted net assets, and (c) reclassifications from (or to) other classes of net assets as a consequence of donor-imposed stipulations, their expiration by passage of time, or their fulfillment and removal by actions of the organization pursuant to those stipulations.

129. Revenues and gains that increase unrestricted net assets of a not-for-profit organization have characteristics similar to those of revenues and gains of business enterprises. Those revenues and gains and the transactions that give rise to them are in many forms and are called by various names—for example, fees for services,

membership dues, unrestricted gifts or bequests, interest income, and gains on sales of marketable securities.

130. Expenses and losses that decrease unrestricted net assets of a not-for-profit organization have characteristics similar to those of expenses and losses of business enterprises. Except for diminishments of donor-restricted contributed assets that decrease either permanently restricted or temporarily restricted net assets, all types of transactions, other events, and circumstances that decrease net assets of an organization are expenses or losses that decrease unrestricted net assets (paragraphs 121 and 125). Those expenses and losses and the transactions that give rise to them are in many forms and are called by various names—for example, cost of services provided, cost of goods sold, salaries and wages, rent, supplies, interest expense, depreciation, flood damage, and gifts to other entities.[51]

131. Reclassifications, although not changing the amount of net assets, may change the amount of unrestricted net assets. Reclassifications more commonly increase rather than decrease unrestricted net assets. Events resulting in the expiration or removal of temporary restrictions result in reclassifications from temporarily restricted net assets that increase unrestricted net assets.

132. A not-for-profit organization's activities that fulfill stipulated conditions and result in removing donor-imposed purpose restrictions on use of donated assets also commonly result in expenses that decrease unrestricted net assets. Activities undertaken pursuant to a specified purpose remove the related restriction, often as the organization pays cash or incurs liabilities to vendors or employees to carry out a stipulated activity (paragraph 115). Those transactions result in expenses either when cash is paid or liabilities are incurred or as the organization uses up assets acquired in the transactions.

133. Information about whether a not-for-profit organization has maintained particular classes of net assets may be more significant than whether it has maintained net assets in the aggregate (paragraph 106). Change in unrestricted net assets for a period indicates whether an organization has maintained the part of its net assets that is fully available—that is, free of donor-imposed restrictions—to support the

---

[51]Information about the service efforts of a not-for-profit organization should focus on how the organization's resources are used in providing different programs or services (Concepts Statement 4, pars. 51-53). Accordingly, it may be useful to group and report separately the costs of providing various services or other activities for each significant program or supporting activity. However, whether expenses and unrestricted losses are reported by program or supporting activity, by kind (such as salaries and wages, rent, supplies, and other purchased services), or otherwise is a display matter beyond the scope of this Statement.

organization's services to beneficiaries in the next period. The combined change in unrestricted net assets and change in temporarily restricted net assets for a period indicates whether an organization has maintained the part of its net assets that is now or can someday be available—that is, free of permanent restrictions—to support its services to beneficiaries in future periods.

ACCRUAL ACCOUNTING AND RELATED CONCEPTS

134. Items that qualify under the definitions of elements of financial statements and that meet criteria for recognition and measurement (paragraph 23) are accounted for and included in financial statements by the use of accrual accounting procedures. Accrual accounting and related concepts are therefore significant not only for defining elements of financial statements but also for understanding and considering other aspects of the conceptual framework for financial accounting and reporting. Paragraphs 135-152 define or describe several significant financial accounting and reporting concepts that are used in this Statement and other concepts Statements.

Transactions, Events, and Circumstances

135. This Statement commonly uses *transactions and other events and circumstances affecting an entity* to describe the sources or causes of changes in assets, liabilities, and equity or net assets. An event is a happening of consequence to an entity. It may be an internal event that occurs within an entity, such as using raw materials or equipment in production, or it may be an external event that involves interaction between an entity and its environment, such as a transaction with another entity, a change in price of a good or service that an entity buys or sells, a flood or earthquake, or an improvement in technology by a competitor.[52] Many events are combinations. For example, acquiring services of employees or others involves exchange transactions, which are external events; using those services, often simultaneously with their acquisition, is part of production, which involves a series of internal events (paragraph 79, footnote 40). An event may be initiated by an entity, such as a purchase of merchandise or use of a building, or it may be partly or wholly beyond the control of an entity and its management, such as an interest rate change, an act of vandalism or theft, the imposition of taxes, or the expiration of a donor-imposed time restriction.

[52] In contrast, APB Statement No. 4, *Basic Concepts and Accounting Principles Underlying Financial Statements of Business Enterprises* (October 1970), paragraph 62, distinguishes external and internal events as follows: External events are "events that affect the enterprise and in which other entities participate," while internal events are "events in which only the enterprise participates." In that classification, so-called acts of God, such as floods and earthquakes, which are external events in this Statement, are internal events.

136. Circumstances are a condition or set of conditions that develop from an event or a series of events, which may occur almost imperceptibly and may converge in random or unexpected ways to create situations that might otherwise not have occurred and might not have been anticipated. To see the circumstance may be fairly easy, but to discern specifically when the event or events that caused it occurred may be difficult or impossible. For example, a debtor's going bankrupt or a thief's stealing gasoline may be an event, but a creditor's facing the situation that its debtor is bankrupt or a warehouse's facing the fact that its tank is empty may be a circumstance.

137. A transaction is a particular kind of external event, namely, an external event involving transfer of something of value (future economic benefit) between two (or more) entities. The transaction may be an exchange in which each participant both receives and sacrifices value, such as purchases or sales of goods or services; or the transaction may be a nonreciprocal transfer in which an entity incurs a liability or transfers an asset to another entity (or receives an asset or cancellation of a liability) without directly receiving (or giving) value in exchange. Nonreciprocal transfers contrast with exchanges (which are reciprocal transfers) and include, for example, investments by owners, distributions to owners, impositions of taxes, gifts, charitable or educational contributions given or received, and thefts.[53]

138. This Statement does not use the term *internal transaction* (which is essentially contradictory). Transferring materials to production processes, using plant and equipment whose wear and tear is represented by depreciation, and other events that happen within an entity are internal events, not internal transactions.

Accrual Accounting

139. Accrual accounting attempts to record the financial effects on an entity of transactions and other events and circumstances that have cash consequences for the entity in the periods in which those transactions, events, and circumstances occur rather than only in the periods in which cash is received or paid by the entity. Accrual accounting is concerned with an entity's acquiring of goods and services and using them to produce and distribute other goods or services. It is concerned with the process by which cash expended on resources and activities is returned as more (or perhaps less) cash to the entity, not just with the beginning and end of that process. It recognizes that the buying, producing, selling, distributing, and other operations of an entity during a period, as well as other events that affect entity performance,

[53]APB Statement 4, par. 62, and APB Opinion No. 29, *Accounting for Nonmonetary Transactions,* beginning with par. 5.

often do not coincide with the cash receipts and payments of the period (FASB Concepts Statement No. 1, *Objectives of Financial Reporting by Business Enterprises,* paragraph 44, and FASB Concepts Statement No. 4, *Objectives of Financial Reporting by Nonbusiness Organizations,* paragraph 50).

140. Thus, accrual accounting is based not only on cash transactions but also on credit transactions, barter exchanges, nonreciprocal transfers of goods or services, changes in prices, changes in form of assets or liabilities, and other transactions, events, and circumstances that have cash consequences for an entity but involve no concurrent cash movement. By accounting for noncash assets, liabilities, revenues, expenses, gains, and losses, accrual accounting links an entity's operations and other transactions, events, and circumstances that affect it with its cash receipts and outlays. Accrual accounting thus provides information about an entity's assets and liabilities and changes in them that cannot be obtained by accounting for only cash receipts and outlays.

Accrual and Deferral (Including Allocation and Amortization)

141. Accrual accounting attempts to recognize noncash events and circumstances as they occur and involves not only accruals but also deferrals, including allocations and amortizations. Accrual is concerned with expected future cash receipts and payments: it is the accounting process of recognizing assets or liabilities and the related liabilities, assets, revenues, expenses, gains, or losses for amounts expected to be received or paid, usually in cash, in the future. Deferral is concerned with past cash receipts and payments—with prepayments received (often described as collected in advance) or paid: it is the accounting process of recognizing a liability resulting from a current cash receipt (or the equivalent) or an asset resulting from a current cash payment (or the equivalent) with deferred recognition of revenues, expenses, gains, or losses. Their recognition is deferred until the obligation underlying the liability is partly or wholly satisfied[54] or until the future economic benefit underlying the asset is partly or wholly used or lost. Common examples of accruals include purchases and sales of goods or services on account, interest, rent (not yet paid), wages and salaries, taxes, and decreases and increases in marketable securities accounted for at

[54]For example, paragraph 79, footnote 40, explains how liabilities that result from customers' cash advances are later satisfied by delivery of goods or services.

lower of cost and market. Common examples of deferrals include prepaid insurance and unearned subscriptions.[55]

142. Allocation is the accounting process of assigning or distributing an amount according to a plan or a formula. It is broader than and includes amortization, which is the accounting process of reducing an amount by periodic payments or write-downs. Specifically, amortization is the process of reducing a liability recorded as a result of a cash receipt by recognizing revenues or reducing an asset recorded as a result of a cash payment by recognizing expenses or costs of production. That is, amortization is an allocation process for accounting for prepayments and deferrals. Common examples of allocations include assigning manufacturing costs to production departments or cost centers and thence to units of product to determine "product cost," apportioning the cost of a "basket purchase" to the individual assets acquired on the basis of their relative market values, and spreading the cost of an insurance policy or a building to two or more accounting periods. Common examples of amortizations include recognizing expenses for depreciation, depletion, and insurance and recognizing earned subscription revenues.

Realization and Recognition

143. Realization in the most precise sense means the process of converting noncash resources and rights into money and is most precisely used in accounting and financial reporting to refer to sales of assets for cash or claims to cash. The related terms *realized* and *unrealized* therefore identify revenues or gains or losses on assets sold and unsold, respectively. Those are the meanings of realization and related terms in the Board's conceptual framework. Recognition is the process of formally recording or incorporating an item in the financial statements of an entity. Thus, an asset, liability, revenue, expense, gain, or loss may be recognized (recorded) or unrecognized (unrecorded). *Realization* and *recognition* are not used as synonyms, as they sometimes are in accounting and financial literature.[56]

---

[55]The expressions *accrued depreciation* or *to accrue depreciation* are sometimes used, but depreciation in present practice is technically the result of allocation or amortization, which are deferral, not accrual, techniques. Conversely, the expressions *unamortized debt discount or premium* and *to amortize debt discount or premium* are sometimes used, but accounting for debt securities issued (or acquired as an investment) at a discount or premium by the "interest" method is technically the result of accrual, not deferral or amortization, techniques (pars. 235-239 of this Statement). The "interest" method is described in APB Opinion No. 12, *Omnibus Opinion—1967,* paragraphs 16 and 17, and APB Opinion No. 21, *Interest on Receivables and Payables,* paragraphs 15 and 16.

[56]Concepts Statement 5 uses the term *recognition* in the same way as does this Statement and distinguishes it from *realization*. It also uses *realized* in the same sense and defines the related concept *realizable* (par. 83 and footnote 50).

Recognition, Matching, and Allocation

144. Accrual accounting recognizes numerous noncash assets, liabilities, and transactions and other events that affect them (paragraphs 139-141). Thus, a major difference between accrual accounting and accounting based on cash receipts and outlays is timing of recognition of revenues, expenses, gains, and losses. Investments by an entity in goods and services for its operations or other activities commonly do not all occur in the same period as revenues or other proceeds from selling the resulting products or providing the resulting services. Several periods may elapse between the time cash is invested in raw materials or plant, for example, and the time cash is returned by collecting the sales price of products from customers. A report showing cash receipts and cash outlays of an enterprise for a short period cannot indicate how much of the cash received is return *of* investment and how much is return *on* investment and thus cannot indicate whether or to what extent an enterprise is successful or unsuccessful. Similarly, goods or services that a not-for-profit organization provides gratis to beneficiaries commonly result from using goods or services acquired with cash received and spent in earlier periods. A report showing cash receipts and outlays of the organization for a short period cannot tell much about the relation of goods or services provided to the resources used to provide them and thus cannot indicate whether or to what extent an organization is successful or unsuccessful in carrying out its service objectives. Cash receipts in a particular period may largely reflect the effects of activities of a business enterprise or a not-for-profit organization in earlier periods, while many of the cash outlays may relate to its activities and efforts expected in future periods.

145. Accrual accounting uses accrual, deferral, and allocation procedures whose goal is to relate revenues, expenses, gains, and losses to periods to reflect an entity's performance during a period instead of merely listing its cash receipts and outlays. Thus, recognition of revenues, expenses, gains, and losses and the related increments or decrements in assets and liabilities—including matching of costs and revenues, allocation, and amortization—is the essence of using accrual accounting to measure performance of entities. The goal of accrual accounting is to account in the periods in which they occur for the effects on an entity of transactions and other events and circumstances, to the extent that those financial effects are recognizable and measurable.

146. Matching of costs and revenues is simultaneous or combined recognition of the revenues and expenses that result directly and jointly from the same transactions or other events. In most entities, some transactions or events result simultaneously in both a revenue and one or more expenses. The revenue and expense(s) are directly related to each other and require recognition at the same time. In present practice,

for example, a sale of product or merchandise involves both revenue (sales revenue) for receipt of cash or a receivable and expense (cost of goods sold) for sacrifice of the product or merchandise sold to customers. Other examples of expenses that may result from the same transaction and be directly related to sales revenues are transportation to customers, sales commissions, and perhaps certain other selling costs.

147. Many expenses, however, are not related directly to particular revenues but can be related to a period on the basis of transactions or events occurring in that period or by allocation. Recognition of those expenses is largely independent of recognition of particular revenues, but they are deducted from particular revenues by being recognized in the same period.[57]

148. Some costs that cannot be directly related to particular revenues are incurred to obtain benefits that are exhausted in the period in which the costs are incurred. For example, salesmen's monthly salaries and electricity used to light an office building usually fit that description and are usually recognized as expenses in the period in which they are incurred. Other costs are also recognized as expenses in the period in which they are incurred because the period to which they otherwise relate is indeterminable or not worth the effort to determine.

149. However, many assets yield their benefits to an entity over several periods, for example, prepaid insurance, buildings, and various kinds of equipment. Expenses resulting from their use are normally allocated to the periods of their estimated useful lives (the periods over which they are expected to provide benefits) by a "systematic and rational" allocation procedure, for example, by recognizing depreciation or other amortization. Although the purpose of expense allocation is the same as that of other expense recognition—to reflect the using up of assets as a result of transactions or other events or circumstances affecting an entity—allocation is applied if causal relations are generally, but not specifically, identified. For example, wear and tear from use is known to be a major cause of the expense called depreciation, but the amount of depreciation caused by wear and tear in a period normally cannot be measured. Those expenses are not related directly to either specific revenues or particular periods. Usually no traceable relationship exists, and they are recognized by allocating costs to periods in which assets are expected to be used and are related only indirectly to the revenues that are recognized in the same period.

---

[57]APB Statement 4 (pars. 154-161) describes "three pervasive expense recognition principles": associating cause and effect, systematic and rational allocation, and immediate recognition. Paragraphs 146-149 of this Statement describe generally the same three bases for recognizing expenses but not in the same order.

Guidance for recognition of expenses and losses, set forth for business enterprises in Concepts Statement 5 (pars. 85-87), is based in large part on the considerations in paragraphs 146-149.

150. Some revenues and gains result from nonreciprocal transfers to an entity from other entities and thus relate to the period in which cash or other assets are received by the entity, or in which its liabilities are reduced. Recognition of those nonreciprocal transfers seldom involves allocation or matching procedures. For example, not-for-profit organizations commonly receive donations in cash, and timing of cash receipts is normally readily verifiable. Similarly, receipts of other assets, including receivables (promises by another entity to pay cash or transfer other assets), or of reductions or remissions of liabilities are also usually readily identifiable with the periods in which they occur, and there is nothing to allocate to other periods.

151. Nonreciprocal transfers to an entity rarely result directly and jointly from the same transactions as expenses. Most contributions and expenses are much more closely related to time periods than to each other. For example, the receipt by a not-for-profit organization of contributed assets that involve donor stipulations restricting their use to particular types of services may be a cause of the expenses incurred in providing those services; however, the receipt of contributed assets—revenues or gains—and the subsequent incurring of liabilities or reduction of assets in providing services—expenses—are separate events recognized in the periods in which they occur.

152. Removal of restrictions on temporarily restricted net assets of a not-for-profit organization is an event that often occurs at the same time as the incurring of particular expenses. The discussion of donor-imposed restrictions in this Statement contemplates that removals of restrictions on net assets—reclassifications—may be shown in financial statements in the same period(s) as the activities that remove the restrictions.

This Statement was adopted by the unanimous vote of the seven members of the Financial Accounting Standards Board:

Donald J. Kirk, *Chairman*
Frank E. Block
Victor H. Brown
Raymond C. Lauver
David Mosso
Robert T. Sprouse
Arthur R. Wyatt

Appendix A

BACKGROUND INFORMATION

153. The need for a conceptual framework for financial accounting and reporting, beginning with consideration of the objectives of financial reporting, is generally recognized. The Accounting Principles Board issued APB Statement No. 4, *Basic Concepts and Accounting Principles Underlying Financial Statements of Business Enterprises,* in 1970. When the Financial Accounting Standards Board came into existence, the Study Group on the Objectives of Financial Statements was at work, and its report, *Objectives of Financial Statements,* was published in October 1973 by the American Institute of Certified Public Accountants. Although that report focused primarily on business enterprises, it also included a brief discussion of "objectives of financial statements for governmental and not-for-profit organizations."

154. The Financial Accounting Standards Board issued a Discussion Memorandum, *Conceptual Framework for Accounting and Reporting: Consideration of the Report of the Study Group on the Objectives of Financial Statements,* dated June 6, 1974, and held a public hearing on September 23 and 24, 1974 on the objectives of financial statements.

155. The Board first concentrated on concepts of financial accounting and reporting by business enterprises and issued three documents on December 2, 1976: *Tentative Conclusions on Objectives of Financial Statements of Business Enterprises,* FASB Discussion Memorandum, *Conceptual Framework for Financial Accounting and Reporting: Elements of Financial Statements and Their Measurement,* and *Scope and Implications of the Conceptual Framework Project.* The same task force, with only one membership change, provided counsel in preparing both Discussion Memorandums. Eleven persons from academe, the financial community, industry, and public accounting served on the task force while the Discussion Memorandums were written.

156. The Board held public hearings (a) August 1 and 2, 1977 on the *Tentative Conclusions on Objectives of Financial Statements of Business Enterprises* and on Chapters 1-5 of the Discussion Memorandum concerning definitions of the elements of financial statements and (b) January 16-18, 1978 on the remaining chapters of the Discussion Memorandum concerning capital maintenance or cost recovery, qualities of useful financial information (qualitative characteristics), and measurement of the elements of financial statements.

157. The Board received 283 written communications on the subject of the August 1977 hearing, of which 221 commented on the elements, and 27 parties presented their views orally and answered Board members' questions at the hearing. The Board issued an Exposure Draft of a proposed Statement of Financial Accounting Concepts, *Objectives of Financial Reporting and Elements of Financial Statements of Business Enterprises,* dated December 29, 1977, and received 135 letters of comment.

158. During 1978, the Board divided the subject matter of the Exposure Draft. One part became FASB Concepts Statement No. 1, *Objectives of Financial Reporting by Business Enterprises,* which was issued in November 1978. A second part became the basis for the revised Exposure Draft, *Elements of Financial Statements of Business Enterprises,* issued December 28, 1979, on which the Board received 92 letters of comment. That Exposure Draft led in December 1980 to FASB Concepts Statement No. 3, *Elements of Financial Statements of Business Enterprises,* following FASB Concepts Statement No. 2, *Qualitative Characteristics of Accounting Information,* which was issued in May 1980.

159. The Board's work on concepts of financial accounting and reporting by not-for-profit organizations began in August 1977. Professor Robert N. Anthony of the Harvard Business School prepared an FASB Research Report, *Financial Accounting in Nonbusiness Organizations,* published in May 1978, which was followed by a related Discussion Memorandum and an Exposure Draft. FASB Concepts Statement No. 4, *Objectives of Financial Reporting by Nonbusiness Organizations,* was issued in December 1980.

160. The four concepts Statements described are part of a single conceptual framework for financial accounting and reporting by all entities. The Board noted in Concepts Statements 2 and 3 its expectation that the qualitative characteristics and definitions of elements of financial statements should apply to both business enterprises and not-for-profit organizations and its intent to solicit views on that matter.

161. The Board issued an Exposure Draft, *Proposed Amendments to FASB Concepts Statements 2 and 3 to Apply Them to Nonbusiness Organizations,* on July 7, 1983. In considering similarities and differences of business enterprises and not-for-profit organizations that may affect qualitative characteristics of accounting information and definitions of elements of financial statements, the Board had the counsel of a task force consisting of 32 members knowledgeable about not-for-profit organizations and their financial reporting. The Board received 74 letters of com-

ment on the Exposure Draft, and 20 parties presented their views orally and answered Board members' questions at public hearings held on November 14 and 15, 1983.

162. That Exposure Draft was in two parts, and the Board made decisions on both. First, it reaffirmed the conclusion of the Exposure Draft that the qualitative characteristics of accounting information set forth in Concepts Statement 2 (relevance, reliability, comparability, and related qualities) apply to not-for-profit organizations as well as to business enterprises. Second, based on suggestions of respondents to the Exposure Draft and on its own further consideration of similarities and differences between business enterprises and not-for-profit organizations, the Board revised the proposed amendments to Concepts Statement 3 and issued a revised Exposure Draft, *Elements of Financial Statements,* on September 18, 1985. The following describe major changes from the 1983 Exposure Draft and identify major changes suggested but not made.

- This Statement does not define as elements of financial statements two that the 1983 Exposure Draft proposed: change in net assets (described as a concept equivalent to comprehensive income of business enterprises) and contributions. Instead, by identifying three broad classes of net assets of not-for-profit organizations—permanently restricted, temporarily restricted, and unrestricted net assets—and changes in those classes, it emphasizes the importance of donor-imposed restrictions on resources contributed to not-for-profit organizations and changes in both the amount and nature of net assets based on the presence or absence of donor restrictions. Numerous respondents, both those interested in not-for-profit organizations and those interested in business enterprises, questioned whether defining contributions separately from revenues and gains, though clearly possible, was either necessary or useful. This Statement notes that inflows of assets in nonreciprocal transfers from nonowners (contributions), like other transactions that increase net assets, result either in revenues (from ongoing major operating activities) or in gains (from peripheral or incidental transactions). It also notes that whether a particular contribution results in a revenue or a gain is often less important than whether it increases permanently restricted, temporarily restricted, or unrestricted net assets.
- A separate diagram now shows interrelationships between sources of changes in net assets of not-for-profit organizations (revenues, expenses, gains, and losses), reclassifications between classes of net assets, and changes in permanently restricted, temporarily restricted, and unrestricted net assets.
- This Statement reaffirms the conclusion in the 1983 Exposure Draft that under the definitions in Concepts Statement 3 (and this Statement) contributions or donations, whether or not subject to donor-imposed restrictions, generally increase net

assets (equity) rather than liabilities. Several respondents had argued that purpose-restricted, and perhaps time-restricted, contributions result in (or should be considered to result in) liabilities.

- This Statement reaffirms the conclusion in the 1983 Exposure Draft that how an asset was acquired and whether and how it will be replaced are not germane to whether or not the entity's using it up results in an expense. Some respondents to the Exposure Draft had suggested that depreciation often should not be an expense (or cost) of a not-for-profit organization, in part because the related assets were, and their replacements are expected to be, funded by contributions or special assessments.
- Some respondents to the 1983 Exposure Draft had suggested that depreciation based on historical cost is not the most relevant way of measuring a not-for-profit organization's cost of using up of long-lived assets. However, how depreciation expense should be measured is a measurement issue beyond the scope of this Statement.
- This Statement takes note of Board decisions on matters that were still under consideration as part of other projects at the time Concepts Statement 3 and the 1983 Exposure Draft were issued, particularly the recognition, measurement, and display matters for business enterprises that are the subjects of Concepts Statement 5.
- Although financial statement display is beyond the scope of this Statement, the Board has attempted to respond at various points to requests by a number of respondents for more explanation of the significance of the proposed definitions for reporting by not-for-profit organizations.

163. The Board received 60 letters of comment on the revised Exposure Draft. Some respondents reiterated the arguments referred to in paragraph 162, while others expressed new concerns. The Board has considered those comments. The following describe and identify changes made to the revised Exposure Draft and identify changes suggested by respondents but not made.

- This Statement reaffirms the conclusion that financial reporting by not-for-profit organizations requires a concept of maintenance of net assets. Some respondents suggested that depreciation is often irrelevant to not-for-profit organizations because the related expenses need not be "matched" with revenues to measure income, which in their view is not important for not-for-profit organizations. However, this Statement describes depreciation as a cost of using assets, not as a technique for "matching" expenses with revenues.
- This Statement reaffirms the conclusion in the Exposure Drafts that most restrictions do not create obligations that qualify as liabilities. The discussion has been expanded (paragraphs 56-58) to clarify the point.

- Some respondents suggested that the revisions to the characteristics of assets and liabilities proposed in the revised Exposure Draft had changed the related definitions and expressed concern about the intent of the revisions. The troublesome aspects of the revisions have been reworded to alleviate those concerns. The revisions to the last sentences in paragraph 26 and in paragraph 36 are meant to avoid circularity in the use of the term *probable* in explaining probable future benefit and sacrifice, and clarify the intended point, that there are ways other than legal enforceability by which an entity may obtain an existing benefit or may be unable to avoid paying an existing obligation.

Appendix B

CHARACTERISTICS OF ASSETS, LIABILITIES, AND EQUITY OR NET ASSETS AND OF CHANGES IN THEM

Purpose and Summary of Appendix

164. This appendix elaborates on the descriptions of the essential characteristics that items must have to qualify under the definitions of elements of financial statements in this Statement. It includes some discussion and illustrations of how to assess the characteristics of items that are potential candidates for formal inclusion in financial statements and in general how to apply the definitions.

165. The remainder of this section briefly illustrates the relationship of the definitions to recognition, measurement, and display issues and the function and some consequences of the definitions. It is followed by a discussion of the characteristics of assets, liabilities, equity of business enterprises, comprehensive income of business enterprises and its components, and net assets and changes in the classes of net assets of not-for-profit organizations.[58] The appendix concludes with a series of examples that are intended to illustrate the meanings of the definitions and the essential characteristics that form them.

166. This Statement emphasizes that the definitions of elements are not intended to answer recognition, measurement, or display questions.[59] The definitions are, however, a significant first step in determining the content of financial statements. They screen out items that lack one or more characteristics of assets, liabilities, revenues, expenses, or other elements of financial statements (paragraphs 22 and 23).

167. Thus, unless an item qualifies as an asset of an entity under the definition in paragraph 25, for example, questions do not arise about whether to recognize it as an asset of the entity, which of its attributes to measure, or how to display it as an asset in the financial statements of the entity. Although items that fail to qualify

[58]As noted in paragraph 50, footnote 26, this Statement often uses *equity* and *net assets* interchangeably but generally applies *equity* to business enterprises and *net assets* to not-for-profit organizations.

[59]Those questions are a subject of FASB Concepts Statement No. 5, *Recognition and Measurement in Financial Statements of Business Enterprises*. Recognition, measurement, and display questions for not-for-profit organizations, and more detailed development of those concepts for all entities, may be the subject of further concepts or standards Statements.

under the definitions of elements during a period do not raise recognition issues, they may nevertheless raise issues about whether and, if so, how and at what amounts they should be disclosed. For example, contingencies that have not yet, and may never, become assets or liabilities may need to be estimated and disclosed. Thus, the first question about each potential candidate for formal inclusion in financial statements is whether it qualifies under one of the definitions of elements; recognition, measurement, and display questions follow.

168. An item does not qualify as an asset or liability of an entity if it lacks one or more essential characteristics. Thus, for example, an item does not qualify as an asset of an entity under the definition in paragraph 25 if (a) the item involves no future economic benefit, (b) the item involves future economic benefit, but the entity cannot obtain it, or (c) the item involves future economic benefit that the entity may in the future obtain, but the events or circumstances that give the entity access to and control of the benefit have not yet occurred (or the entity in the past had the ability to obtain or control the future benefit, but events or circumstances have occurred to remove that ability). Similarly, an item does not qualify as a liability of an entity under the definition in paragraph 35 if (a) the item entails no future sacrifice of assets, (b) the item entails future sacrifice of assets, but the entity is not obligated to make the sacrifice, or (c) the item involves a future sacrifice of assets that the entity will be obligated to make, but the events or circumstances that obligate the entity have not yet occurred (or the entity in the past was obligated to make the future sacrifice, but events or circumstances have occurred to remove that obligation).

169. This appendix contains numerous examples of items that commonly qualify as assets or liabilities of an entity under the definitions in this Statement. It also includes several illustrations showing that items that may not qualify as assets may readily qualify as reductions (valuation accounts) of liabilities and that items that may not qualify as liabilities may readily qualify as reductions (valuation accounts) of assets. The following examples illustrate items that do not qualify as assets or liabilities of an entity under the definitions: (a) "dry holes" drilled by an exploration enterprise that has not yet discovered hydrocarbon, mineral, or other reserves are not assets (except to the extent of salvageable materials or equipment) because they provide no access to probable future economic benefit;[60] (b) estimated possible casualty losses from future floods or fires are not liabilities or impairments of assets because an event incurring a liability or impairing an asset has not occurred; (c) inventories or depreciable assets required (but not yet ordered) to replace similar items that are being or have been used up are not assets because no future economic benefits have been acquired, and the requirement to sacrifice assets to obtain them is not a liability

[60]Paragraph 247 notes an aspect of the cost of some "dry holes" in different circumstances.

because the entity is not yet obligated to sacrifice assets in the future; (d) deferrals relating to assets no longer held or liabilities no longer owed—such as a deferred loss on selling an asset for cash or a deferred gain on settling a liability for cash—are not assets or liabilities because they involve no future economic benefit or no required future sacrifice of assets; (e) receipts of grants of cash or other assets with no strings attached do not create liabilities because the entity is not required to sacrifice assets in the future; (f) other receipts of cash in return for which an entity is in no way required to pay cash, transfer other assets, or provide services do not create liabilities because the entity is not presently obligated to sacrifice assets in the future;[61] (g) "know-how" of NASA or other governmental agencies placed in the public domain is not an asset of an entity unless the entity spends funds or otherwise acts to secure benefits not freely available to everyone; (h) estimated losses for two years from a decision to start up a new product line next year are not liabilities because the entity is not legally, equitably, or constructively obligated to sacrifice assets in the future; and (i) "stock dividends payable" are not liabilities because they do not involve an obligation to make future sacrifices of assets.

170. The Board expects most assets and liabilities in present practice to continue to qualify as assets or liabilities under the definitions in this Statement. That expectation is supported by the examples in the preceding paragraph as well as by those throughout this appendix. The Board emphasizes that the definitions in this Statement neither require nor presage upheavals in present practice, although they may in due time lead to some evolutionary changes in practice or at least in the ways certain items are viewed. They should be especially helpful, however, in understanding the content of financial statements and in analyzing and resolving new financial accounting issues as they arise.

Characteristics of Assets

171. Paragraph 25 defines assets as "probable future economic benefits obtained or controlled by a particular entity as a result of past transactions or events." Paragraphs 26-34 amplify that definition. The following discussion further amplifies it and illustrates its meaning under three headings that correspond to the three essential

[61]Examples (e) and (f) describe receipts of assets in nonreciprocal transfers to an entity, for example, contributions. Although restrictions may place limits on assets received, most donor-imposed restrictions do not create obligations that qualify as liabilities of the recipient. Moreover, the transaction necessarily is an exchange rather than a nonreciprocal transfer if an entity receives assets and incurs liabilities in the same transaction. Although restrictions on the use of donated assets may lead to the future use of cash (or other assets) to provide stipulated services, that future use of cash is not a required "sacrifice" of assets. Rather, it generally is a future exchange of assets to purchase goods or services from suppliers or employees (pars. 56-58, 137, and 150 and 151).

characteristics of assets described in paragraph 26: future economic benefits, control by a particular entity, and occurrence of a past transaction or event.

Future Economic Benefits

172. Future economic benefit is the essence of an asset (paragraphs 27-31). An asset has the capacity to serve the entity by being exchanged for something else of value to the entity, by being used to produce something of value to the entity, or by being used to settle its liabilities.

173. The most obvious evidence of future economic benefit is a market price. Anything that is commonly bought and sold has future economic benefit, including the individual items that a buyer obtains and is willing to pay for in a "basket purchase" of several items or in a business combination. Similarly, anything that creditors or others commonly accept in settlement of liabilities has future economic benefit, and anything that is commonly used to produce goods or services, whether tangible or intangible and whether or not it has a market price or is otherwise exchangeable, also has future economic benefit.[62] Incurrence of costs may be significant evidence of acquisition or enhancement of future economic benefits (paragraphs 178-180).

174. To assess whether a particular item constitutes an asset of a particular entity at a particular time requires at least two considerations in addition to the general kinds of evidence just described: (a) whether the item obtained by the entity embodied future economic benefit in the first place and (b) whether all or any of the future economic benefit to the entity remains at the time of assessment.

175. Uncertainty about business and economic outcomes often clouds whether or not particular items that might be assets have the capacity to provide future economic benefits to the entity (paragraphs 44-48), sometimes precluding their recognition as assets. The kinds of items that may be recognized as expenses or losses rather than as assets because of uncertainty are some in which management's intent in taking certain steps or initiating certain transactions is clearly to acquire or enhance future economic benefits available to the entity. For example, business enterprises engage in research and development activities, advertise, develop markets, open new branches or divisions, and the like, and spend significant funds to do so. The uncertainty is not about the intent to increase future economic benefits but about whether and, if so, to what extent they succeeded in doing so. Certain

[62]Absence of a market price or exchangeability of an asset may create measurement and recognition problems, but it in no way negates future economic benefit that can be obtained by use as well as by exchange.

expenditures for research and development, advertising, training, start-up and preoperating activities, development stage enterprises, relocation or rearrangement, and goodwill are examples of the kinds of items for which assessments of future economic benefits may be especially uncertain.

176. Since many of the activities described in the preceding paragraph involve incurring costs, the distinction between the items just listed and assets, such as prepaid insurance and prepaid rent, that are described in paragraph 181 is often difficult to draw because the two groups tend to shade into each other. Indeed, the distinction is not based on the definition of assets in paragraph 25 but rather on the practical considerations of coping with the effects of uncertainty. If research or development activities or advertising results in an entity's acquiring or increasing future economic benefit, that future economic benefit qualifies as an asset as much as do the future benefits from prepaid insurance or prepaid rent. The practical problem is whether future economic benefit is actually present and, if so, how much—an assessment that is greatly complicated by the feature that the benefits may be realized far in the future, if at all.

177. Most assets presently included in financial statements qualify as assets under the definition in paragraph 25 because they have future economic benefits. Cash, accounts and notes receivable, interest and dividends receivable, investments in securities of other entities, and similar items so obviously qualify as assets that they need no further comment except to note that uncollectible receivables do not qualify as assets. Inventories of raw materials, supplies, partially completed product, finished goods, and merchandise likewise obviously fit the definition as do productive resources, such as property, plant, equipment, tools, furnishings, leasehold improvements, natural resource deposits, and patents. They are mentioned separately from cash, receivables, and investments only because they have commonly been described in accounting literature as "deferred costs" or occasionally as "deferred charges" to revenues. The point requires noting because comments received on the Discussion Memorandum and earlier Exposure Drafts have manifested some misunderstanding: some respondents apparently concluded that all or most deferrals of costs were precluded by the definition of assets.

Assets and Costs

178. An entity commonly incurs costs to obtain future economic benefits, either to acquire assets from other entities in exchange transactions or to add value through operations to assets it already has (paragraph 32). An entity acquires assets in exchanges with other entities by sacrificing other assets or by incurring liabilities to transfer assets to the other entity later. An entity also incurs a cost when it uses an

asset in producing or distributing goods or services—future economic benefits are partially or wholly used up to produce or acquire other assets, for example, product in process, completed product, or receivables from customers.

179. Although an entity normally incurs costs to acquire or use assets, costs incurred are not themselves assets. The essence of an asset is its future economic benefit rather than whether or not it was acquired at a cost. However, costs may be significant to applying the definition of assets in at least two ways: as evidence of acquisition of an asset or as a measure of an attribute of an asset.

180. First, since an entity commonly obtains assets by incurring costs, incurrence of a cost may be evidence that an entity has acquired one or more assets, but it is not conclusive evidence. Costs may be incurred without receiving services or enhanced future economic benefits. Or, entities may obtain assets without incurring costs—for example, from investment in kind by owners or contributions of securities or buildings by donors. The ultimate evidence of the existence of assets is the future economic benefit, not the costs incurred.

181. Second, cost may measure an attribute of future economic benefit. Costs of assets such as inventories, plant, equipment, and patents are examples of costs or unamortized costs of future benefits from present practice, as are prepayments such as prepaid insurance and prepaid rent, which are unamortized costs of rights to receive a service or use a resource.

182. Losses have no future economic benefits and cannot qualify as assets under the definition in paragraph 25. Stated conversely, items that have future economic benefits are not in concept losses, although practical considerations may sometimes make it impossible to distinguish them from expenses or losses.

Control by a Particular Entity

183. Paragraph 25 defines assets in relation to specific entities. Every asset is an asset of some entity; moreover, no asset can simultaneously be an asset of more than one entity, although a particular physical thing or other agent that provides future economic benefit may provide separate benefits to two or more entities at the same time (paragraph 185). To have an asset, an entity must control future economic benefit to the extent that it can benefit from the asset and generally can deny or regulate access to that benefit by others, for example, by permitting access only at a price.

184. Thus, an asset of an entity is the future economic benefit that the entity can control and thus can, within limits set by the nature of the benefit or the entity's right

to it, use as it pleases. The entity having an asset is the one that can exchange it, use it to produce goods or services, exact a price for others' use of it, use it to settle liabilities, hold it, or perhaps distribute it to owners.

185. The definition of assets focuses primarily on the future economic benefit to which an entity has access and only secondarily on the physical things and other agents that provide future economic benefits. Many physical things and other agents are in effect bundles of future economic benefits that can be unbundled in various ways, and two or more entities may have different future economic benefits from the same agent at the same time or the same continuing future economic benefit at different times. For example, two or more entities may have undivided interests in a parcel of land. Each has a right to future economic benefit that may qualify as an asset under the definition in paragraph 25, even though the right of each is subject at least to some extent to the rights of the other(s). Or, one entity may have the right to the interest from an investment, while another has the right to the principal. Leases are common examples of agreements that unbundle the future economic benefits of a single property to give a lessee a right to possess and use the property and give a lessor a right to receive rents and a right to the residual value. Moreover, a mortgagee may also have a right to receive periodic payments that is secured by the leased property.

Control and Legal Rights

186. As some of the preceding discussion indicates, an entity's ability to obtain the future economic benefit of an asset commonly stems from legal rights. Those rights share the common feature of conferring ability to obtain future economic benefits, but they vary in other ways. For example, ownership, a contract to use, and a contract to receive cash confer different rights.

187. Although the ability of an entity to obtain the future economic benefit of an asset and to deny or control access to it by others rests generally on a foundation of legal rights, legal enforceability of a right is not an indispensable prerequisite for an entity to have an asset if the entity has the ability to obtain and control the benefit in some other way. For example, exclusive access to future economic benefit may be maintained by keeping secret a formula or process.

Noncontrolled Benefits

188. Some future economic benefits cannot meet the test of control. For example, public highways and stations and equipment of municipal fire and police departments may qualify as assets of governmental units but they cannot qualify as assets

of other entities under the definition in paragraph 25. Similarly, general access to things such as clean air or water resulting from environmental laws or requirements cannot qualify as assets of individual entities, even if the entities have incurred costs to help clean up the environment.

189. Those examples should be distinguished from similar future economic benefits that an individual entity can control and thus are its assets. For example, an entity can control benefits from a private road on its own property, clean air it provides in a laboratory or water it provides in a storage tank, or a private fire department or a private security force, and the related equipment probably qualifies as an asset even if it has no other use to the entity and cannot be sold except as scrap. Equipment used to help provide clean air or water in the general environment may provide future economic benefit to the user, even if it has no other use and cannot be sold except as scrap. Moreover, a specific right to use a public highway from which the licensee might otherwise be excluded—for example, a license to operate a truck on the highways within a state—may have future economic benefit to the licensee even though it does not keep everyone else off the highway. Similarly, riparian rights and airspace rights may confer future economic benefits on their holders even though they do not keep others' boats off the river or prevent airplanes from flying overhead.

Occurrence of a Past Transaction or Event

190. The definition of assets in paragraph 25 distinguishes between the future economic benefits of present and future assets of an entity. Only present abilities to obtain future economic benefits are assets under the definition, and they become assets of particular entities as a result of transactions or other events or circumstances affecting the entity. For example, the future economic benefits of a particular building can be an asset of a particular entity only after a transaction or other event—such as a purchase or a lease agreement—has occurred that gives it access to and control of those benefits. Similarly, although an oil deposit may have existed in a certain place for millions of years, it can be an asset of a particular entity only after the entity either has discovered it in circumstances that permit the entity to exploit it or has acquired the rights to exploit it from whoever had them.

191. Since the transaction or event giving rise to the entity's right to the future economic benefit must already have occurred, the definition excludes from assets items that may in the future become an entity's assets but have not yet become its assets. An entity has no asset for a particular future economic benefit if the transactions or events that give it access to and control of the benefit are yet in the future. The corollary is that an entity still has an asset if the transactions or events that use

up or destroy a particular future economic benefit or remove the entity's access to and control of it are yet in the future. For example, an entity does not acquire an asset merely by budgeting the purchase of a machine and does not lose an asset from fire until a fire destroys or damages some asset.

Characteristics of Liabilities

192. Paragraph 35 defines liabilities as "probable future sacrifices of economic benefits arising from present obligations of a particular entity to transfer assets or provide services to other entities in the future as a result of past transactions or events." Paragraphs 36-43 amplify that definition. The following discussion further amplifies that definition and illustrates its meaning under three headings that correspond to the three essential characteristics of liabilities described in paragraph 36: required future sacrifice of assets, obligation of a particular entity, and occurrence of a past transaction or event.

Required Future Sacrifice of Assets

193. The essence of a liability is a duty or requirement to sacrifice assets in the future. A liability requires an entity to transfer assets, provide services, or otherwise expend assets to satisfy a responsibility to one or more other entities that it has incurred or that has been imposed on it.

194. The most obvious evidence of liabilities are contracts or other agreements resulting from exchange transactions and laws or governmental regulations that require expending assets to comply. Although receipt of proceeds is not conclusive evidence that a liability has been incurred (paragraph 198), receipt of cash, other assets, or services without an accompanying cash payment is often evidence that a liability has been incurred. Evidence of liabilities may also be found in declarations of dividends, lawsuits filed or in process, infractions that may bring fines or penalties, and the like. Reductions in prices paid or offered to acquire an enterprise or a significant part of it to allow for items that a buyer must assume that require future transfers of assets or providing of services also may indicate the kinds of items that qualify as liabilities. Moreover, liabilities that are not payable on demand normally have specified or determinable maturity dates or specified events whose occurrence requires that they must be settled, and absence of a specified maturity date or event may cast doubt that a liability exists.

195. To assess whether a particular item constitutes a liability of a particular entity at a particular time requires at least two considerations in addition to the general kinds of evidence just described: (a) whether the entity incurred a responsibility to sacrifice

assets in the future and (b) whether all or any of the responsibility remains unsatisfied at the time of assessment.

196. Most liabilities presently included in financial statements qualify as liabilities under the definition in paragraph 35 because they require an entity to sacrifice assets in the future. Thus, accounts and notes payable, wages and salaries payable, long-term debt, interest and dividends payable, and similar requirements to pay cash so obviously qualify as liabilities that they need no further comment. Responsibilities such as those to pay pensions, deferred compensation, and taxes and to honor warranties and guarantees also create liabilities under the definition. That they may be satisfied by providing goods or services instead of cash, that their amounts or times of settlement must be estimated, or that the identity of the specific entities to whom an entity is obligated is as yet unknown does not disqualify them under the definition, although some may not be recognized because of uncertainty or measurement problems (paragraphs 44-48).

197. Deposits and prepayments received for goods or services to be provided—"unearned revenues," such as subscriptions or rent collected in advance—likewise qualify as liabilities under the definition because an entity is required to provide goods or services to those who have paid in advance. They are mentioned separately from other liabilities only because they have commonly been described in the accounting literature and financial statements as "deferred credits" or "reserves." Comments on the Discussion Memorandum and earlier Exposure Drafts have manifested some misunderstanding: some respondents apparently concluded that all or most "deferred credits" and "reserves" were precluded by the definition of liabilities.

Liabilities and Proceeds

198. An entity commonly receives cash, goods, or services by incurring liabilities (paragraph 38), and that which is received is often called proceeds, especially if cash is received. Receipt of proceeds may be evidence that an entity has incurred one or more liabilities, but it is not conclusive evidence. Proceeds may be received from cash sales of goods or services or other sales of assets, from cash contributions by donors, or from cash investments by owners, and entities may incur liabilities without receiving proceeds, for example, by imposition of taxes. The essence of a liability is a legal, equitable, or constructive obligation to sacrifice economic benefits in the future rather than whether proceeds were received by incurring it. Although proceeds received may be a useful attribute in measuring a liability incurred, proceeds themselves are not liabilities.

Obligation of a Particular Entity

199. Paragraph 35 defines liabilities in relation to specific entities. A required future sacrifice of assets is a liability of the particular entity that must make the sacrifice.

200. To have a liability, an entity must be obligated to sacrifice its assets in the future—that is, it must be bound by a legal, equitable, or constructive duty or responsibility to transfer assets or provide services to one or more other entities. Not all probable future sacrifices of economic benefits (assets) are liabilities of an entity. For example, an entity's need to replace merchandise sold or raw materials or equipment used up, no matter how pressing, does not by itself constitute a liability of the entity because no obligation to another entity is present.

201. Most obligations that underlie liabilities stem from contracts and other agreements that are enforceable by courts or from governmental actions that have the force of law,[63] and the fact of an entity's obligation is so evident that it is often taken for granted. To carry out its operations, an entity routinely makes contracts and agreements that obligate it to repay borrowing, to pay suppliers and employees for goods and services they provide, to provide goods or services to customers, or to repair or replace defective products sold with warranties or guarantees. Governmental units also routinely assess tax obligations against business enterprises and some not-for-profit organizations, and courts may impose obligations for damages or fines.

202. Equitable or constructive obligations may underlie liabilities as well as those that are legally enforceable. Legal obligations are much more common, and their existence may be more readily substantiated, but other kinds of obligations are sometimes liabilities. For example, the question, which has resulted in differences of opinion, of the extent to which future payments under a lease agreement are legally enforceable against lessees is not necessarily significant in determining whether the obligations under lease agreements qualify as liabilities.

---

[63]Contracts and agreements and enforceability of agreements and statutes are necessary parts of the environment in which business and other economic activities and financial reporting take place. Business and other economic activities in the United States depend on flows of money and credit, and the fact that the participants largely keep their promises to pay money or provide goods or services is a necessary stabilizing factor. But the definitions in this Statement are not legal definitions and do not necessarily agree with legal definitions of the same or related terms (which have a propensity to have diverse meanings, often depending on the context or the branch of law that is involved). Nor is existence of a legally enforceable obligation inevitably required for an entity to have a liability (pars. 36-40).

203. An entity may incur equitable or constructive obligations by actions to bind itself or by finding itself bound by circumstances rather than by making contracts or participating in exchange transactions. An entity is not obligated to sacrifice assets in the future if it can avoid the future sacrifice at its discretion without significant penalty. The example of an entity that binds itself to pay employees vacation pay or year-end bonuses by paying them every year even though it is not contractually bound to do so and has not announced a policy to do so has already been noted (paragraph 40). It could refuse to pay only by risking substantial employee-relations problems.

204. Most liabilities are obligations of only one entity at a time. Some liabilities are shared—for example, two or more entities may be "jointly and severally liable" for a debt or for the unsatisfied liabilities of a partnership. But most liabilities bind a single entity, and those that bind two or more entities are commonly ranked rather than shared. For example, a primary debtor and a guarantor may both be obligated for a debt, but they do not have the same obligation—the guarantor must pay only if the primary debtor defaults and thus has a contingent or secondary obligation, which ranks lower than that of the primary debtor.

205. Secondary, and perhaps even lower ranked, obligations may qualify as liabilities under the definition in paragraph 35, but recognition considerations are highly significant in deciding whether they should formally be included in financial statements because of the effects of uncertainty (paragraphs 44-48). For example, the probability that a secondary or lower ranked obligation will actually have to be paid must be assessed to apply the definition.

Occurrence of a Past Transaction or Event

206. The definition of liabilities in paragraph 35 distinguishes between present and future obligations of an entity. Only present obligations are liabilities under the definition, and they are liabilities of a particular entity as a result of the occurrence of transactions or other events or circumstances affecting the entity.

207. Most liabilities result from exchange transactions in which an entity borrows funds or acquires goods or services and agrees to repay borrowing, usually with interest, or to pay for goods or services received. For example, using employees' services obligates an entity to pay wages or salaries and usually fringe benefits.

208. In contrast, the acts of budgeting the purchase of a machine and budgeting the payments required to obtain it result in neither acquiring an asset nor in incurring a liability. No transaction or event has occurred that gives the entity access to or con-

trol of future economic benefit or obligates it to transfer assets or provide services to another entity.

209. Many agreements specify or imply how a resulting obligation is incurred. For example, borrowing agreements specify interest rates, periods involved, and timing of payments; rental agreements specify rentals and periods to which they apply; and royalty agreements may specify payments relating to periods or payments relating to production or sales. The occurrence of the specified event or events results in a liability. For example, interest accrues with the passage of time (that is, providing loaned funds for another hour, day, week, month, or year), while royalties may accrue either with the passage of time or as units are produced or sold, depending on the agreement.

210. Transactions or events that result in liabilities imposed by law or governmental units also are often specified or inherent in the nature of the statute or regulation involved. For example, taxes are commonly assessed for calendar or fiscal years, fines and penalties stem from infractions of the law or failure to comply with provisions of laws or regulations, damages result from selling defective products, and restoring the land after strip-mining the mineral deposit is a consequence of removing the ground cover or overburden and ore. For those imposed obligations, as for obligations resulting from exchange transactions, no liability is incurred until the occurrence of an event or circumstance that obligates an entity to pay cash, transfer other assets, or provide services to other entities in the future.

211. A liability once incurred by an entity remains a liability until it is satisfied in another transaction or other event or circumstance affecting the entity. Most liabilities are satisfied by cash payments. Others are satisfied by the entity's transferring assets or providing services to other entities, and some of those—for example, liabilities to provide magazines under a prepaid subscription agreement—involve performance to earn revenues. Liabilities are also sometimes eliminated by forgiveness, compromise, incurring another liability, or changed circumstances.

Characteristics of Equity of Business Enterprises

212. Paragraph 49 defines equity or net assets as "the residual interest in the assets of an entity that remains after deducting its liabilities." Characteristics of equity of business enterprises are briefly discussed under two headings: residual interest, and invested and earned equity. Although *capital* is not a precise term in referring to equity because it is also applied to assets and liabilities in various ways, it is used in this discussion because *capital* is part of so many terms commonly used to describe aspects of equity of business enterprises; for example, investments by owners are

commonly called capital contributions, distributions to owners are commonly called capital distributions, and discussions of comprehensive income and its components often refer to capital maintenance. (The distinguishing characteristics of net assets of not-for-profit organizations are discussed in paragraphs 50-53 and 90-106.)

Residual Interest

213. Equity in a business enterprise is the ownership interest, and its amount is the cumulative result of investments by owners, comprehensive income, and distributions to owners. That characteristic, coupled with the characteristic that liabilities have priority over ownership interest as claims against enterprise assets, makes equity not determinable independently of assets and liabilities. Although equity can be described in various ways, and different recognition criteria and measurement procedures can affect its amount, equity always equals net assets (assets minus liabilities). That is why it is a residual interest.

Invested and Earned Equity

214. Equity is defined only in total in this Statement. Although equity of business enterprises is commonly displayed in two or more classes, usually based on actual or presumed legal distinctions, those classes may not correspond to the two sources of equity: investments by owners and comprehensive income. For example, a traditional classification for corporate equity is capital stock, other contributed capital, and retained or undistributed profit, with the first two categories described as invested or contributed capital and the third described as earned capital or capital from operations. That distinction holds reasonably well in the absence of distributions to owners or stock dividends; and cash dividends or dividends in kind that are "from profit" may not cause significant classification problems. However, transactions and events such as stock dividends (proportional distributions of an enterprise's own stock accompanied by a transfer of retained or undistributed profit to capital stock and other contributed capital) and reacquisitions and reissues of ownership interests (commonly called treasury stock transactions in corporations) mix the sources and make tracing of sources impossible except by using essentially arbitrary allocations. Thus, categories labeled invested or contributed capital or earned capital may or may not accurately reflect the sources of equity of an enterprise. However, those problems are problems of measurement and display, not problems of definition.

Characteristics of Comprehensive Income of Business Enterprises and Its Components

215. Paragraph 70 defines comprehensive income as "the change in equity of a business enterprise during a period from transactions and other events and circumstances from nonowner sources." It adds that "it includes all changes in equity during a period except those resulting from investments by owners and distributions to owners." Comprehensive income comprises four basic components—revenues, expenses, gains, and losses—that are defined in paragraphs 78-89.

216. The diagram in paragraph 64 shows that comprehensive income and investments by and distributions to owners account for all changes in equity (net assets) of a business enterprise during a period. The sources of comprehensive income are therefore significant to those attempting to use financial statements to help them with investment, credit, and similar decisions about the enterprise, especially since various sources may differ from each other in stability, risk, and predictability. Users' desire for information about those sources underlies the distinctions between revenues, expenses, gains, and losses as well as other components of comprehensive income that result from combining revenues, expenses, gains, and losses in various ways (paragraphs 73-77).

217. The principal distinction between revenues and expenses on the one hand and gains and losses on the other is the distinction between an entity's ongoing major or central operations and its peripheral and incidental transactions and activities. Revenues and expenses result from an entity's productive efforts and most of its exchange transactions with other entities that constitute the entity's ongoing major or central operations. The details vary with the type of entity and activities involved. For example, a manufacturing or construction enterprise buys or contracts to use labor, raw materials, land, plant, equipment, and other goods and services it needs. Its manufacturing or construction operations convert those resources into a product—output of goods—that is intended to have a greater utility, and therefore a higher price, than the combined inputs. Sale of the product should therefore bring in more cash or other assets than were spent to produce and sell it. Other kinds of enterprises earn more cash or other assets than they spend in producing and distributing goods or services through other kinds of operations—for example, by buying and selling goods without changing their form (such as retailers or wholesalers), by providing one or more of a wide variety of services (such as garages, professional firms, insurance companies, and banks), or by investing in securities of other entities (such as mutual funds, insurance companies, and banks). Some enterprises simultaneously engage in many different ongoing major or central activities.

218. Most entities also occasionally engage in activities that are peripheral or incidental to their ongoing major or central operations. For example, many entities invest in securities of other entities to earn a return on otherwise idle assets (rather than to control or influence the other entities' operations). Moreover, all entities are affected by price changes, interest rate changes, technological changes, thefts, fires, natural disasters, and similar events and circumstances that may be wholly or partly beyond the control of individual entities and their managements. The kinds of events and circumstances noted in this paragraph are commonly sources of gains and losses. Of course, the distinction between revenues and gains and between expenses and losses depends significantly on the nature of an entity and its activities (paragraphs 87 and 88).

Interest in Information about Sources of Comprehensive Income

219. Information about various components of comprehensive income is usually more useful than merely its aggregate amount to investors, creditors, managers, and others who are interested in knowing not only that an entity's net assets have increased (or decreased) but also *how* and *why.* The amount of comprehensive income for a period can, after all, be measured merely by comparing the ending and beginning equity and eliminating the effects of investments by owners and distributions to owners, but that procedure has never provided adequate information about an entity's performance. Investors, creditors, managers, and others need information about the causes of changes in assets and liabilities.

220. As the preceding paragraphs imply, financial accounting and reporting information that is intended to be useful in assessing an enterprise's performance or profitability focuses on certain components of comprehensive income. Ways of providing information about various sources of comprehensive income are matters of display that are beyond the scope of this Statement. Pertinent issues involve questions such as: Should all components of comprehensive income be displayed in a single financial statement or in two or more statements and, if the latter, which statements should be provided? What level of aggregation or disaggregation is needed for revenues, expenses, gains, and losses? Which intermediate components or measures resulting from combining those elements should be emphasized and which, if any, should be emphasized to the extent of being the "bottom line" of a financial statement? Which, if any, intermediate component or components should be designated as *earnings*? Should some components of comprehensive income be displayed as direct increases or decreases of equity (net assets)?[64]

[64]Concepts Statement 5 addresses many of those matters and notes that those matters may be developed further at the standards level.

Characteristics of Net Assets and Changes in the Classes of Net Assets of Not-for-Profit Organizations

221. Paragraph 49 defines equity or net assets as "the residual interest in the assets of an entity that remains after deducting its liabilities." This Statement defines net assets of not-for-profit organizations in total and divides it into three classes—permanently restricted net assets, temporarily restricted net assets, and unrestricted net assets—based on the presence or absence of donor-imposed restrictions and the nature of those restrictions. The two restricted classes of net assets at any time reflect existing limits on the organization's use of assets resulting from donor stipulations. When the limiting conditions are met, expire, or are withdrawn, temporarily restricted net assets are reclassified as unrestricted net assets. Characteristics of net assets of a not-for-profit organization and the interests in information about changes in the classes of net assets are briefly discussed in the following paragraphs.

Residual Interest

222. Net assets in a not-for-profit organization is the cumulative result of changes in permanently restricted, temporarily restricted, and unrestricted net assets, each of which, in turn, is the result of revenues, gains, expenses, and losses and of reclassifications within net assets. That characteristic, coupled with the characteristic that net assets is subject to the priority of liabilities as claims against organization assets, makes net assets not determinable independently of assets and liabilities. Although equity or net assets can be described in various ways, and different recognition criteria and measurement procedures can affect its amount, it is always the amount that remains after deducting liabilities from assets.That is why it is a residual interest.

Interest in Information about Changes in Classes of Net Assets

223. Resource providers are interested in knowing not only that a not-for-profit organization's net assets has increased (or decreased) but also *how* and *why.* That stems from the common interests of contributors, creditors, and others who provide resources to not-for-profit organizations in information about the services those organizations provide, their efficiency and effectiveness in providing those services, and their continuing ability to provide those services. Some resource providers, such as contributors and members, may be interested in that information as a basis for assessing how well the organization has met its objectives and for determining whether to continue their support. Other resource providers, such as lenders, suppliers, and employees, view a not-for-profit organization as a source of payment for

the cash, goods, or services they supply and accordingly are interested in assessing the organization's ability to generate the cash needed for timely payment of the organization's obligations to them.[65]

224. Because the use of resources provided to not-for-profit organizations is often restricted by providers to a particular purpose or time, information about the restrictions on the use of resources and the amounts and kinds of inflows and outflows of resources that change its net assets is usually more useful to present and potential resource providers than merely the amount of change in net assets. The amount of change in net assets for a period can be measured by comparing the ending and beginning net assets, but that procedure alone does not provide adequate information for assessing (a) the services a not-for-profit organization provides, (b) its ability to continue to provide those services, or (c) how managers have discharged their stewardship responsibilities to contributors and others for use of its resources entrusted to them, all of which are important in assessing an organization's performance during a period.

225. Information about purpose restrictions may help assess the organization's ability to provide particular types of services or to make cash payments to creditors. Similarly, information about time restrictions may help creditors and others assess whether an organization has sufficient resources to provide future services or to make cash payments when due. Information about the amounts and kinds of changes in those restrictions is useful in assessing the extent to which activities of a not-for-profit organization during a period may have drawn upon resources obtained in past periods or have added resources for use in future periods.

226. Information about permanent restrictions is useful in determining the extent to which an organization's resources may not be a source of cash for payments to present or prospective lenders, suppliers, or employees. Thus, information that distinguishes permanently restricted resource inflows from other kinds of changes in an organization's net assets is useful in identifying the resource inflows that are not directly available for providing its services or cash for paying creditors in that (or any

[65]Concepts Statement 4, par. 30. Paragraphs 29, 31, and 32 also discuss the interest of other types of users of financial information, including those having specialized needs and those of internal users, such as managers and governing bodies, and explain that special-purpose reports and detailed information often required by those types of users is beyond the scope of general-purpose external financial reporting.

other) period (even though they may be a source of future income or other continuing economic benefits).[66]

227. Information about the change in unrestricted net assets for a period is a useful indicator of whether an organization's activities have drawn upon, maintained, or added to the part of its net assets that is fully available—that is, free of donor-imposed restrictions—to support the organization's operating activities. Information about the combined change in unrestricted net assets and in temporarily restricted net assets for a period indicates whether an organization has maintained the part of its net assets that is now or, at some time will be, available to support its operating activities.

228. As the preceding paragraphs suggest, financial reporting information that is intended to be useful in assessing a not-for-profit organization's performance focuses on information about changes in the three classes of a not-for-profit organization's net assets, classes based on the effects of donor-imposed restrictions.[67] Ways of presenting information about the various sources of those changes—revenues, expense, gains, and losses—and of changes in donor-imposed restrictions on net assets—reclassifications—are matters of display rather than problems of definition, and thus are beyond the scope of this Statement. Pertinent issues for later study involve questions such as: Should changes in classes of net assets be displayed in a single financial statement or in two or more statements? What level of aggregation or disaggregation is needed for revenues, expenses, gains, or losses? How should reclassifications of temporarily restricted net assets that become unrestricted be displayed?

---

[66]Permanently restricted resource inflows (for example, endowment contributions) are sometimes said to resemble the "capital" inflows of a business enterprise—investments by its owners. However, as this Statement indicates, characteristics of and changes in net assets of not-for-profit organizations and equity of business enterprises are often more different than similar. For example, unlike investments by owners, donations of assets with permanent restrictions are not a source of cash for payment to creditors. Furthermore, the rights of owners and donors are fundamentally different. A not-for-profit organization that accepts a permanently restricted contribution is obligated only to comply with the restriction. It generally operates for the benefit of the recipients of its services—not for the financial benefit of its donors.

[67]Donors that provide restricted resources may have specific interests in how those resources are used. Information focused on donor-imposed restrictions may be useful to them; however, broad distinctions are not intended to provide external users with assurance that managers have exercised their responsibilities in the manner specifically designated by a particular resource provider. General purpose external financial reporting can best meet the need for information about managers' special responsibilities by disclosing any failures to comply with restrictions that may impinge on an organization's financial performance or on its ability to continue to provide a satisfactory level of services (Concepts Statement 4, par. 41).

Examples to Illustrate Concepts

229. The following paragraphs illustrate some possible applications of the definitions and related concepts. Two cautions apply. First, although the points involved are conceptually significant, they may be practically trivial—that is, the results may appear to make little difference in practice. However, since this Statement is part of the Board's conceptual framework project, it is intended to emphasize concepts and sound analysis and to foster careful terminology, classification, and disclosure. The illustrations are meant to focus on substance rather than form. They illustrate, among other things, (a) that the presence or absence of future economic benefit rather than whether or not an entity incurred a cost ultimately determines whether it has a particular kind of asset, (b) that the presence or absence of a legal, equitable, or constructive obligation entailing settlement by future sacrifice of economic benefit (assets) rather than whether or not an entity received proceeds ultimately determines whether it has a particular kind of liability, and (c) that debit balances are not necessarily assets and credit balances are not necessarily liabilities.

230. Second, the examples used are intended to illustrate concepts and are not intended to imply that the accounting illustrated or the display described should necessarily be adopted in practice. Statements of Financial Accounting Standards, not Statements of Financial Accounting Concepts, establish generally accepted accounting principles. Decisions about what should be adopted in practice involve not only concepts but also practical considerations, including the relative benefits and costs of procedures and the reliability of measures. For example, some of the kinds of items illustrated are significantly affected by the uncertainty that surrounds the activities of business enterprises and not-for-profit organizations (paragraphs 44-48), and those effects should be considered in applying the definitions in this Statement.

231. A particular item to which the definitions may be applied may belong to either of two groups of elements:

First Group	Second Group
an asset,	a liability,
a reduction of a liability (liability valuation),[68]	a reduction of an asset (asset valuation),[68]
an expense, or	a revenue, or
a loss.	a gain.

[68]Valuation accounts are part of the assets or liabilities to which they pertain and are neither assets nor liabilities in their own right (pars. 34 and 43). That distinction is significant in several of the examples.

(None of the examples involves investments by owners or distributions to owners, and only the last one involves equity; those elements are therefore omitted from the two groups.) The nature of the elements and the relations between them dictate that the same item can be, for example, either an asset or an expense or either a liability or a gain, but the same item cannot be, for example, either an asset or a liability or either an expense or a gain. (Those who are familiar with the mechanics of accounting will recognize that the first group includes "debits" and the second group includes "credits.") Thus, to apply the definitions involves determining the group to which an item belongs and the element within the group whose definition it fits.[69]

Deferred Gross Profit on Installment Sales

232. Deferred gross profit on installment sales falls into the second group. It is neither a revenue nor a gain; the recognition basis that results in deferred gross profit (in substance a cash receipts basis) permits no revenue or gain to be recognized at the time of sale, except to the extent of gross profit in a down payment. Designating the amount as "deferred gross profit" also indicates that it is not now a revenue or gain, although it may be in the future.

233. Nor is the deferred gross profit a liability. The selling entity is not obligated to pay cash or to provide goods or services to the customer, except perhaps to honor a warranty or guarantee on the item sold, but that is a separate liability rather than part of the deferred gross profit. The deferred gross profit resulted because of doubt about the collectibility of the sales price (installment receivable), not because of cash payments or other asset transfers that the seller must make.

234. The essence of the installment sale transaction (using the recognition basis involved) is that the sale resulted in an increase in installment receivables and a decrease in inventory of equal amounts—the receivable reflects the unrecovered cost of the inventory sold. Gross profit (revenue less the related cost of goods sold) is recognized as cash is collected on the installment receivable, and the receivable continues to reflect the unrecovered cost—as it should using a cash-receipts basis of recognition—if the deferred gross profit is deducted from it. Thus, no matter how it is displayed in financial statements, deferred gross profit on installment sales is conceptually an asset valuation—that is, a reduction of an asset.

[69]The examples generally concern transactions and other events of business enterprises and are expressed in business terms. Since not-for-profit organizations may have similar transactions (except those related to ownership interests and perhaps those related to income taxes) these examples and the concepts they illustrate relate to those organizations as well.

Debt Discount, Premium, and Issue Cost

235. Unamortized or deferred debt discount belongs to the first group (paragraph 231) and was long commonly reported as an asset and amortized to interest expense by straight-line methods. APB Opinion No. 21, *Interest on Receivables and Payables,* changed that practice by requiring debt discount to be (a) deducted directly from the liability (as a "valuation account") and (b) "amortized" by the "interest" method using the effective interest or discount rate implicit in the borrowing transaction. That accounting reports the liability at the present value of the future cash payments for interest and maturity amount, discounted at the effective rate (which is higher than the nominal rate specified in the debt agreement), and reports interest expense at an amount determined by applying the effective rate to the amount of the liability at the beginning of the period.

236. The definitions in this Statement support the accounting required by Opinion 21. The debt discount is not an asset because it provides no future economic benefit. The entity has the use of the borrowed funds but it pays a price for that use—interest. A bond discount means that the entity borrowed less than the face or maturity amount of the debt instrument and therefore pays a higher actual (effective) interest rate than the rate (nominal rate) specified in the debt agreement. Conceptually, debt discount is a liability valuation—that is, a reduction of the face or maturity amount of the related liability.

237. Debt issue cost also falls into the first group of elements and is either an expense or a reduction of the related debt liability. Debt issue cost is not an asset for the same reason that debt discount is not—it provides no future economic benefit. Debt issue cost in effect reduces the proceeds of borrowing and increases the effective interest rate and thus may be accounted for the same as debt discount. However, debt issue cost may also be considered to be an expense of the period of borrowing.

238. Unamortized or deferred debt premium is the exact counterpart of unamortized or deferred debt discount, and Opinion 21 requires counterpart accounting. Unamortized debt premium is not itself a liability—it has no existence apart from the related debt—and is accounted for under the Opinion by being (a) added directly to the related liability and (b) "amortized" by the "interest" method using the effective interest or discount rate implicit in the borrowing transaction. The lower interest rate and lower interest cost result because the proceeds of borrowing exceeded the face or maturity amount of the debt. Conceptually, debt premium is a liability valuation, that is, an addition to the face or maturity amount of the related liability.

239. Terms such as *unamortized or deferred discount or premium* and *to amortize discount or premium* are carry-overs from the days when debt discount was considered to be an amortizable asset (paragraph 235) and do not describe accurately either the assets or liabilities and events involved or the interest method of accounting for them. Paragraphs 141 and 142 of this Statement define and describe accrual, deferral, and amortization. A simple example shows the distinction described in footnote 55: ". . . accounting for debt securities issued (or acquired as an investment) at a discount or premium by the 'interest' method is technically the result of accrual, not deferral or amortization, techniques."

> The proceeds are $87 (ignoring debt issue costs) if a 2-year debt security with a $100 face amount and 7 percent interest (payable annually) is issued to yield 15 percent. The interest method gives this accounting (all amounts are rounded to nearest dollar) if the usual valuation account—debt discount—is omitted.

1/1/X1		
Cash	$87	
Debt payable		$87

12/31/X1			**12/31/X2**		
Interest expense	$13		Interest expense	$14	
Interest payable (.15 × $87)		$13	Interest payable [.15 × ($87 + $6)]		$ 14
Interest payable	$ 7		Debt payable	$87	
Cash		$ 7	Interest payable	20	
			Cash		$107

Thus, despite references to the *interest method of amortization* in Opinion 21 and APB Opinion No. 12, *Omnibus Opinion—1967,* the interest method that both Opinions describe is straightforward accounting for cash receipts and payments and accrual of interest expense and interest payable at the effective rate. It involves neither deferring costs nor amortizing deferred costs. Similarly, accounting for investments in debt securities by the interest method involves accruing interest income and receivable but involves no deferrals or amortizations.[70]

Deferred Income Tax Credits

240. One view of deferred income tax credits—the liability method—is that they are taxes payable in future periods, that is, they are obligations of an entity that entail future cash payments. Another view—the net-of-tax method—is that they are valuations related to the effects of taxability and tax deductibility on individual assets. Deferred tax credits belong in the second group (paragraph 231), and the two views just noted exhaust the possibilities—deferred tax credits cannot be revenues, or gains.[71] Both the liability method and the net-of-tax method are compatible with the definitions in this Statement.

241. Only the deferred method that is prescribed by APB Opinion No. 11, *Accounting for Income Taxes,* does not fit the definitions. Deferred income tax credits are neither liabilities nor reductions of assets in Opinion 11. That Opinion rejects the liability method and specifically denies that deferred tax credits are "payables in the usual sense" (paragraph 57). The Opinion also proscribes the net-of-tax method. It requires accounting for deferred tax credits as "tax effects of current timing differences [that] are deferred currently and allocated to income tax expense of future periods when the timing differences reverse" (paragraph 23) rather than either as accrued taxes to be paid in future periods when the timing differences reverse or as reductions in related assets.[72]

---

[70]The proceeds are $114.50 if the example is changed to a 15 percent security issued to yield 7 percent. Interest income and receivable accrued is $8.00 (.07 × $114.50) for the first year and $7.50 [.07 × ($114.50 − $7.00)] for the second. Accounting for cash received is:

12/31/X1			12/31/X2		
Cash	$15.00		Cash	$115.00	
Interest receivable		$8.00	Interest receivable		$ 7.50
Investment		7.00	Investment		107.50

[71]Deferred tax charges are not discussed separately in this Statement. However, they are assets (prepaid taxes) in the liability method and reductions of related liabilities in the net-of-tax method.

[72]Some proponents of the deferred method hold that it is actually a variation of the net-of-tax method despite rejection of that method in Opinion 11. They view the deferred tax charges and credits as the separate display of the effects of interperiod tax allocation instead of as reductions of the related assets, liabilities, revenues, expenses, gains, and losses. They argue that separate display is necessary or desirable, but it is a matter of "geography" in financial statements rather than a matter of the nature of deferred income tax credits.

242. The compatibility of two of the three most widely suggested methods of accounting for tax effects of timing differences with the definitions in this Statement (and a possible compatible rationale for the results of the third method) is noted because several comments on the Discussion Memorandum and 1977 Exposure Draft had concluded, some with dismay and some with satisfaction, that the definitions ruled out deferred tax accounting or interperiod income tax allocation. However, the definitions are neutral on that recognition question: they affect only the method of allocation and neither require tax allocation nor rule it out.

Deferred Investment Tax Credits

243. Deferred investment tax credits were created by APB Opinion No. 2, *Accounting for the "Investment Credit,"* and the concept of deferred investment tax credits in that Opinion is the basis of this example. Those deferred credits fall into the second group (paragraph 231) and are not revenues, or gains. Deferred investment tax credits differ from deferred income tax credits in lacking a characteristic of liabilities that deferred income tax credits may have: deferred investment tax credits do not involve an obligation to pay taxes or otherwise sacrifice assets in the future. Conceptually, if investment tax credits are to be deferred and amortized over the life of the related assets, they are reductions of the acquisition costs of assets, not liabilities.

244. The Accounting Principles Board concluded in Opinion 2 that an investment tax credit was in substance a reduction of the cost of the related asset acquired and thereby a reduction of depreciation expense over the life of the asset rather than a reduction of income tax expense for the period of acquisition. The APB therefore concluded that "reflection of the allowable credit as a reduction in the net amount at which the acquired property is stated (either directly or by inclusion in an offsetting account)" was "preferable in many cases," and it permitted accounting for the credit as "deferred income" (a deferred credit) only if it were amortized over the productive life of the property (Opinion 2, paragraph 14). In other words, a deferred investment tax credit could be displayed as if it were a liability, and its amortization could be displayed as a reduction of income tax expense, but it must be accounted for as a reduction of an asset.[73]

---

[73]The definitions in this Statement do not bear on the question of whether an investment tax credit should be accounted for by the "deferral and amortization" method (which is described in this paragraph) or the "flow-through" method (which the Board also accepted in APB Opinion No. 4, *Accounting for the "Investment Credit,"* [amending Opinion 2]). That issue involves whether the tax credit reduces the cost of the asset and depreciation over its life or reduces income tax expense in the period of acquisition, which is a recognition or measurement question. The existence of an asset from whose cost the credit may be deducted is not in doubt.

245. The issue of whether the tax credit is a liability (deferred credit) or a reduction of the assets acquired is a significant conceptual question with a much less significant practical effect. Indeed, some consider the matter trivial because it does not affect reported profit. The issue of whether the investment tax credit is an asset valuation or a liability focuses, however, directly on the heart of the definition of liabilities. The essence of a liability is a legal, equitable, or constructive obligation to sacrifice economic benefits (assets) in the future, and a deferred investment tax credit based on the analysis in Opinion 2 wholly lacks that characteristic. If, therefore, liabilities were defined in a way that those deferred investment tax credits could qualify as liabilities, the concept would have virtually no meaning—almost any credit balance would qualify as a liability. A definition must set limits to be useful, and a definition broad enough to include deferred investment tax credits would be of little or no help in determining whether any other particular item was a liability of a particular entity.

Deferred Costs of Assets

246. Accountants, and others, are accustomed to describing costs incurred as assets, but costs incurred are at best evidence of the existence of assets (paragraphs 178-180). They result in assets only if an entity acquires or increases future economic benefits available to it in exchange transactions or through production. Once that conceptual point is made, however, it is obvious that cost incurred (acquisition cost or sometimes "historical cost") is commonly the attribute that is measured in financial reporting for many assets. Thus, inventories, plant, equipment, land, and a host of other future economic benefits are now represented in financial statements by some variation of costs incurred to acquire or make them.

247. Other "deferred costs" that are not themselves assets may be costs of the kinds of assets of an entity described in the preceding paragraph. For example, a procedure so long established that it rarely rates a second thought is to account for the costs (less salvage value, if any) of units normally spoiled in producing a product as additional costs of the salable units produced. Similarly, although a "dry hole" cannot by itself qualify as an asset, except perhaps for some salvageable materials or equipment, the costs of drilling a dry hole may be part of the cost of developing the future economic benefits of a mineral deposit that has been discovered.[74] Or, the legal and other costs of successfully defending a patent from infringement are "deferred legal costs" only in the sense that they are part of the cost of retaining and obtaining the future economic benefit of the patent.

[74]"The cost of a development well [in contrast to that of an exploratory well] is a part of the cost of a bigger asset—a producing system of wells and related equipment and facilities intended to extract, treat, gather, and store known reserves" (FASB Statement No. 19, *Financial Accounting and Reporting by Oil and Gas Producing Companies,* par. 205). The "full-costing" method incorporates the same notion—costs of dry holes are not themselves assets but are costs of mineral deposits.

248. The examples in the preceding paragraph illustrate costs that are accounted for in current practice as costs of other assets rather than as assets by themselves. The examples in this and the next two paragraphs illustrate costs that are of the same general nature but have sometimes been accounted for, and are commonly described, as if they were themselves assets. For example, entities that incur relocation, repair, training, advertising, or similar costs usually receive services (that is, something of value) in exchange for cash paid or obligations incurred. The question that needs to be answered to apply the definition of assets is whether the economic benefit received by incurring those costs was used up at the time the costs were incurred or shortly thereafter or future economic benefit remains at the time the definition is applied. Costs such as those of relocation, repair, training, or advertising services do not *by themselves* qualify as assets under the definition in paragraph 25 any more than do spoiled units, dry holes, or legal costs. The reason for considering the possibility that they might be accounted for as if they were assets stems from their possible relationship to future economic benefits.

249. Costs incurred for services such as research and development, relocation, repair, training, or advertising relate to future economic benefits in one of two ways. First, costs may represent rights to unperformed services yet to be received from other entities. For example, advertising cost incurred may be for a series of advertisements to appear in national news magazines over the next three months. Those kinds of costs incurred are similar to prepaid insurance or prepaid rent. They are payments in advance for services to be rendered to the entity by other entities in the future. Second, they may represent future economic benefit that is expected to be obtained within the entity by using assets or in future exchange transactions with other entities. For example, prerelease advertising of a motion picture may increase the future economic benefits of the product, or repairs may increase the future economic benefits of a piece of equipment. Those kinds of costs may be accounted for as assets either by being added to other assets or by being disclosed separately. If costs are to be included in assets because they enhance future economic benefits of two or more assets, the only practical alternative to arbitrarily allocating them to those other assets may be to show them as separate assets.

250. The examples do not, of course, preclude accounting for the kinds of costs involved as expenses of the period in which they are incurred. Many, perhaps most, will not be shown as assets at all for practical reasons stemming from considerations of uncertainty or measurement (paragraphs 44-48 and 175 and 176).

Estimated Loss on Purchase Commitments

251. Estimated loss on purchase commitments belongs in the second group of elements (paragraph 231). It is not a revenue or gain because it results from a loss. It is at best part of a liability and is not *by itself* an obligation to pay cash or otherwise sacrifice assets in the future. There is no asset from which it may be a deduction in present practice. Thus, it seems not to fit in the second group, after all. That predicament results, however, because estimated loss on purchase commitments is the recorded part of a series of transactions and events that are mostly unrecorded.

252. A purchase commitment involves both an item that might be recorded as an asset and an item that might be recorded as a liability. That is, it involves both a right to receive assets and an obligation to pay.[75] A decrease in the price that leaves the committed buyer in the position of now being able to buy the assets cheaper were it not committed to buy them at the former, higher price does not by itself create an obligation that was not already present. If both the right to receive assets and the obligation to pay were recorded at the time of the purchase commitment, the nature of the loss and the valuation account that records it when the price falls would be clearly seen. The obligation to pay has been unaffected by the price decrease—the full amount must be paid if the assets are accepted upon delivery, or damages must be paid if the assets are not accepted. However, the future economic benefit and value of the right to receive the assets has decreased because the market value of the assets to be received has declined, and the estimated loss on purchase commitment is in concept a reduction of that asset.

253. As long as the commitment transaction remains unrecorded, however, the only way to recognize the loss on the commitment is to do as is done in current practice—to recognize the valuation account for estimated loss on purchase commitments and include it among the assets or liabilities. Although it can be deducted from assets in some way, even though the asset to which it applies is not recorded, it is now sometimes shown among the liabilities.

Minority Interests and Stock Purchase Warrants

254. Minority interests in net assets of consolidated subsidiaries do not represent present obligations of the enterprise to pay cash or distribute other assets to minority

[75]Whether those rights and obligations might be accounted for as assets and liabilities is a question of recognition, criteria for which are established by Concepts Statement 5 and may be developed further as they are applied at the standards level. Although the definitions in this Statement do not exclude the possibility of recording assets and liabilities for purchase commitments, the Statement contains no conclusions or implications about whether they should be recorded.

stockholders. Rather, those stockholders have ownership or residual interests in components of a consolidated enterprise. The definitions in this Statement do not, of course, preclude showing minority interests separately from majority interests or preclude emphasizing the interests of majority stockholders for whom consolidated statements are primarily provided. Stock purchase warrants are also sometimes called liabilities but entirely lack the characteristics of liabilities. They also are part of equity.

Examples Do Not Govern Practice

255. The Board reiterates that the examples in paragraphs 232-254 are intended to illustrate the definitions and related concepts, not to establish standards for accounting practice (paragraph 230). The examples are intended to help readers understand the essential characteristics of the definitions and related concepts and thereby to help them understand the definitions in this Statement.

Summary Index of Concepts Defined or Discussed

In addition to defining 10 elements of financial statements and 3 classes of net assets (of not-for-profit organizations) and changes in those classes during a period, this Statement defines or discusses other concepts, terms, or phrases that are used in the definitions or explanations or that are otherwise related to those elements and classes. This index identifies the paragraphs in which those elements and classes and certain other significant concepts, terms, or phrases are defined or discussed.

	Paragraph Numbers
Accrual	141
Accrual accounting	134, 139-141, 145
Allocation	142, 149-150
Amortization	142, 149
Articulation	20-21, 64, 107
Assets	25-34, 64-65, 107-108, 171-191
Attributes measured	(footnote 37) 73
Capital maintenance	71-72, 103-106
Change in permanently restricted net assets	107-110, 117-122, 226
Change in temporarily restricted net assets	107-110, 117-118, 123-126, 225
Change in unrestricted net assets	107-110, 117-118, 127-133, 227
Changes in classes of net assets of not-for-profit organizations	107-110, 117-133, 223-228
Changes in financial position	(footnote 13) 20
Circumstances	136
Classes of net assets of not-for-profit organizations	91-94, 101-102, 221
Comprehensive income of business enterprises	64-65, 70-77, 215-220
Constructive obligations	(footnote 22) 35, 40, (footnote 28) 57, 202-203
Cost	(footnote 19) 26
Deferral	141-142
Distributions to owners	64-69
Donor-imposed restrictions	56-58, 95-102
Earnings	(footnote 1) 1
Economic resources	11-15, 27-31
Elements of financial statements	5-7
Entity	24
Equitable obligations	(footnote 22) 35, 40, (footnote 28) 57, 202-203
Equity of business enterprises	49-55, 60-65, 212-214
Equity or net assets	49-65, (footnote 26) 50, 90-110, 212-214, 221-222

Paragraph Numbers

Events 135-138
Exchange transactions 137
Expenses 64-65, 80-81, 87-89, 107-113, 215-220
External events 135, 137
Financial position .... (footnote 13) 20
Fund balance .... (footnote 45) 91
Future economic benefit 26-30, 172-173
Gains 64-65, 82-89, 107-113, 215-220
Internal events 135, 138
Internal transactions 138
Investments by owners 64-69
Item (contrast with *element*) 5-7
Liabilities 35-43, 54-59, 64-65, 107-108, 192-211
Losses 64-65, 82-89, 107-113, 215-220
Maintenance of net assets 71-72, 103-106
Matching of costs and revenues 146
Measurement .... 22, (footnote 37) 73
Net assets of not-for-profit organizations 49-53, 56-58, 90-110, 221-222
Net assets or equity .... 49-65, (footnote 26) 50, 90-110, 212-214, 221-222
Nonreciprocal transfers .... 137, 150-151, (footnote 61) 169
Not-for-profit organizations (distinguishing characteristics of) .. (footnote 8) 12, 90
Obligations .... (footnote 22) 35, 36-40, 193-194, 200-203
Other entities 24
Ownership interest 49-55, 60-65, 212-214
Permanently restricted net assets 91-92, 95-102, 107-110, 221
Permanent restrictions 98-100
Prepayments 141
Probable .... (footnote 18) 25, (footnote 21) 35, 46
Production .... 30, (footnote 33) 65, (footnote 38) 74, (footnote 40) 79, (footnote 50) 112
Profit and loss .... (footnote 9) 16
Realization 143
Realized 143
Reclassifications (not-for-profit organizations) 107-110, 114-116, 152
Recognition 22, 143
Residual interest 49-50, 90, 212-213, 221-222
Resources (economic) 11-15, 27-31
Restricted or restrictions (not-for-profit organizations) 91-93, 95-102, 221

Paragraph
Numbers

Revenues 64-65, 78-79, 87-89, 107-113, 215-220
Service potential (synonym for *future economic benefit*) 26-30, 172-173
Service-providing efforts ....(footnote 50) 112
Systematic and rational allocation......................................149
Temporarily restricted net assets 91, 93, 95-102, 107-110, 221
Temporary restrictions 98-100
Transactions 135, 137
Unrealized...143
Unrestricted net assets...........................91, 94, 107-110, 221
Valuation accounts 34, 43

AMENDMENT OF FASB CONCEPTS STATEMENT NO. 2, QUALITATIVE CHARACTERISTICS OF ACCOUNTING INFORMATION

As discussed in Appendix A (paragraphs 160-162) the Board has reaffirmed the conclusion that the qualitative characteristics of accounting information set forth in Concepts Statement 2 (relevance, reliability, comparability, and related qualities) apply to both not-for-profit organizations and business enterprises. Accordingly, paragraph 4 and footnote 2 of Concepts Statement 2 are superseded and replaced by the following:

> 4. The qualities of information discussed in this Statement apply to financial information reported by business enterprises and by not-for-profit organizations. Although the discussion and the examples in this Statement are expressed in terms commonly related to business enterprises, they generally apply to not-for-profit organizations as well. "Objectives of financial reporting by business enterprises," "investors and creditors," "investment and credit decisions," and similar terms are intended to encompass their counterparts for not-for-profit organizations, "objectives of financial reporting by not-for-profit organizations," "resource providers," "resource allocation decisions," and similar terms.[2]

[2]This paragraph is as amended by FASB Concepts Statement No. 6, *Elements of Financial Statements* (December 1985).

TOPICAL INDEX

ACCOUNTING CHANGES
Relation to Consistency.............CON2, ¶122
ACCOUNTING PRINCIPLES AND METHODS
Choice of........................CON2, ¶6-20
ACCRUAL
Definition........................CON6, ¶141
ACCRUAL BASIS OF ACCOUNTING
Allocation and Amortization......CON6, ¶141-142
Compared to Cash Basis.............CON4, ¶50
............................CON6, ¶139-140
............................CON6, ¶144-145
Deferral.......................CON6, ¶141-142
Definition.....................CON6, ¶139-141
Description....................CON6, ¶134-142
Elements of Financial Statements..CON6, ¶134-152
Enterprise Performance...........CON1, ¶44-48
Not-for-Profit Organizations.........CON4, ¶50
Relation to Matching of Costs and Revenues
............................CON6, ¶145-151
Transactions, Events, and Circumstances
............................CON6, ¶135-138
ALLOCATION OF COSTS
See Accrual Basis of Accounting
Definition........................CON6, ¶142
Matching of Costs and Revenues......CON6, ¶149
AMORTIZATION
See Depreciation
Definition........................CON6, ¶142
Matching of Costs and Revenues......CON6, ¶149
Methods for Debt Discount.......CON6, ¶235-239
Recognition Guidance...............CON5, ¶86
ARTICULATION
Definition........................CON6, ¶20-21
ASSETS
Characteristics...................CON6, ¶26-31
............................CON6, ¶171-191
Control by Entity...............CON6, ¶183-189
Criteria for Recognition............CON5, ¶58-65
............................CON5, ¶67-69
............................CON5, ¶73-77
Definition........................CON6, ¶25-31
Elements of Financial Statements....CON6, ¶25-34
Future Economic Benefits.............CON6, ¶28
............................CON6, ¶172-182
Items Not Qualified as..............CON6, ¶169
Measurement of..................CON5, ¶67-69
Past Transactions...............CON6, ¶190-191
Qualification as....................CON6, ¶168
................................CON6, ¶174
Recognition of Changes in.........CON5, ¶88-90
Relation to Control.............CON6, ¶183-189
Relation to Costs...............CON6, ¶178-182
Relation to Future Economic Benefits
............................CON6, ¶190-191
Service Potential...................CON6, ¶28
Transactions and Events Affecting...CON6, ¶32-33
Uncertainty of Recognition.........CON6, ¶44-48
ATTRIBUTES
See Measurement
BALANCE SHEET
See Statement of Financial Position
BARTER (TRANSACTIONS)
Guidance in Recognizing Revenues and Gains
................................CON5, ¶84
BIAS
Definition.....................CON2, Glossary
Relation to Representational Faithfulness
............................CON2, ¶77-78
BUDGETS
Not-for-Profit Organizations...........CON4, ¶9
............................CON4, ¶21-22
BUSINESS ENTERPRISE
Cash Flow Prospects................CON1, ¶39
Compared to Not-for-Profit Organizations
................................CON4, ¶6-9
............................CON4, ¶14-22
Earning Process..................CON1, ¶42-48
Performance Measurement.........CON1, ¶42-55
Return on Investment................CON1, ¶45
BUSINESS ENTERPRISE OBJECTIVES
Compared to Not-for-Profit Organizations' Objectives.......................CON4, ¶67
CAPITAL
Description........................CON6, ¶212
CAPITAL MAINTENANCE
Concepts, Physical Capital and Financial Capital
............................CON5, ¶45-48
............................CON6, ¶71-72
Maintenance of Net Assets
. . Not-for-Profit Organizations...CON6, ¶103-106
. . Relation to Price-Level Changes....CON6, ¶71
Relation to Return on Investment (Business Enterprises).......................CON6, ¶71
CASH
Medium of Exchange................CON1, ¶10
................................CON6, ¶29
CASH BASIS OF ACCOUNTING
Compared to Accrual Basis of Accounting
................................CON4, ¶50
............................CON6, ¶139-140
............................CON6, ¶144-145
CASH FLOWS
See Recognition and Measurement in Financial Statements
Information Useful in Assessing.....CON1, ¶37-39
Performance Measurement.........CON1, ¶43-49
Relation to Earnings...............CON1, ¶43-49
Statement of.....................CON5, ¶52-54
Users' Needs for Information..........CON1, ¶25
................................CON1, ¶30
CATCH-UP ADJUSTMENT
See Cumulative Accounting Adjustments
CHANGES IN FINANCIAL POSITION
See Statement of Financial Position
Definition..........................CON6, ¶20
CIRCUMSTANCES
Definition.........................CON6, ¶136
COMMITMENTS
Purchase, Losses, Qualification as a Liability
............................CON6, ¶251-253
Recognition of Executory Contracts
............................CON6, ¶251-253

COMPARABILITY
Accounting for Similar Circumstances..CON2, ¶16
As a Quality....................CON2, ¶111-119
Between Enterprises
. . Primary Qualitative Characteristic
........................CON2, ¶111-122
. . Definition.................CON2, Glossary
Primary Qualitative Characteristic.CON2, ¶111-122
COMPENSATION TO EMPLOYEES: DEFERRED
Qualification as a Liability...........CON6, ¶196
COMPLETENESS
Definition.....................CON2, Glossary
Relation to Representational Faithfulness
..............................CON2, ¶79-80
COMPREHENSIVE INCOME
See Earnings
See Investments: Marketable Securities
See Losses
See Revenues
Change in Term from Concepts Statement 1
.................................CON5, ¶11
Characteristics....................CON6, ¶73-77
............................CON6, ¶215-218
Component of Full Set of Financial Statements
.................................CON5, ¶13
Components......................CON6, ¶73-77
Definition.........................CON6, ¶70
Display Issues.....................CON6, ¶220
Element of Financial Statements.....CON6, ¶70-77
Equivalent Terms...................CON5, ¶40
Financial Capital Concept..........CON6, ¶71-72
Information about Sources...........CON6, ¶219
Nonowner Changes in Equity (or Equivalent Term)
.................................CON5, ¶40
Relation to Price-Level Changes.....CON6, ¶73-75
Relation to Profit and Loss...........CON6, ¶16
Relationship between Earnings and Comprehensive Income........................CON5, ¶42-44
Statement of Comprehensive Income
. . Complementary Relationship to Other Financial Statements....................CON5, ¶24
. . Statement of Earnings and Comprehensive Income....................CON5, ¶30-32
CONCEPTUAL FRAMEWORK
As Basis for Standards.................CON1, ¶3
History of Need for...............CON1, ¶57-60
Not-for-Profit Organizations..........CON4, ¶1-2
Relation to Current Value.............CON1, ¶2
Relation to Financial Accounting Standards
..................................CON1, ¶3
CONSERVATISM
Definition.....................CON2, Glossary
Recognition Implication for Earnings...CON5, ¶50
Relation to Reliability.............CON2, ¶91-97
CONSISTENCY
Accounting for Similar Circumstances..CON2, ¶16
Definition.....................CON2, Glossary
Relation to Comparability........CON2, ¶120-122
Relation to Conservatism...........CON2, ¶91-97
CONSTRUCTIVE OBLIGATIONS
Definition..........................CON6, ¶40
CONSUMPTION OF BENEFITS
Guidance in Applying Recognition Criteria to Expenses.........................CON5, ¶86
CONTRACTOR ACCOUNTING: CONSTRUCTION-TYPE CONTRACTS
Revenue Recognition Concept.........CON5, ¶84
CONTROL (OF ASSETS)
By a Particular Enterprise........CON6, ¶183-189
Future Economic Benefits
. . Relation to Legal Rights.......CON6, ¶186-189
CONVERTIBLE DEBT
Characteristics......................CON6, ¶55
COST
Definition..........................CON6, ¶26
COST-BENEFIT RELATIONSHIP
In FASB Standards..............CON2, ¶143-144
Not-for-Profit Organizations, Financial Information ....CON4, ¶28
Of Providing Information.......CON2, ¶133-144
CREDITORS
Information Needs..................CON1, ¶41
CUMULATIVE ACCOUNTING ADJUSTMENTS
Catch-Up Adjustment................CON5, ¶34
Definition.........................CON5, ¶42
Description........................CON5, ¶43
Illustration of Relationship to Earnings.CON5, ¶44
CURRENT MARKET VALUE
Recognition and Measurement
. . Measurement Attribute.........CON5, ¶67-69
CURRENT (REPLACEMENT) COST
Recognition and Measurement
. . Measurement Attribute............CON5, ¶67
..............................CON5, ¶69
DEBT DISCOUNT
Qualification as an Asset.........CON6, ¶235-236
DEBT ISSUE COST
Characteristics.....................CON6, ¶237
DEBT PREMIUM
Qualification as an Asset.............CON6, ¶238
DECISION USEFULNESS
Assessing Services and Ability to Provide Services
.............................CON4, ¶38-39
Decision Makers and Their Characteristics
.............................CON2, ¶36-39
Not-for-Profit Organizations, Resource Allocation Decisions......................CON4, ¶35-37
Relation to Qualitative Characteristics
.............................CON2, ¶36-39
Role of Decision Making...........CON2, ¶27-31
DEFERRAL
Definition.........................CON6, ¶141
DEFERRED COSTS
Qualification as Assets...............CON6, ¶177
...........................CON6, ¶246-250
DEFERRED CREDITS
Qualification as Liabilities...........CON6, ¶197
DEFERRED INCOME TAX CREDITS
Qualification as Liabilities.......CON6, ¶240-242

DEFINITIONS
See Terminology
DEPOSITS
Qualification as Liabilities............CON6, ¶197
DEPRECIATION
Recognition Guidance................CON5, ¶86
DEVELOPMENT WELLS
Qualification as an Asset.............CON6, ¶247
DISCLOSURE
See Management
DISCOUNTED PRESENT VALUE OF FUTURE CASH FLOWS
See Present Value
DISPLAY
Financial Statements...............CON5, ¶13-14
Relation to Elements of Financial Statements
...............................CON6, ¶22-23
Reporting Comprehensive Income.....CON6, ¶220
DISTRIBUTIONS TO OWNERS
Characteristics....................CON6, ¶68-69
Definition..........................CON6, ¶67
Statement of Investments by and....CON5, ¶55-57
EARNING POWER
Performance Measurement.........CON1, ¶47-48
...............................CON1, ¶51
...............................CON5, ¶28
EARNINGS
Change in Use of Term from Concepts Statement 1
...............................CON5, ¶11
Description and Evolution of Concept
...............................CON5, ¶33-38
Enterprise Performance............CON1, ¶42-48
Measurement.....................CON1, ¶45-48
Recognition Implications...........CON5, ¶49-51
Relation to Cash Flows.............CON1, ¶43-49
Relation to Comprehensive Income..CON5, ¶42-44
...............................CON6, ¶1
...............................CON6, ¶72
ECONOMIC RESOURCES
Allocation in the Economy..........CON1, ¶12-16
Discussion.......................CON6, ¶11-15
...............................CON6, ¶27-31
Information about................CON1, ¶40-41
Not-for-Profit Organizations........CON4, ¶43-54
ELEMENTS OF FINANCIAL STATEMENTS
See Assets
See Expenses
See Gains
See Investments by Owners
See Liabilities
See Not-for-Profit Organizations
See Revenues
Accrual Basis of Accounting......CON6, ¶134-152
Articulation.....................CON6, ¶20-21
Characteristics and Examples.....CON6, ¶164-255
Definition..........................CON6, ¶5
Elements
. . Assets.......................CON6, ¶25-34
. . Comprehensive Income..........CON6, ¶70-77
. . Equity or Net Assets...........CON6, ¶49-59

ELEMENTS OF FINANCIAL STATEMENTS—continued
. . Expenses.....................CON6, ¶80-81
. . Gains and Losses..............CON6, ¶82-89
. . Investments by and Distributions to Owners
...............................CON6, ¶66-69
. . Liabilities.....................CON6, ¶35-43
. . Revenues.....................CON6, ¶78-79
Examples......................CON6, ¶229-255
Financial Representations.............CON6, ¶5-7
Relation to Objectives of Financial Reporting
...............................CON6, ¶9-19
Relation to Qualitative Characteristics.CON6, ¶9-19
Relation to Recognition, Measurement, and Display
...............................CON5, ¶64
...............................CON6, ¶22-23
Uncertainty.....................CON6, ¶44-48
ENTITY
Description.........................CON6, ¶24
EQUITABLE OBLIGATIONS
Description.....................CON6, ¶202-203
EQUITY (OR NET ASSETS)
Characteristics
. . Business Enterprises............CON6, ¶50-51
...............................CON6, ¶60-63
...............................CON6, ¶212-214
. . Not-for-Profit Organizations.......CON6, ¶52
...............................CON6, ¶90-102
...............................CON6, ¶221-222
Definition.........................CON6, ¶49
Difference between Equity and Liabilities
...............................CON6, ¶55-59
Elements of Financial Statements....CON6, ¶49-59
Interrelation with Liabilities.........CON6, ¶54-59
Invested and Earned (Business Enterprises)
...............................CON6, ¶214
Recognition of Events Affecting.....CON5, ¶59-60
Relation to Assets..............CON6, ¶107-108
Relation to Comprehensive Income..CON6, ¶64-65
Relation to Residual Interest...........CON6, ¶49
Residual or Ownership Interest........CON6, ¶213
Sources of Changes In.............CON6, ¶64-65
...............................CON6, ¶107-108
Transactions and Events Affecting.CON6, ¶107-110
ESTIMATES
Relation to Reliability..............CON2, ¶72-78
Use in Financial Statements...........CON1, ¶21
EVENTS AND TRANSACTIONS
Affecting Assets..................CON6, ¶32-33
Asset and Liability Changes.........CON5, ¶59-60
. . Recognition Criteria............CON5, ¶88-90
. . Description.................CON6, ¶135-138
Exchange Transactions...............CON6, ¶137
External Events....................CON6, ¶135
...............................CON6, ¶137
Internal Events....................CON6, ¶135
...............................CON6, ¶138
Internal Transactions................CON6, ¶138
Nonreciprocal Transfers..............CON6, ¶137
...............................CON6, ¶150-151

EXCHANGE TRANSACTIONS
Description........................CON6, ¶137
EXPENSES
Characteristics........................CON6, ¶81
Component of Comprehensive Income
..............................CON6, ¶73-77
..............................CON6, ¶215-220
Definition........................CON6, ¶80
Elements of Financial Statements....CON6, ¶80-81
Not-for-Profit Organizations......CON6, ¶111-113
Recognition Criteria, Guidance in Application
. . Loss or Lack of Future Benefit...CON5, ¶85-87
. . Relation to Losses.............CON6, ¶87-89
FEEDBACK VALUE
Component of Relevance...........CON2, ¶51-52
Definition......................CON2, Glossary
FINANCIAL FLEXIBILITY
Definition........................CON5, ¶24
Use of Statement of Cash Flows in Assessing
..............................CON5, ¶52
Use of Statement of Financial Position in Assessing
..............................CON5, ¶29
FINANCIAL POSITION
Definition........................CON6, ¶20
FINANCIAL REPORTING
Accrual Basis of Accounting......CON6, ¶134-152
Character and Limitations of Information Provided
..............................CON1, ¶17-23
Characteristics.....................CON1, ¶5-8
Compared to Management Reporting...CON1, ¶27
Conservatism....................CON2, ¶91-97
General Purpose External Reporting, Objectives
..............................CON1, ¶28-31
Information about Claims on Resources, Changes
..............................CON1, ¶40-41
Information about Economic Resources, Changes
..............................CON1, ¶40-41
Limitations Due to Nonrecognition.....CON6, ¶48
Limitations of Information.........CON1, ¶17-23
Neutrality of Information.............CON1, ¶33
Not-for-Profit Organizations........CON4, ¶43-55
Not-for-Profit Organizations, Characteristics and Limitations....................CON4, ¶23-28
Nonfinancial Information.............CON1, ¶7
Objectives.......................CON1, ¶32-54
Relation to Financial Statements.......CON1, ¶5-8
Relation to Recognition in Financial Statements
..............................CON5, ¶5-9
Relevant Information...............CON1, ¶36
Role in Decision Making...........CON2, ¶27-31
FINANCIAL STATEMENTS
See Recognition and Measurement in Financial Statements
Attribute to Be Measured, Definition....CON1, ¶2
Characteristics of.................CON1, ¶17-23
General Purpose External..........CON1, ¶28-30
Historic Reporting Norms.............CON1, ¶6
Limitations......................CON1, ¶17-23
Management Performance, Limitations
..............................CON1, ¶53-54
FUTURE ECONOMIC BENEFITS
Discussion........................CON6, ¶26-30
..............................CON6, ¶172-182
Relation to Assets..............CON6, ¶190-191
GAINS
See Recognition and Measurement in Financial Statements
Characteristics....................CON6, ¶84-89
Component of Comprehensive Income
..............................CON6, ¶73-77
Elements of Financial Statements....CON6, ¶82-89
Holding...........................CON6, ¶71
Operating vs. Nonoperating
. . Business Enterprises...............CON6, ¶86
. . Not-for-Profit Organizations.....CON6, ¶87-89
..............................CON6, ¶111-113
Recognition Criteria
. . Guidance in Application........CON5, ¶83-84
Relation to Revenues..............CON6, ¶87-89
Unrealized........................CON6, ¶143
GENERAL PURPOSE EXTERNAL FINANCIAL REPORTING
See Financial Reporting
See Recognition and Measurement in Financial Statements
HISTORICAL COST FINANCIAL STATEMENTS
Conceptual Framework................CON1, ¶2
HISTORICAL COST (HISTORICAL PROCEEDS)
Recognition and Measurement
. . Measurement Attribute.........CON5, ¶67-69
HOLDING GAINS (LOSSES)
Recognition and Measurement in Financial Statements
. . Financial Capital Maintenance......CON5, ¶48
INCOME
Measurement.....................CON1, ¶45-48
INFLATION
Relation to Measurement.............CON5, ¶72
Relation to Recognition...............CON5, ¶71
INFORMATION BIAS
Relation to Neutrality.............CON2, ¶99-100
INSTALLMENT SALES
Deferred Gross Profit, Qualification as a Liability
..............................CON6, ¶232-234
INTERNAL EVENTS AND TRANSACTIONS
See Events and Transctions
INVENTORY
Measurement Attributes Used
. . Historical Cost, Current Cost, Net Realizable Value........................CON5, ¶67
INVESTMENTS BY OWNERS
Characteristics.......................CON6, ¶68
Definition..........................CON6, ¶66
Element of Financial Statements.......CON5, ¶13
..............................CON6, ¶66-69
Statement of......................CON5, ¶55-57
INVESTMENTS: MARKETABLE SECURITIES
Comprehensive Income, Inclusion of Some Changes in Market Value in ....CON5, ¶42

Measurement Attribute Used for Some Securities, Current Market Value..............CON5, ¶67

INVESTMENT TAX CREDITS

Deferred, Qualification as a Liability ....CON6, ¶243-245

INVESTORS

Information Needs..................CON1, ¶41
Interest in Financial Reporting......CON1, ¶32-39

LIABILITIES

Characteristics....................CON6, ¶36-40
............................CON6, ¶192-211
Criteria for Recognition............CON5, ¶58-65
..............................CON5, ¶67-69
..............................CON5, ¶73-77
Definition.........................CON6, ¶35
Elements of Financial Statements....CON6, ¶35-43
Future Sacrifice of Assets.........CON6, ¶193-198
Interrelation with Equity...........CON6, ¶54-59
Items Not Qualified as..............CON6, ¶169
Measurement of..................CON5, ¶67-69
Obligations of a Particular Enterprise ....CON6, ¶199-205
Past Transactions................CON6, ¶206-211
Proceeds.........................CON6, ¶198
Qualification as....................CON6, ¶168
Recognition of Changes in..........CON5, ¶88-90
Relation to Equity (Net Assets) Changes ....CON6, ¶107-108
Transactions and Events Affecting...CON6, ¶41-42
Uncertainty of Recognition.........CON6, ¶44-48
Valuation Accounts.................CON6, ¶43

LICENSES

Qualification as Assets..............CON6, ¶189

LIQUIDITY

Definition.........................CON5, ¶24
Information about..................CON1, ¶49
Not-for-Profit Organizations..........CON4, ¶54
Use of Statement of Cash Flow in Assessing ....CON5, ¶29
Use of Statement of Financial Position in Assessing ....CON5, ¶29

LOSSES

Characteristics....................CON6, ¶84-89
Component of Comprehensive Income ....CON6, ¶73-77
............................CON6, ¶215-220
Definition.........................CON6, ¶83
Elements of Financial Statements....CON6, ¶83-89
Holding...........................CON6, ¶71
Not-for-Profit Organizations......CON6, ¶111-113
Operating vs. Nonoperating...........CON6, ¶86
Purchase Commitments
. . Qualification to Be Included as ....CON6, ¶251-253
Recognition Criteria
. . Guidance in Application..........CON5, ¶85
. . Guidance in Application, Loss or Lack of Future Benefit.................CON5, ¶87
Relation to Expenses..............CON6, ¶87-89

MANAGEMENT

Need for Operational Information......CON1, ¶27
Relation to Enterprise Performance..CON1, ¶50-53
Reporting..........................CON1, ¶54
. . Not-for-Profit Organizations.......CON4, ¶55
Stewardship.....................CON1, ¶50-53
. . Not-for-Profit Organizations.....CON4, ¶40-42

MATCHING OF COSTS AND REVENUES

Consumption of Benefits.............CON5, ¶86
Guidance in Applying Recognition Criteria to Expenses.........................CON5, ¶85
Relation to Accrual Basis of Accounting ....CON6, ¶145-151

MATERIALITY

Definition.....................CON2, Glossary
Description....................CON2, ¶123-132
Quantitative Considerations.......CON2, ¶161-170
SEC Regulations...............CON2, ¶161-162
Threshold for Recognition............CON5, ¶63

MEASUREMENT

Attributes.......................CON5, ¶65-70
. . Current Market Value............CON5, ¶67
. . Current Replacement Cost.........CON5, ¶67
. . Historical Cost/Historical Proceeds.CON5, ¶67
. . Net Realizable (Settlement) Value....CON5, ¶67
. . Present (or Discounted) Value of Future Cash Flows........................CON5, ¶67
Cost-Benefit Constraints..............CON5, ¶63
Criteria
. . Asset and Liability Changes, Use of Current Prices ....CON5, ¶90
Current Market Value................CON5, ¶67
.................................CON5, ¶69
Current (Replacement) Cost...........CON5, ¶69
Description.........................CON1, ¶2
............................CON5, ¶65-72
Elements Definitions.................CON5, ¶64
Materiality Threshold................CON5, ¶63
Measurability Criterion...............CON5, ¶65
Monetary Unit and Measurement Scale ....CON5, ¶71-72
Relation to Elements of Financial Statements ....CON6, ¶22-23
Relation to Recognition, Measurement, and Display ....CON6, ¶23

MINORITY INTERESTS

Qualification as a Liability...........CON6, ¶254

MONEY

Medium of Exchange................CON6, ¶29

NET ASSETS

Not-for-Profit Organizations
. . Change in Permanently Restricted Net Assets ....CON6, ¶119-122
. . Change in Temporarily Restricted Net Assets ....CON6, ¶123-126
. . Change in Unrestricted Net Assets ....CON6, ¶127-133
. . Changes in Classes...........CON6, ¶117-133
........................CON6, ¶223-227
. . Characteristics................CON6, ¶90-102

NET ASSETS—continued
.... CON6, ¶221-222
. . Classes .... CON6, ¶91-102
. . Display Issues .... CON6, ¶228
. . Donor Imposed Restrictions.... CON6, ¶95-102
. . Reclassifications .... CON6, ¶114-116
. . Restrictions Affect Net Assets Rather Than Particular Assets .... CON6, ¶101-102
. . Restrictions, Information About
.... CON6, ¶224-227
. . Removal of Restrictions on Temporarily Restricted Net Assets .... CON6, ¶152
. . Revenues, Gains, Expenses, Losses
.... CON6, ¶111-113
. . Temporary and Permanent Restrictions
.... CON6, ¶98-100
. . Transactions and Events that Change (Net Assets) .... CON6, ¶107-110

NET REALIZABLE VALUE
Recognition and Measurement
. . Measurement Attribute .... CON5, ¶67

NEUTRALITY
Definition .... CON2, Glossary
Financial Reporting .... CON1, ¶33
Relation to Relevance and Reliability
.... CON2, ¶98-110

NOMINAL DOLLAR ACCOUNTING
Measurement Scale .... CON5, ¶71-72

NONBUSINESS ORGANIZATIONS
See Not-for-Profit Organizations

NONMONETARY TRANSACTIONS
Guidance in Recognizing Revenues and Gains
.... CON5, ¶84

NONOWNER CHANGES IN EQUITY
See Comprehensive Income

NONRECIPROCAL TRANSFERS
Definition .... CON6, ¶137
Description .... CON6, ¶150-151

NOTES TO FINANCIAL STATEMENTS
Relation to Recognition in Financial Statements
.... CON5, ¶7-9

NOT-FOR-PROFIT ORGANIZATIONS
Accrual vs. Cash Basis of Accounting...CON4, ¶50
Budgets .... CON4, ¶21-22
Characteristics .... CON4, ¶6-9
Characteristics of Information Provided
.... CON4, ¶23-28
Comparison to Business Enterprise Objectives
.... CON4, ¶67
Comparison with Business Enterprise..CON4, ¶6-9
.... CON4, ¶14-22
Donations, Restricted
. . Relation to Equity (Net Assets) and Liabilities
.... CON6, ¶56-59
Economic Resources, Obligations, Net Resources and Changes in Them .... CON4, ¶43-54
Elements of Financial Statements
. . Applicability .... CON6, ¶1-2

NOT-FOR-PROFIT ORGANIZATIONS
—continued
Environmental Context, Objectives..CON4, ¶13-22
Examples .... CON4, ¶7-8
General Purpose External Financial Reporting
.... CON4, ¶10-12
Grants .... CON4, ¶6
Information Useful in Assessing Services and Ability to Provide Service .... CON4, ¶38-39
Information Useful in Making Resource Allocation Decisions .... CON4, ¶35-37
Limitations of Information Provided
.... CON4, ¶23-28
Liquidity .... CON4, ¶54
Management Stewardship .... CON4, ¶40-42
Managers' Explanations and Interpretations
.... CON4, ¶55
Nature of Resources .... CON4, ¶14-22
Nonapplicability of Recognition and Measurement Concepts .... CON5, ¶4
Nonbusiness Organizations
. . Change in Terminology .... CON6, ¶2
Objectives of Financial Reporting .... CON1, ¶1
.... CON4, ¶10-12
.... CON4, ¶33-55
Objectives, Qualitative Characteristics and Elements .... CON6, ¶9-19
Organization Performance .... CON4, ¶47-53
Relation to State and Local Governmental Units
.... CON6, ¶2
.... CON4, ¶3-5
Resources: Budgetary Appropriations...CON4, ¶21
State and Local Governmental Units...CON4, ¶3-5
.... CON4, ¶51-53
.... CON4, ¶65-66
.... CON6, ¶2
Types of Users .... CON4, ¶29-32

OBJECTIVES OF FINANCIAL REPORTING
Accrual Accounting and Cash Flows.CON1, ¶44-49
Amount, Timing, and Uncertainty of Cash Receipts
.... CON1, ¶37-39
Business Estimates by Users .... CON1, ¶48
Characteristics and Limitations ...... CON1, ¶17-23
Comparison between Not-for-Profit and Business Enterprises .... CON4, ¶67
Description .... CON1, ¶32-54
Earnings and Enterprise Performance
.... CON1, ¶44-48
Environmental Context .... CON1, ¶9-16
Financial Reporting, General Purpose External
.... CON1, ¶28-31
Information for Users .... CON1, ¶34-36
Liquidity, Solvency, and Funds Flow.... CON1, ¶49
Management Performance .... CON1, ¶50-53
Management Reporting .... CON1, ¶54
Not-for-Profit Organizations .... CON4, ¶1
.... CON4, ¶10-12
.... CON4, ¶33-55

OBJECTIVES OF FINANCIAL REPORTING—continued
Relation to Elements of Financial Statements ....CON6, ¶9-19
Relation to Qualitative Characteristics ....CON2, ¶21-26
Relation to Recognition and Measurement ....CON5, ¶10-12
Resources, Claims and Changes in Them ....CON1, ¶40-41
Users, Interests....CON1, ¶24-27

OBLIGATIONS
Definition....CON6, ¶35
Description....CON6, ¶200-205
Not-for-Profit Organizations....CON4, ¶43-54

OPERATING CYCLE
Description....CON1, ¶39

OTHER MEANS OF FINANCIAL REPORTING
Relation to Recognition in Financial Statements ....CON5, ¶7-9

PERFORMANCE
Not-for-Profit Organizations....CON4, ¶47-53

PRECISION
Relation to Representational Faithfulness ....CON2, ¶72-76

PREDICTIVE VALUE
Definition....CON2, ¶53-55
....CON2, Glossary

PREFERRED STOCK
Characteristics....CON6, ¶55

PREPAYMENTS
Qualification as Assets....CON6, ¶176

PRESENT VALUE
Recognition and Measurement
. . Measurement Attribute....CON5, ¶67

PRICE LEVEL CHANGES
Monetary Unit or Measurement Scale
. . Effect on....CON5, ¶71-72
Relation to Capital Maintenance....CON6, ¶71
Relation to Comprehensive Income..CON6, ¶73-75

PRIOR PERIOD ADJUSTMENTS
Exclusion from Earnings for the Current Period ....CON5, ¶34

PROBABLE
Definition....CON6, ¶25
....CON6, ¶35

PROFIT AND LOSS
Definition....CON6, ¶16
Relation to Comprehensive Income....CON6, ¶16

QUALITATIVE CHARACTERISTICS
Choice between Accounting Methods.CON2, ¶6-20
Comparability....CON2, ¶111-122
Conservatism....CON2, ¶91-97
Costs and Benefits....CON2, ¶133-144
Decision Making....CON2, ¶36-39
Exposure Draft Comments and Responses ....CON2, ¶152-160
Glossary of Terms....CON2, Glossary

QUALITATIVE CHARACTERISTICS—continued
Hierarchy of Accounting Qualities...CON2, ¶32-45
Materiality....CON2, ¶123-132
Nature of Accounting Choices....CON2, ¶6-20
Neutrality....CON2, ¶98-110
Recognition Criteria Derived from....CON5, ¶61
Relation to Elements of Financial Statements ....CON6, ¶9-19
Relation to Objectives of Financial Reporting ....CON2, ¶21-26
Relation to Role of Decision Making.CON2, ¶27-31
Relative Importance and Trade-Offs.CON2, ¶42-45
Relevance....CON2, ¶46-57
Reliability....CON2, ¶58-97
Representational Faithfulness....CON2, ¶63-80
Timeliness....CON2, ¶56-57
Understandability....CON2, ¶40-41
Verifiability....CON2, ¶81-89

REALIZATION
Definition....CON6, ¶143
Revenues and Gains
. . Guidance in Applying Recognition Criteria ....CON5, ¶83-84

RECOGNITION
See Recognition and Measurement in Financial Statements
Cost-Benefit Constraints....CON5, ¶63
Criteria....CON5, ¶62
. . Asset and Liability Changes....CON5, ¶85-88
. . Asset and Liability Changes, Use of Current Prices....CON5, ¶90
. . Fundamental....CON5, ¶63-64
. . Guidance in Application to Components of Earnings....CON5, ¶83-84
. . Guidance in Application to Revenues and Gains ....CON5, ¶83-84
. . Purposes....CON5, ¶59-60
. . Relevance....CON5, ¶73-74
. . Reliability....CON5, ¶75-77
. . Structure....CON5, ¶61-62
Definition....CON5, ¶6
....CON6, ¶143
Discussion....CON5, ¶58
Elements Definitions....CON5, ¶64
Financial Reporting....CON5, ¶5-6
Limitations....CON6, ¶48
Purchase Commitments....CON6, ¶251-253
Purposes....CON5, ¶59-61
Relation to Elements of Financial Statements ....CON6, ¶22-23
Relation to Measurement and Display...CON6, ¶23
Relation to Uncertainties....CON6, ¶48

RECOGNITION AND MEASUREMENT IN FINANCIAL STATEMENTS
See Measurement
See Recognition
Articulation of....CON5, ¶14
Definition
. . Earned....CON5, ¶83

RECOGNITION AND MEASUREMENT IN FINANCIAL STATEMENTS—continued
. . Financial Capital Maintenance Concept ....CON5, ¶47
. . Financial Flexibility...............CON5, ¶24
. . Liquidity.......................CON5, ¶24
. . Physical Capital Maintenance Concept ....CON5, ¶47
. . Realized or Realizable............CON5, ¶83
Financial Statements
. . Articulation.......................CON5, ¶5
............................CON5, ¶12
............................CON5, ¶23
. . Cash Flows during the Period.......CON5, ¶13
. . Classification and Aggregation in ....CON5, ¶20-22
. . Complementary Nature of.......CON5, ¶23-24
. . Comprehensive Income.........CON5, ¶39-41
. . Comprehensive Income (Total Nonowner Changes in Equity) for the Period.CON5, ¶13
. . Cumulative Accounting Adjustments ....CON5, ¶42-44
. . Details of Display Not Addressed...CON5, ¶14
. . Earnings.....................CON5, ¶33-38
. . Earnings (Net Income) for the Period ....CON5, ¶13
. . Financial Capital Maintenance...CON5, ¶45-48
. . Financial Position.................CON5, ¶13
. . Full Set of....................CON5, ¶13-14
. . Gains and Losses.................CON5, ¶43
. . General Purpose Financial Statements and Individual Users.............CON5, ¶15-16
. . Individual.......................CON5, ¶25
. . Investments by and Distributions to Owners during the Period..............CON5, ¶13
. . Net Income, Relation to Earnings ....CON5, ¶33-35
. . Notes to Financial Statements and Supplementary Information ......CON5,¶7-9
. . Other Nonowner Changes in Equity.CON5, ¶43
. . Recognition Implications of Earnings ....CON5, ¶49-51
. . Relation to Other Means of Financial Reporting ....CON5, ¶7-9
. . Statement of Cash Flows, Nature and Recognition Considerations....CON5, ¶52-54
. . Statement of Financial Position, Nature and Recognition Considerations....CON5, ¶26-29
. . Statement of Investments by and Distributions to Owners: Nature, Recognition ....CON5, ¶55-57
. . Statements of Earnings and Comprehensive Income: Nature; Recognition .CON5, ¶30-51
. . Usefulness of Financial Statements, Individually and Collectively.............CON5, ¶17-19
Gains and Losses..................CON5, ¶42
Not-for-Profit Organizations
. . Nonapplicability to................CON5, ¶4
. . Objectives of Financial Reporting, Relationship ....CON5, ¶10-12

RECOGNITION AND MEASUREMENT IN FINANCIAL STATEMENTS—continued
. . Other Nonowner Changes in Equity, Description....................CON5, ¶43

RELEVANCE
Criterion for Recognition.............CON5, ¶74
Definition......................CON2, Glossary
Feedback Value..................CON2, ¶51-52
Predictive Value..................CON2, ¶53-55
Primary Qualitative Characteristic...CON2, ¶46-57
Relation to Neutrality............CON2, ¶98-110
Relation to Reliability................CON2, ¶90
Relation to Timeliness.............CON2, ¶56-57
Role in Financial Reporting...........CON1, ¶36

RELIABILITY
Criterion for Recognition...........CON5, ¶75-77
Definition......................CON2, Glossary
Degree of.......................CON2, ¶65-71
Financial Statements, Nature of Audit...CON1, ¶8
Precision and Uncertainty..........CON2, ¶72-76
Primary Qualitative Characteristic...CON2, ¶58-97
Relation to Conservatism..........CON2, ¶91-97
Relation to Neutrality............CON2, ¶98-110
Relation to Relevance................CON2, ¶90
Relation to Representational Faithfulness ....CON2, ¶63-80
Relation to Substance vs. Form.......CON2, ¶160
Relation to Uncertainty............CON6, ¶45-48
Relation to Verifiability.............CON2, ¶81-89

REPLACEMENT COST
See Measurement

REPRESENTATIONAL FAITHFULNESS
Definition......................CON2, Glossary
Relation to Bias...................CON2, ¶77-78
Relation to Completeness..........CON2, ¶79-80
Relation to Precision...............CON2, ¶72-76
Relation to Reliability..............CON2, ¶63-80
Relation to Uncertainties...........CON2, ¶72-76

RESEARCH AND DEVELOPMENT
Qualification as an Asset............CON6, ¶176

RESERVES
Qualification as Liabilities...........CON6, ¶197

RESIDUAL INTEREST
Characteristics....................CON6, ¶49-53
................................CON6, ¶213
................................CON6, ¶222

RESTRICTED FUNDS
Not-for-Profit Organizations..........CON4, ¶21
................................CON4, ¶46
Relation to Net Assets...............CON6, ¶191

RETURN ON INVESTMENT
Accrual vs. Cash Basis of Accounting ....CON1, ¶45-48
Prospects for.....................CON1, ¶37-39
Relation to Capital Maintenance.......CON6, ¶71

REVENUE RECOGNITION
Guidance for Applying Recognition Criteria ....CON5, ¶84

REVENUES
Characteristics......................CON6, ¶79
Component of Comprehensive Income
..............................CON6, ¶73-77
Definition.........................CON6, ¶78
Element of Financial Statements.....CON6, ¶78-81
Guidance in Applying Recognition Criteria
..............................CON6, ¶87-89
Not-for-Profit Organizations......CON6, ¶111-113
Relation to Gains.................CON6, ¶87-89
SERVICE EFFORTS AND ACCOMPLISHMENTS
Not-for-Profit Organizations........CON4, ¶51-53
SERVICE POTENTIAL
Definition.........................CON6, ¶28
Discussion........................CON6, ¶26-30
..............................CON6, ¶172-173
SOLVENCY
Information about..................CON1, ¶49
STANDARDS, FINANCIAL ACCOUNTING
Relation to Concepts.................CON1, ¶3
STATE AND LOCAL GOVERNMENTAL UNITS
Application of Conceptual Framework...CON6, ¶2
..............................CON4, ¶65-66
Contributions.......................CON4, ¶6
Relation to Not-for-Profit Organizations
..............................CON4, ¶3-5
..............................CON6, ¶2
STATEMENT OF CASH FLOWS
Description, Nature and Recognition Considerations ....CON5, ¶26-29
Description and Recognition Considerations
..............................CON5, ¶52-54
STATEMENT OF FINANCIAL POSITION
Component of Full Set of Financial Statements
..............................CON5, ¶13
Definition.........................CON6, ¶20
Description, Nature and Recognition Considerations ....CON5, ¶26-29
STATEMENT OF INVESTMENTS BY AND DISTRIBUTIONS TO OWNERS
Component of Full Set of Financial Statements
..............................CON5, ¶13
Description, Nature and Recognition Considerations ....CON5, ¶55-57
STATEMENTS OF EARNINGS AND COMPREHENSIVE INCOME
See Comprehensive Income
Description, Nature and Recognition Considerations ....CON5, ¶30-41
Relationship between Earnings and Comprehensive Income........................CON5, ¶42-44
STOCK PURCHASE WARRANTS
Qualification as a Liability...........CON6, ¶254
SUBSCRIPTIONS
Qualification as Liabilities............CON6, ¶197
SUBSTANCE VS. FORM
Relation to Reliability...............CON2, ¶160
SUPPLEMENTAL FINANCIAL INFORMATION
Relation to Recognition in Financial Statements
..............................CON5, ¶7-9

TERMINOLOGY
Accrual........................CON6, ¶139-141
Allocation.........................CON6, ¶142
Amortization.......................CON6, ¶142
Articulation.....................CON6, ¶20-21
Assets.............................CON6, ¶25
Attribute(s).....................CON6, ¶65-67
Bias..........................CON2, Glossary
Capital Maintenance.................CON6, ¶71
Changes in Financial Position..........CON6, ¶20
Change in Permanently Restricted Net Assets
..............................CON6, ¶119
Change in Temporarily Restricted Net Assets
..............................CON6, ¶123
Change in Unrestricted Net Assets.....CON6, ¶127
Circumstances (Affecting an Entity)...CON6, ¶136
Comparability..................CON2, Glossary
Completeness...................CON2, Glossary
Comprehensive Income...............CON6, ¶70
Conservatism...................CON2, Glossary
Consistency....................CON2, Glossary
Constructive Obligations.............CON6, ¶40
Cost..............................CON6, ¶26
Cumulative Accounting Adjustments...CON5, ¶42
Deferral..........................CON6, ¶141
Distributions to Owners..............CON6, ¶67
Earned............................CON5, ¶83
Earnings..........................CON5, ¶33
Economic Resources.................CON6, ¶27
Elements of Financial Statements........CON6, ¶5
Entity............................CON6, ¶24
Equitable Obligations................CON6, ¶40
Equity..........................CON6, ¶49-50
Events...........................CON6, ¶135
Exchange (Exchange Transactions)....CON6, ¶137
Expenses..........................CON6, ¶80
Feedback Value.................CON2, Glossary
Financial Capital Maintenance Concept.CON5, ¶47
..............................CON6, ¶71-72
Financial Flexibility..................CON5, ¶24
Financial Position...................CON6, ¶20
Funds or Fund Balances..............CON6, ¶91
Future Economic Benefits.............CON6, ¶28
..............................CON6, ¶172
Gains.............................CON6, ¶82
Internal Events....................CON6, ¶135
..............................CON6, ¶138
Internal Transactions................CON6, ¶138
Investments by Owners...............CON6, ¶66
Liabilities.........................CON6, ¶35
Liquidity..........................CON5, ¶24
Loss..............................CON6, ¶16
Losses............................CON6, ¶83
Maintenance of Net Assets...........CON6, ¶105
Materiality....................CON2, Glossary
Net Assets.......................CON6, ¶49-50
Neutrality.....................CON2, Glossary
Nonreciprocal Transfer(s)............CON6, ¶137
Obligations........................CON6, ¶35
Permanently Restricted Net Assets......CON6, ¶92
Physical Capital Maintenance Concept..CON5, ¶47

TERMINOLOGY—continued
Predictive Value................CON2, Glossary
Probable..........................CON6, ¶25
..................................CON6, ¶35
Profit..............................CON6, ¶16
Realization.........................CON6, ¶143
Realized, Realizable.................CON5, ¶83
..................................CON6, ¶143
Recognition..........................CON5, ¶6
..................................CON6, ¶143
Relevance......................CON2, Glossary
Reliability.....................CON2, Glossary
Representational Faithfulness.....CON2, Glossary
Revenue...........................CON6, ¶78
Service Potential....................CON6, ¶28
Service Providing Efforts............CON6, ¶112
Temporarily Restricted Net Assets......CON6, ¶93
Timeliness.....................CON2, Glossary
Transaction........................CON6, ¶137
Uncertainty........................CON6, ¶44
Understandability...............CON2, Glossary
Unrealized.........................CON6, ¶143
Unrestricted Net Assets...............CON6, ¶94
Valuation Allowances.................CON6, ¶34
Verifiability....................CON2, Glossary

TIMELINESS
Definition......................CON2, Glossary
Relation to Usefulness and Relevance
..............................CON2, ¶56-57

TRANSFERS, NONRECIPROCAL
See Nonmonetary Transactions

UNCERTAINTIES
Effects of.......................CON6, ¶44-48
Relation to Assets..................CON6, ¶175
Relation to Recognition of Assets and Liabilities
..................................CON6, ¶48
Relation to Reliability.............CON6, ¶45-48
Relation to Representational Faithfulness
..............................CON2, ¶72-76

UNDERSTANDABILITY
Definition......................CON2, Glossary
User-Specific Characteristic.........CON2, ¶40-41

UNEARNED REVENUES
Qualification as Liabilities...........CON6, ¶197

UNREALIZED
Definition.........................CON6, ¶143

USEFULNESS
Choice between Accounting Methods...CON2, ¶17
..............................CON2, ¶10-11
..............................CON2, ¶14-15
Financial Statements
. . Classification and Aggregation in
..............................CON5, ¶20-22
Financial Statements, Individually and Collectively
..............................CON5, ¶17-19
Information for Assessing Cash Flow Prospects
..............................CON1, ¶37-39
Information for Investment and Credit Decisions
..............................CON1, ¶34-36
Relation to Timeliness.............CON2, ¶56-57

USERS OF FINANCIAL INFORMATION
Description......................CON1, ¶24-27
External Users...................CON1, ¶25-27
General Purpose Financial Statements
..............................CON5, ¶15-16
..............................CON5, ¶28-30
Management........................CON1, ¶27
Not-for-Profit Organizations........CON4, ¶29-32
Understanding Financial AccountingCON2, ¶36-41

VALUATION ACCOUNTS
Definition.........................CON6, ¶34
..................................CON6, ¶43

VERIFIABILITY
Component to Reliability..........CON2, ¶81-89
Definition......................CON2, Glossary